ARCANA IX

ARCANA IX
MUSICIANS ON MUSIC

EDITED BY
JOHN ZORN

HIPS ROAD 2021

Book design by Heung-Heung Chin.

First published in 2021
ISBN 978-09788337-2-5
ISBN 0-9788337-2-4
Printed on acid-free paper
Printed and bound in the United States of America

Hips Road
200 East 10th Street #126
New York, NY 10003
http://www.tzadik.com

Distributed to the trade by D.A.P. / Distributed Art Publishers
75 Broad Street, Suite 630
New York, NY 10004

Orders: (800) 338-2665 Tel: (212) 627-1999
Fax: (212) 627-9484

CONTENTS

PREFACE

JOHN ZORN

"Certum est quia impossibilie est."
—Tertullian, c.160–225

At the publication of each new volume of *Arcana*, I vow it will be the last; but then a few years roll by, amazing new musicians enter my field of vision, and editing a new volume of *Arcana* becomes not only an idea—it becomes an imperative. One thing that really riles me is people with resources and opportunities that do not take responsibility. These books are not published because I *want* to put them out—they are published because they *must* come out. The responsibility involved outweighs any other consideration.

Filled with honesty, passion, wisdom and imagination, *Arcana IX* is another beautiful collection of writings on and about music. Featuring thirty-three different authors, it presents a rich and diverse cross section of creative minds, all active today and at different stages of their artistic development. Ranging in age from their early 20s to their 70s, the musicians represented here all excel in their chosen fields and hail from the worlds of jazz, classical, film soundtracks, rock, improvisation, sound design, engineering, critical theory and more. What ties them all together is the miracle of an open mind. We all believe in music; in truth; in the power of art to heal and help a world that has always needed help and healing.

It is my sincere wish that the articles, essays and critical papers you read in this latest installment of *Arcana* will open some exciting new worlds for you; will stimulate and inspire; will unlock doors and overturn preconceptions; will raise some questions and give you the courage to take a risk—because one cannot transcend anything without leaving safe ground—and the world only moves forward through lofty work and heroic accomplishment.

ONWARD!

—John Zorn, *NYC 2019*

ARCANA IX

CHAPTER
1

FROM THE RIDICULOUS TO THE SUBLIME

Danny Kaye Meets the Interval Machine

BRUCE ACKLEY

It is impossible to predict which early childhood events will turn out to be life-altering, particularly for artists who truck with invisible ephemera. Seemingly banal experiences can surprisingly open pathways to the profound. I mean, how could my decades-long life in music have been ignited by Danny Kaye's *The Little Fiddle*? And how did singing Palestrina lead me to Steve Lacy and to Rova?

Although I can't pinpoint exactly when Kaye's tomfoolery entered my life, or how his 78 found its way into our household, *The Little Fiddle* was in heavy rotation on our family console hi-fi before I was five. Released the year I was born, Kaye's madcap mini-drama filled me with absolute glee. I memorized the sung scenes he created to imitate the instruments of the orchestra, and parroted his every vocal escapade. To the dismay of older sister, Kaye's insane fiddlesticks had me tearing around our house for years, making whatever sounds I could tease out of my voice. Almost 70 years later, Kaye's genius still resonates in my head, and my frenzied vocalizing now dances on the bell of my soprano saxophone.

My eventual gravitation to the straight horn was certainly presaged by my love for singing soprano as a boy in choir and in school. Seeming to prefigure the musical direction I would later take, my father had sung in a male vocal sextet in the 1930s—six voices, no rhythm section. He and I sang in the choir together, my dad a bass/baritone, and me a soprano before adolescence descended to lower my voice. I loved to soar, singing the highest lines of that early music in Latin, the inevitable loss of the high register affecting me profoundly. But, those experiences singing 16th century part-music, particularly in Palestrina's complex style, ultimately kindled in me a desire to play in wind ensembles.

Contemporaneously, my 6th grade teacher led us in singing the songs from *The Sound of Music*, which included the iconic *My Favorite*

Things. And she invited my classmate Billy Beaver to do a show-and-tell for us on alto sax. Seeing and hearing the saxophone in action made a deep impression on me—Billy even wore puss print pants for his solo show. But, I couldn't even imagine myself playing. Yet.

My parents often listened to jazz records at home—Billie, Duke, Ella and others, and it was around this time that I discovered my dad's old 78s—mostly 1920s Chicago jazz and boogie-woogie piano. Throughout that following summer when I was 11, my pal Eddie and I would play chess, listening to *Darktown Strutter's Ball*, *Indiana*, *Crazeology*, and *Maple Leaf Rag*. Eddie played trumpet and ecstatically heralded every solo, but I was already listening for the saxophone, influenced by our classmate's horn playing.

Fast forward to 1963. In the summers of my high school years I worked picking corn for a professorial and crotchety farmer, Old Man Bailey. He raised hybrid produce to sell to suburbanites in the rural outskirts of Detroit, employing local teenagers for a dollar an hour to do the labor. It was during that summer, riding in the tractor's flatbed after the day's harvest, I learned a co-worker a few years my senior dug jazz. And of course, I announced that I too was into jazz—a vague and unformed notion to me at that point.

I eagerly accepted my corn-picking jazz buddy's invitation to his parents' place to check out some sides. We listened for hours, but I can only remember hearing Les McCann's funky *Plays the Shampoo*, and the record that changed everything for me—Coltrane's *My Favorite Things*. I was mesmerized looking at the straight horn Trane holds on that iconic blue cover. I remember wondering if it was an oboe, and was promptly informed he was playing a soprano saxophone. The title track resonated deeply with me, having sung it endlessly in class. Thanks to that afternoon's session, Coltrane's music and the soprano would become life-long obsessions. Yet, it wouldn't be until I was 22 that I got my first horn.

My passion for music continued to deepen, yet I opted to study painting and photography in college. Through mutual friends I got to know Tom Braund, an iconoclastic painter-educator who taught high school art and music and had access to instruments. Although I was focused on getting a soprano, he kindly offered to provide me a 1920s era Buescher C melody saxophone (pitched a major second above the tenor) to get me started. Tom referred to the horn as the silver bullet, and told me, "Go play that thing for a month and then come back and let's jam", which of course I did.

After buying my first soprano, a Couf Superba II, Tom and I, along with an assortment of musicians, played several nights a week—everything freely improvised. Living in a repurposed dentist's office above a noisy laundromat, I was able to practice daily without distraction. When Tom played me Sidney Bechet's *Summertime* recording, another world opened up. Bechet's thick and storied sound washed over me, an approach with the horn so distinct from Trane's almost cubistic-lined soprano. And soon, Wayne Shorter's lush and pastoral playing, so much a part of Miles' evolving music, was also on my radar. I began to sense there were other practitioners out there I would find equally intriguing, as I continued to diligently pursue my craft.

Important to me among the many ideas forming then, were two primary tenets learned in my time as a visual artist: the importance of the discipline of daily practice; and the concept that a creative work must be made with authenticity, be self-referential, and come with its own inherent laws. I departed Detroit, fortified with these seminal improvising experiences and percolating ideals about creativity.

I hitchhiked across the country during the summer of 1971, traveling alone with minimal clothing, a few books and my horn, arriving in San Francisco at journey's end. The following few years were characterized by deep turmoil. I was held at knife point and had my horn stolen soon after arriving. Although this wrenching violation was both frightening and heartbreaking, I remained undeterred. I soon acquired a beautiful Selmer tenor that I traded for a less coveted, but soulful sounding, vintage soprano. The person on the other end of that bargain was quite happy to get away with such a sought after tenor, but I was psyched to have the soprano back in my life. That late '20s King was my instrument for the next 5 years.

It was then that I first read about Steve Lacy and heard him on Cecil Taylor's version of *Things Ain't What They Used to Be*. Issued on Taylor's 1961 *New York City R&B* album, Lacy was allotted a brief solo, and you can pick his soprano out of the ensemble cadenza at the end of the track, spiraling high above the clouds. Those singular moments captured on the Taylor LP grabbed me and Lacy's contribution hasn't let go nearly five decades later. Hearing his mastery of the high horn, while working to develop my own soprano sound, left me spellbound.

In the early '70s the great jazz re-issue project was yet to be launched, and Steve Lacy albums were scarce. Some older recordings were in circulation, and those in the know had a few, or had cassette tapes of them. But, by 1975 both new recordings and re-issued Lacy LPs were proliferating. Since I was concentrating exclusively on the straight horn, hearing each new record was like school for me and those in my circle. In fact, it was *School Days*, along with his record with Don Cherry, *Evidence*, where I was able to really focus on his concept. The tone, the range, the phrasing, the incredible swing and imagination! And his extended interview with Ron Welburn, published in the journal, *The Grackle*, in the fall of 1976, provided important context for this world of soprano magic Lacy was creating. Ideas expressed there matched what I was hearing come through his horn—his thought was consistent, original, and moving. I found his insistence on making connections between music and visual art, comedy, writing, theatre, poetics, wildlife, politics and daily life essential, and his remarkable dedication to the art of performance infinitely inspirational.

Friends and early Lacy acolytes I encountered were horn players Phillip Johnston, Leora Barish, Larry Ochs and John Zorn. What drew me, and I suspect the others, to Lacy's music was his being unbounded by conventions of the celebrated jazz of the time. I found Steve's music a doorway to traverse, an opening to new possibilities. Following that opening's path led to points of departure, just as the study of Thelonious Monk's entire canon had for Lacy.

Soprano player Barish and I made a commitment to daily practice sessions to see what we could create on two straight horns. We discussed the instrument, sound, composition, improvisation, and listened to and talked about Lacy. We explored alternatives to what had previously made sense, imagining more personal and less traditional rules for improvising, or no rules. Those sessions further crystalized my dedication to the straight horn, and illustrated the value of consistent and concentrated effort.

It was in 1975 that the poet and playwright Ntozake Shange took me to hear Jon Raskin playing at the Yardbird, a bar on San Francisco's Divisadero Street. That night he was smoking on soprano, and I was soon to learn what I heard at the Yardbird was only the tip of the iceberg. Jon and I connected, leading to the formation of the large ensemble Continuum.

Members of that band soon opened the Blue Dolphin, a collectively run neighborhood performance space in the Castro district. Shows there included a range of local improvisers, as well as touring players, Oliver Lake, Julius Hemphill, Wadada Leo Smith, Eugene Chadbourne and others. With this and other venues emerging, new improvising groups were forming. The Dolphin became a hub for adventurous players and listeners, where a free exchange of ideas helped to initiate an important era in Bay Area improvised music.

Without a doubt my early singing experiences informed my desire to play in horns-only groups, like my first band in Detroit. And for 3 years in San Francisco I teamed up with Lewis Jordan on alto, and George Sams on trumpet, to form the Sound Clinic. That band developed an original repertoire that blended improvisation and composition in seamless and compelling ways. I was also having parallel discussions with Larry Ochs, whom I had already worked with for several years, about forming a saxophone quartet as a vehicle for creating composed works for improvisation.

When I was approached to put together a group to perform at an improvising music festival in late 1977, I immediately called on Larry and Jon with the saxophone quartet in mind, and of course both were on board. We discovered a kindred spirit in alto player Andrew Voigt and asked him to join us, with Raskin taking up the baritone, Ochs on tenor and me on soprano. 10 years later, with Rova firmly established, Steve Adams replaced Andrew to form the group's present-day configuration.

That model of daily work applied to our nameless quartet during that formative period. We met each morning to rehearse at the Blue Dolphin to work through sketches, ideas, concepts, full blown compositions, and to improvise, explore and discuss. Those sessions established a foundation the quartet would build on over time, and led to our first recording dates in 1978.

In the saxophone quartet I once again assumed the high voice in the choir, the altissimo range of the horn especially attracting me. I had been fascinated with Lacy's ability to take the horn to the stratosphere, and for several years I worked on the horn's upper register. Hearing his composition *Moon*, on the solo LP *Stalks*, made me aware of what was possible—four full octaves, in tune, with deep rich tone. Extending the horn's range was just one of the many ways the four of us were resisting the confines of traditional saxophone technique and the accepted conventions of jazz-based improvisation.

While the quartet commenced preliminary steps to becoming an active ensemble, I took on a new project with guitarist Eugene Chadbourne. Eugene had a long-standing dream of forming a two horn/two guitar quartet to be known as Twins. He and Zorn were both living in New York at the time, playing together incessantly. Eugene cooked up a plan for them to come to the west coast to meet up with guitarist Henry Kaiser and me, making Twins a reality. The concept was that we would rehearse, record and perform together for a month.

The work was challenging, and required a dramatic shift in how I approached improvising. With the exception of one by me, we concentrated on compositions by the New Yorkers. Zorn's pieces were magnificent and complex, compelling us to deal on multiple strategic levels at once, while Chadbourne's were more playful, almost slapstick, and had their own unique logic and rules of engagement. Performance required undistracted attention to every detail, and monster chops. I often felt in over my head, yet was utterly charged to be doing Twins.

That collaboration had a lasting impact on my outlook about music, improvisation, performance, and the value friendship and trust can bring to risk-taking projects. Our time together revealed a great deal that remains a part of my musical DNA, resonating for years after, and significantly influencing my eventual contributions to the saxophone quartet.

Always running in the background during Twins was our shared fascination with Steve Lacy's music. Chadbourne had met Lacy in Canada and was taken with both his music and his persona. And John, Henry and I were avidly listening to everything we could find. Simultaneously, the saxophone quartet was also investigating and absorbing Lacy's ideas—both for his improvisational creativity, and for his compositional inventiveness.

It is no surprise that the aesthetic direction of Rova was in part informed by our relationship with Lacy's recordings. His soprano-driven output included pieces that influenced how we were hearing things, and also expanded considerations for organizing music as a group. Especially impressive were his '70s masterpieces: *Solo Concert* (recorded in Avignon in 1972), *Saxophone Special*, *Lapis*, *Clangs*, and *Straws*. From solo soprano, to sax quartet plus electronics, to percussion-horn duos, as well as recordings with different instrumentation on each track, the breadth and scope of these releases was without parallel in jazz. In 1982, at Lacy's suggestion while hanging with him in Paris, Rova embarked on a project to create an album of his music, arranged by Rova. *Favorite Street*, released on the Italian Black Saint label in 1984, chronicles seven lesser-known pieces by the maestro, each prepared by Rova members with separate and unique concerns important to the arranger, intoning that precept of originality and authenticity. A lot of thinking, labor and love went into remaking each Lacy composition, and our engagement with this venture continues to affect our work decades later.

I have been especially enchanted with Lacy's solo playing, which I witnessed live several times. Each experience demonstrated the power of his iconoclastic voice, and laid bare the mechanics of creating solo work—from the rigor of memorizing complex lines to the relaxed and committed posture that allowed him to deliver disciplined and carefully-honed improvisations, without the constraints or benefits of a supporting cast.

The isolated soprano echoed the solitude of my own practice and connected me to that boyhood passion for singing. With characteristic humor, while trading touring woes, Lacy shared a story of playing a concert for an audience of one. I asked him about the group. He said it was a solo concert. I wryly asked if he played two sets. "Of course", he replied. His commitment to the work, regardless of the size of the audience, resonated with me: commercial concerns sidelined in favor of a dedicated desire to create and discover. For, even though a reliable and consistent audience can dictate the economics of the art, my life of music making largely operates independent of practicality.

My enduring investigations with the soprano—playing with Rova, alone, and with countless other artists—has brought me immense pleasure and feelings of awe, while still challenging me to the core. 50 years after first picking it up, the soprano saxophone engages me at the heart of this mysterious process of discovery, and enables me to broadcast findings to the world. As I offer deep bows of gratitude to Danny Kaye, Palestrina, Lacy, and Coltrane, I can exclaim that this interval machine, as Lacy referred to the soprano, continues to reveal endless delights.

—San Francisco, November 2019

CHAPTER 2

IN SEARCH OF SACRED SPACE

JOHN LUTHER ADAMS

A young composer and I were sitting on a bench in Central Park, talking about music. He asked me about form.

"I want my music to be intensely sensuous", I said. "But I also want it to be rigorously formal."

"Why?" he asked.

"Form gives the music a deeper coherence. It also protects the music against the bad taste of the composer!"

He laughed.

I added: "But recently I've begun to relax a little in my obsession with form..."

"Then what will take the place of form?" Without hesitating I replied: "Space."

It was a prescient question, and my answer surprised me a bit. I wasn't entirely sure what I meant, but it had the ring of truth. And it got me thinking.

When I was 21, I became captivated by the songs of birds. In the woods and fields of rural Georgia, I began trying to write down what I heard. Before long I had a collection of miniature portraits, a bit like pages in a musical field guide to the birds. But that wasn't enough. I wanted to evoke something of the magic that I felt listening to the birds in the places where they sang. So to my first settings of birdsongs, scored for piccolos, I added parts for percussion—rattles, sizzle cymbals, woodblocks, bells and the like—that I imagined as the wind, the rain, the light and the weather. This was the beginning a lifelong exploration of place and space in music.

The following year, in Alaska, I experienced landscape on a scale I'd never known. Enthralled, I began to sketch out broad harmonic fields that I hoped would echo those sprawling expanses of mountains and glaciers, forest and tundra. Eventually those sketches became an orchestral work titled *A Northern Suite.* From the subtitle—*Tone Paintings of Alaska*—it was clear that I was thinking of this music in a pictorial way. And for more than a decade, in works such as *Night Peace* and *The Far Country of Sleep,* I continued this kind of landscape painting in music.

There was a profoundly romantic dimension to this early passion for place, fueled by my reading of Thoreau and Muir, and by contemporary writers like Annie Dillard and Barry Lopez. I found special inspiration in the poetry of John Haines. And when I was not yet 30, I had the extraordinary good fortune to begin a long, close friendship with John, working with him on *Forest Without Leaves* (1984)—a choral work grounded in his cycle of poems about humanity's inextricable roots in the earth.

Several years later I ventured to combine the poetic and the pictorial in *Earth and the Great Weather* (1991). This "sonic geography of the Arctic" mixes instrumental music for strings and percussion with sounds recorded in the landscapes of the North. But the real conceptual ground of this work was a series of *Arctic Litanies*—found poems composed from indigenous names for places, plants, birds and the seasons. Spoken and sung in the Gwich'in and Iñupiat languages, these words seemed to me to come directly out of the earth itself, and to constitute an authentic poetry of place.

Yet music is not poetry or painting. And even while I was painting musical landscapes, I was committed first and foremost to music as *sound.* I wanted my landscapes to have depth. I wanted the listener to be able to enter into, to *inhabit* those musical spaces.

Early on I'd encountered Henry Cowell's visionary book *New Musical Resources.* In the chapter on rhythm Cowell proposes nothing less than a unified field theory of music—compositions that encompass not only tonal harmonies but also rhythmic harmonies derived from the whole-number relationships of the natural harmonic series.

Most Western music is constrained by regular meter and a single audible pulse. But ever since my days as a rock 'n' roller this has struck me as curiously two-dimensional. In the works of Conlon Nancarrow and Johannes Ockeghem, I found inspiring models from the 20th and the 15th centuries of multi-temporal music. And for decades now most of my own music has encompassed three, four or more different tempos simultaneously. Somewhere along the way it occurred to me that these tempo layers could allow me to create a larger sense of musical space.

Beginning with *Clouds of Forgetting, Clouds of Unknowing* (1996), and continuing with *In the White Silence* (1998), and *For Lou Harrison* (2004), I employed large-scale, multi-dimensional orchestral textures in an effort to move beyond landscape painting. In this music I wanted to create inherently *musical* landscapes that immerse and envelope the listener. Yet even as the music became less pictorial, I was still enamored of color.

We often speak of sound in visual terms. Timbre—the unique sonic profile that allows us to distinguish one instrument from another—we call "tone color". I love working with the broad palette of acoustic instruments, mixing their colors in different ways. I also enjoy creating new colors with electronic media.

But beyond timbre, I also think of *harmony* as color, and over the decades my music has traversed a wide territory of harmonic colors. When I'm working in standard 12-tone equal temperament, I usually mix my colors from the interval of a Perfect 5th (or its inversion, the Perfect 4th)—superimposing that single interval on itself in varied ways to create chords, clouds and fields of distinctive harmonic hues.

I also work frequently in non-tempered tunings derived from the harmonic series and its theoretical inversion, the sub-harmonic series. Digital media make it relatively easy to explore unfamiliar harmonic territory, and in electronic works such as *Veils and Vesper* (2006), *The Place Where You Go to Listen* (2007), and *The Wind Garden* (2017), I've worked with a wide range of new harmonic colors. Over time, some of those new harmonies have found their way back into works for human performers and acoustic instruments.

As I became less interested in painting musical landscapes, I began to study the non-representational art of Mark Rothko, Jackson Pollock, Helen Frankenthaler and Barnett Newman, as well as the history of color theory. This led me to a compose a series of "color field" pieces, beginning with *The Light That Fills the World*, and continuing with *Dark Wind, The Farthest Place*, and *The Immeasurable Space of Tones* (all completed in 2001). This music is composed from long clouds of harmony and timbre, moving slowly in multiple tempos—rising and falling, merging and dissolving, drifting together and drifting apart. At the time, this sounded radically new. I wasn't even sure it was music. Yet ironically, over the years these pieces that I originally conceived as floating fields of color have come to sound melodic, almost songlike, to me.

While I was working on my "color field" series I also composed *Red Arc/Blue Veil* for piano, mallet percussion instruments and electronic sounds. Inspired by the forms and colors of the aurora borealis, *Red Arc* was the first piece in which I created an "aura" of electronic sounds derived directly from the acoustic instruments. This "aura" allowed me to create an almost orchestral field of sound, while the "live" musicians animated the surface with touch.

Following *Red Arc*, I've employed auras in a number of other pieces, including *The Light Within, Four Thousand Holes* and *Ilimaq* (Spirit Journey). This technique has also influenced the sound of my music even when a composition doesn't include an electronic aura. In *Dark Waves* I embedded an electronic aura within the sound of a full symphony orchestra. But in *Become Ocean,* I decided to dispense with the electronic sounds and compose the aura directly into the orchestra.

As John Cage observed, most of what we hear around us most of the time is noise. When we try to ignore it, it disturbs us. But when we listen to noise with our full attention, we find it fascinating. So what happens when we invite noise into our music? Suddenly the whole world becomes music.

In this spirit, I began work on *Strange and Sacred Noise*—a concert length cycle of pieces for percussion quartet, celebrating elemental violence in nature. In my travels throughout Alaska I'd experienced howling storms, raging wildfires, and glaciers crashing into the sea. I'd also been reading books about chaos theory, which inspired me to imagine a kind of "sonic geometry"—sounding fractal forms with noise.

Strange and Sacred Noise roars, howls and thunders. But it evokes the unbounded spaces of the natural world within the enclosed space of a concert hall or theater. In fact this music relies on four walls, a ceiling and floor to saturate the acoustic space with sound and overload our psychoacoustic perceptions, provoking us to hear things that aren't really there.

One section of *Noise* is scored for four tam-tams. When I first heard this piece, amid the dense waves of broadband noise, I clearly heard voices—like a choir of spirits singing long, wordless tones. I promptly dubbed these "angel voices". And I wanted to hear them alone.

In Papua New Guinea when a Kaluli songmaker searches for a new song, he will sometimes camp by a waterfall or a running stream. It's said that all the songs in the world are contained in the noise of the water. And the songmaker listens carefully, sometimes for days, until he hears the voice of his new song. All broadband noise contains within it pure tone. And the complex sonorities of percussion instruments conceal choirs of inner voices.

In *The Mathematics of Resonant Bodies* (2002) my search would be to find and reveal those voices. Working with a recording of those tam-tams from *Strange and Sacred Noise*, I filtered out most of the noise until all that was left was that choir of angel voices. This became the point of departure for an exploration of the inner resonances, the sonic spaces hidden within noise.

I continued by composing a complete cycle of new pieces for percussion quartet. Then I assembled recordings of those pieces and then began filtering—selectively erasing them, as I'd done previously with the tam-tams. The result was a series of "auras" derived from the inner resonance of the instruments themselves. As the final step, I composed a series of solo parts to be performed within these sonic fields.

For years I had been working with the *idea* of space and place, imagining each new composition as its own metaphorical space and place. But the time came when this was no longer enough. In a sense, my music was becoming less painterly and more sculptural.

My continuing interest in visual art led me to the so-called "Light and Space" artists who came of age in southern California in the 1960s and '70s. I found the light art of James Turrell, and the perceptual art of Robert Irwin especially compelling. And I began dreaming of musical equivalents to their immersive visual environments. If their basic materials were light and space, mine were sound and space. And just as they were creating the physical spaces in which their work is experienced, I wanted not only to compose the music but also to design the space in which it was performed and heard—whether indoors or outdoors.

The Place Where You Go to Listen is a small room at the Museum of the North in Fairbanks—an interior space that echoes the music of the larger world around it. Inside this room the rhythms of night and day, the phases of the moon, the seismic movements of the earth and the dance of the aurora borealis are all transformed into sound and light.

Loudspeakers all around the room—in the walls, in the ceiling and near the floor—allowed me to place the sounds relative to one another in a way that echoes the geographic locations of those vibrations from the outside world. After working inside this immersive space for more than 2 years, I became more aware than ever of the flatness of hearing music played on a proscenium stage in a conventional concert hall. And I began to think about utilizing those spaces in a fuller, more dynamic way.

In *Become Ocean* (2014) a full symphony orchestra is deployed in three different ensembles separated as widely as possible. Each of these groups has its own distinctive instrumental and harmonic coloration, and each moves at its own tempo.

Become River (2014) is scored for a smaller orchestra, turned upside down. Rather than their usual position near the edge of the stage, the violins are seated far upstage and elevated, and the entire ensemble is raked. Over the course of 20 minutes three different musical streams moving at different speeds flow downstream, from high sounds to low—taking the listener on a musical journey from the headwaters to the edge of the sea.

Become Desert (2017) is a 40-minute symphonic work that completes a trilogy that I didn't set out to write. In all three of these works, space is a fundamental compositional element. I'm not speaking only of poetic or metaphorical space, but also of the physical, acoustic and volumetric space of the musical ensemble and the place in which the music is heard.

For decades now, one of the most fundamental questions I ask myself when I begin a new composition is: "What are the instruments?" With *Become Desert,* this became two questions: "What are the instruments? And where are they located?"

For a long time I pondered the floor plan, the physical deployment of the instrumental and vocal choirs within and around the performance space. Ultimately I decided to disperse the strings all over the stage, with four harps and four percussionists interspersed among them.

The other four choirs are elevated on high risers, in balconies, lofts or boxes around the performance space. Upstage, a choir of sixteen woodwinds and a percussionist playing crotales (antique cymbals) is elevated as high as possible above the strings. A choir of eight horns and a percussionist playing chimes is elevated on one side of the space. A choir of four trumpets and four trombones and a percussionist playing chimes is elevated on the other side of the space. And a choir of singers and handbells is elevated at the rear of the space.

Only when I arrived at this layout, only when I could begin to hear this sonic space in my mind was I ready to begin writing the score.

For decades my music had been inspired by the outdoors, but it was almost always performed indoors. Then I heard *Strange and Sacred Noise* performed outdoors, and everything changed.

It was in the Anza-Borrego desert of southern California. I settled in to listen to what I thought of as my big, powerful piece performed in a stunningly beautiful natural setting. But in all that sprawling space, a lot of it just blew away in the wind, and I realized that it was time for me to make music conceived from the outset to be heard out of doors.

The result was *Inuksuit* (2008) for nine to ninety-nine percussionists, which was inspired by the stone sentinels constructed over the centuries by the Inuit in the windswept expanses of the Arctic.

Inuksuit is a concert-length work in which the performers are widely dispersed and move throughout a large outdoor area. The listeners, too, may move around freely and discover their own individual listening points. Every performance of *Inuksuit* is unique, in response to the topology, vegetation and acoustics of the performance site. This is music as a kind of echolocation or GPS, a vehicle for reminding us where we are, and how we fit in with the never-ending music of the world around us—in the hope of transforming seemingly empty space into more deeply experienced *place*.

Composing *Inuksuit* in my cabin studio in Alaska with the image of those solitary stone figures standing on the tundra, I imagined each performing musician and each individual listener as a solitary figure in a vast enveloping landscape. I thought this was a piece about solitude. It was only when I heard the first performances of *Inuksuit* that I realized that this is a piece about community. Although the experience of each solitary listener is unique, out of the experience of shared solitude an extraordinary sense of community emerges.

In a relatively brief time *Inuksuit* has taken on a robust life of its own, independent of the composer. From the Canadian Rockies to New York City, from Europe to Australia, from Hong Kong to Valparaiso, people around the world have utilized *Inuksuit* to celebrate their own communities and their unique places on the planet. One of the most extraordinary performances was given by musicians on both sides of border between Tijuana, Mexico and San Diego in the United States. For an hour or so, as the music sounded, the looming wall that divides the two countries seemed to disappear. Before the performance began, the percussionist and conductor Steven Schick looked through the wire mesh of the wall and said to his fellow musicians on the other side: "Con la música nunca se puede dividirnos." ("With music, we can never be divided.")

Following *Inuksuit,* I've gone on to compose the choral/orchestral work *Sila: The Breath of the World* (2013), and *Across the Distance* (2015)—an outdoor work for a large ensemble of horns. I've also returned to my original point of departure with *Ten Thousand Birds* (2014) for performance outdoors in locations where the same species of birds included in the score are present on the performance site.

The Wind Garden (2017) is my first work employing electronic sounds to sound outdoor space. This is a musical composition in the form of a landscape. Composed with and within a eucalyptus grove on the campus of the University of California San Diego. Creating *The Wind Garden* involved not only composing the sounds, but also designing the landscape.

Hidden in the trees are thirty-two small loudspeakers. Attached to the highest branches are thirty-two accelerometers that measure the movements of the trees in the wind. As the velocity of the wind increases, the amplitude of the sounds grows louder. And as the velocity of the wind diminishes, their amplitude grows softer. Occasionally, when there is no wind in a particular tree, the sounds from that tree fall silent.

In midday the sounds in the grove are high and bright. At night they are lower and darker. On overcast days all the sounds are more subdued. And the sounds of summer are generally brighter than the sounds of winter. Throughout the day and throughout the year, at every moment the sounds in the grove seem to rise and fall with the wind.

The artist Robert Smithson is perhaps best known for his earthwork *Spiral Jetty,* which curls gently out into the Great Salt Lake. In his brief, explosively creative life, Smithson made works both on the land and in art galleries. The outdoor works he called "sites", and the indoor works he called "non-sites".

In Smithson's lexicon, non-sites are fragments of land, removed from the places from which they came. In a non-site, we feel the absence of the original place, and our own remove from it. Sites, by contrast, are authentic places. In a site, we feel ourselves present in a place in which (to paraphrase Pascal) the center is everywhere, and the circumference is nowhere.

Today, in this time when we humans have become a dominant geological force, we are creating for ourselves a world in which there are fewer and fewer sites, and more and more non-sites. We seek refuge in the comfort of partitions—in the rectilinear geometry of our houses and buildings, and by carving up the landscape into ever-diminishing rectangles and squares.

We know this cannot continue. There are simply too many of us to live so heavily on the earth. But what can we do? How do we get from where we are to where we need to be?

This is a perilous moment in the history of our species. If we don't know where we are, we don't know who we are or where we are going. Lost and wandering on the edge of our own extinction, perhaps we need new maps to help us find our way—to rediscover and re-consecrate our sites, to reclaim and re-inhabit our non-sites.

As present-day geographers have observed, maps are not objective representations. They are propositions. Historically, maps evolved in conjunction with the rise of nation states. Maps are tools that we use to diminish and control the land and its inhabitants, both human and other-than-human. Throughout history, people have used maps to prosecute wars against one another and against the earth.

But maps can also help us understand more deeply the places we inhabit. And if we better understand where we are, we may better understand who we are, and how best to live.

In the Name of the Earth (2018), a large-scale work for massed human voices, is my musical map of North America—a refutation and a counterproposal to the official maps of state highway departments and the corporate worldview of Google, a celebration of this beautiful continent where the only real borders are watersheds and coastlines.

As in *Earth and the Great Weather* many years ago, my texts for *In the Name* are litanies of names—the names of mountain peaks and ranges, rivers and glaciers, forests and plains and deserts—in English and Spanish, and the older indigenous names that reverberate like words spoken by the earth itself.

By singing these names, I hope to draw music not only from my own imagination, but also from the older, deeper music of this continent.

Katadhin, Agiocochook, Yuhaihaskun, Absaroka, Uncompaghre, Culebra.

Citlatépetl, Tajumuleo, Usumacinta, Popocatépetl, Nevado, Sonora.

Tahoma, Klickitat, Wy'east, Shasta, Mojave, Toomanguya.

Iliamna, Tsalxhaan, ShaaTlein, Ahtna, Dinadhi, Igikpak, Kuukpak...

The resonance of these names invokes the presence and the memory of the people who have inhabited this continent since long before the arrival of Europeans. In the poetry of these names I listen for spirits that are still present on the land, and echoes of how it was before the rise of nation states. But there is no turning back. And my real work is to give voice to a vision of how our world might be after their fall.

As I write now (in early 2019), I'm immersed in composing *Crossing Open Ground*—a new outdoor work for woodwinds, brass and percussion. I've borrowed the title from a book by my friend Barry Lopez. As Lopez observes: "*Each place on Earth goes deep. Some vestige of the old, now seemingly eclipsed place is always there to be had.*"

In this spirit, *Crossing Open Ground* invites us to experience the older, deeper resonances of place—wherever we may be—and to practice walking as a form of resistance and hope. From the freedom marchers of the civil rights movement to the refugees from Central America currently seeking asylum in the United States, walking is an expression of devotion and an assertion of freedom—a transgression of the borders we construct to separate ourselves from one another, and from our true nature as thinking animals and citizens of the earth.

In this time when we humans have become a geologic force, most of us live in increasingly homogenous environments, and in the amorphous non-places of "cyberspace". Searching for real experiences in real places, we travel to far-flung destinations, where we make photographs of ourselves to prove that we were there. But it's increasingly rare that we are fully present *anywhere*, and the knowledge that we truly belong to a place eludes many of us. Growing from my own deep desire to feel at home in the world, *Crossing Open Ground* is a ceremony of rediscovery, re-consecration and re-inhabitation of place—wherever we may be.

While *Inuksuit* and my previous outdoor works all utilize timelines, *Crossing Open Ground* does not. The notation for this music is arrayed in a series of twenty-seven "stations", showing not *when*, but rather *where* the notes are played. The exact moments at which the sounds occur are determined the breath of each musician, and by the topography of the site.

Composing this music requires me to think more deeply about the orchestration of space.

And a performance will last as long as it takes all the musicians to move from one side of the space to the other.

For more than four decades now I've explored these and other manifestations of musical space and place. My journey continues, and I hope to continue composing music specifically for outdoor performance for years to come. But what is this obsession all about?

Each musician follows her or his own individual path from station to station—playing, walking, playing again, and walking on...

As an artist, I see myself as a worker for a culture I will never live to inhabit, in a society that may never come to be. And I know that I'm not alone. All over the world there are artists and scientists, teachers and activists, people in every field of labor who, each in their own way, are working in the belief that the only possible future for our human species is to discover a new way of being on this earth. Together and alone, we are doing our best to imagine and to create new cultures and new societies to come after the inevitable collapse of the global monoculture that is driving us toward oblivion. We are working as if our survival depended on it because, very likely, it does.

Music is my way of understanding the world, of knowing where I am and how I fit in. This isn't just an emotional, a psychological need. It's a spiritual hunger—a search for the sacred. Yet in these troubled times, in a secular society in decline, what does that mean? Just what if anything is sacred anymore?

Composers from Johann Sebastian Bach to Arvo Part have found courage and musical inspiration in their faith. So do I. Although I don't follow any established religious tradition, the practice of my art is the practice of my faith. However my faith is not in the church. It is in the earth.

For me, the earth itself is sacred. The natural world is an inexhaustible source of inspiration and music. Whether in the Arctic or the desert, most of my works have begun with some small epiphany, some moment of grace that I've experienced outdoors, in what I call "the real world".

Music for me is a form of prayer. It is a call to attention, an invitation to enter into sacred space, to be more deeply aware, to feel the presence of mysteries larger and older and deeper than I can fathom. In my work I aspire to discover new musical spaces that invite us to lose ourselves, to step out of time as we usually experience it.

In *Parsifal,* Gurnemanz sings: "...here time becomes space." Or as Samuel Beckett puts it: "Time has turned into Space and there will be no more Time."

The book of *Revelation* is filled with apocalyptic visions of the end of time. But even as human society seems to be rushing headlong toward oblivion, I hold no dreams of escaping via messiahs or spaceships. My deepest longing is to be fully present in the fullness of the present moment in *this* world, here on this beautiful stone spinning in space that is the only home I will ever know.

I find something like a credo in the words of the poet Pedro Salinas: *Earth. Nothing more.*
Earth. Nothing less.
And let that be enough for you.

CHAPTER
3

ONE APPROACH TO IMPROVISATION (OR) POSSIBLE PERCEIVED DNA OF ALL MUSIC

Words About Sound that Hopefully Inspire Thoughts to Create Sound

JIM BLACK

The year 2020 marks a 30-year anniversary for myself recording, touring, and performing improvisation-based music across the planet. It also marks 30 years of attempting to teach, speak about, or more aptly "share" music with other musicians around the world in the form of private lessons, single-day to week-long workshops, and academic classroom courses in the university setting. For the last 15 years I've found that teaching or "sharing" music with others has been the most effective fuel for myself to power on into the next decade's worth of touring, composing, and improvising. Having to coalesce and clarify my thoughts and ideas to coherently hand them off to other artists in a practical and useable manner has been the ultimate challenge for myself as an eternal student and continually developing artist in this field.

Challenges

I participated in an incredibly missed summer music meeting/workshop in Salzburg, Austria from 2004–2009—the Jazz and Improvised Music School, led by the generous human being Peter Herbert. What struck me as remarkable was the radical age range of the attendees and their wildly different experience levels, let alone instrumentation—not your average jazz camp.

So imagine your ensemble for the week features two 17-year-old drummers (one that has only played "free" and the other only knows how to "rock"), a 15-year-old bluegrass mandolin virtuoso, a 30-year-old classical cellist that has never played in time without a conductor, a 16-year-old punk rock guitarist, a 19-year-old vocalist that has only sung jazz standards, and a 63-year-old retired dentist who now wants to be Stan Getz on baritone sax…and this ensemble has to perform a concert together in four days.

Around the same time, I had been playing around in a software program attempting to get my computer to improvise and generate some listenable music. Eventually I came to realize that I would have to program it, or teach it *what* music was essentially, one idea at a time. Perhaps an answer for my ensemble dilemma could be discovered here.

I began asking very simple questions regarding the nature of improvisation, not about the emotions, inspirations, or motives but what are the exact building blocks of improvisation? This led to much larger and all-encompassing ideas: What are the common threads or connections found in all music? Which elements of music do all types of music have in common? Could you construct a DNA map of what makes up musical improvisation? What are the perceivable conditions for music?

Immediately I lost interest in getting the laptop to improvise, instead I turned the experiment on myself while considering the needs of my students: How does one improvise? How does one compose? How do we *hear* music?

I needed to find a concept, method, or a guide that was easy to teach, easy to memorize, fast to implement, and that would inspire and not bury the musical personalities of the people I was working with to help them improvise. Years were spent test driving these ideas on my students around the world, my helpful unknowing guinea pigs...so what follows is part of what I put together for my students, and one that I use as well if my spirit goes blank, my inspiration runs dry, and I need to restart the creative flow in my brain.

Disclaimer: if the following sounds too didactic, simple, or cerebral then excellent, it's supposed to; it's designed to produce immediate results, for all levels of experience and ages.

It's easy enough to memorize, remember, recall and utilize spontaneously.

AND... is obviously just one person's opinion about how all "this" *might* work.

The following chart is written from the perspective of the improviser, or more accurately "spontaneous composer..."

or ultimately and unavoidable by nature, "composer."

One Approach to Improvisation (or) Possible Perceived DNA of All Music

Listening outward... and inward...

Mood, Vibe, Atmosphere, Intention the "why?" and "what?"—your story—the creative spark

Silence and the use of space—the photographic negative of sound—the "contrast" of audio.

THE 5 COMMON ELEMENTS OF MUSIC

FORM
The **shape** from when the music begins to the end—visual and **graphic**—the journey for the listener... the idea of **transition**

After silence...
sound on/off—for how long?
Shape/envelope of sound—ADSR
The idea of sonic **translation**

SOUND
Tone, **color**, timbre—character of sound
Your sonic fingerprint—**touch**

RHYTHM
Consistent/clocklike ranging to **Inconsistent**/rubato/random/different rates of **flow**

MELODY
The single **line** or idea

HARMONY
More than one sound/tone/voice/counterpoint/**sound on sound**/layering

To these 5 common **elements** we can apply, **create**, invent, **imagine**, interpret, layer, modify, and **translate** with these **ideas** →

OTHER IDEAS
↓

Soulfulness
Styles
Surprise
Extremes
Subtleties
Anger
Bliss
Mystery
Irony
Fantasy
Meditate
Illusion
Dream...

Sparse	↔	Dense
Tension	↔	Release
Relaxed	↔	Intense
Straight	↔	Swung
Single Layer	↔	Stacked
Clean	↔	Distorted
Muted	↔	Open
Minimal	↔	Maximal
Single Tonality	↔	Poly Tonality
Mono	↔	Stereo
Static	↔	Dynamic
Broken	↔	Whole
Question	↔	Answer
Beautiful	↔	Ugly
Happy	↔	Sad
Simple	↔	Complex
Clear	↔	Opaque
Predictable	↔	Random
Whisper	↔	Scream
Converse	↔	Preach
Insecure	↔	Confident
Calm	↔	Chaos
Emotional	↔	Disengaged

Explanation of the Chart

Three considerations before sound, before improvisation begins:

Listening—outwardly at all times, and at the same time inwardly to ask...

What is the **Mood, Vibe,** or **Atmosphere** of what I want to create?

What is my **Intention**, or **Idea**?

What do I want to say? Do I have a **story** to tell?

The idea of **Silence**—or perceived silence, negative space, absence of sound....at all times to be considered and respected equally as any other sonic idea.

Improv begins:

Form—starts being written when we say the music begins/ends.

Sound on/sound off—What is the **timbral** quality of the sound you want to make?

What is the **shape** of the sound you want to make?

What is its envelope? What kind of attack? Does it decay and/or sustain?

Length of the sound? How does the sound release?

More than one sound or idea creates some sort of **Rhythm**, ranging from absolutely consistent to extremely random.

More than one change of timbre, frequency, pitch will suggest a type of **Melody**.

More than one sound at a time will suggest a type of **Harmony.**

(Arguably a single tone can be described as harmonic, etc., but for all practical and functional purposes the idea of **sound on sound** and its implications is what I am concerned with here: chords, polyphony, **counterpoint**, solo vs. accompaniment, any ideas layered upon a type of drone or harmonic pad, ad infinitum.)

One can then transform these **five elements** in the left-hand column of the chart using the full spectrum of one or more of the **ideas** suggested here in the right-hand column; obviously these are just a few of the infinite number of ideas one could imagine.

Any and every kind of music could be plugged into this chart and you could then analyze the various parameters and measure the amount or weight given to each element and idea, etc. to give a descriptive picture of the music.

Strong Thoughts: A Partial Walkthrough of the Chart

I love **listening** to sound. This analysis of music presented here is based *solely* upon what the ears hear and how we can apply a modicum of critical thought to help understand and find common relationships within sound to perceive/construct any type of music. What I find so unifying about this paradigm is that it transcends location, culture, race, gender, and class distinction. It forces us to jettison our stereotypes of who or what created the music... until we see or get to find out *exactly* who or what created it, which implies we are not only concerned with sound anymore; sound loses its innocence at this point and music becomes something beyond the ears.

Blindfold tests are hysterical. Most people can't listen to more than 10 seconds of music before they demand to know who it is; we can't completely judge it, categorize it—we immediately grasp to make social sense of it. We are almost truly lost in sound in those moments, and music for a brief moment renders the listener disoriented and almost weightless.

There is no mention of "what" to play on the chart. It's the improviser's job to provide all ideas, content, attitude, and soul to the music. This is where the creators' cultures, experiences, and **stories** are all important. The improviser's **taste** is what ultimately defines what we hear, and how the listeners will receive it based upon their tastes.

That's why "free" music is such a misnomer. There is no free... you have to make decisions and take responsibility for every **sound** and **space** you make in the music once it begins; owning your ideas even if they are thoughtless or random—you still take responsibility for creating them. There is only the sense of "free"... free "to do" what you like or hear, most definitely.

As an educator I will never tell a student *what* to play, that's not my job. I can only advise them on how to play what they want more effectively, or at least try to. If every person is a unique human being, which implies everybody has their own unique sound, ideas, and music waiting to hatch from inside themselves, then the teacher or advisor has to be careful at times not to crush the students potential and personal musical soul from emerging; because most likely the teacher will not recognize this new sound or attitude, as it is something *new*, they will tend to see it as something "wrong" perhaps or "not applicable here." I know plenty of stories of educators labeling students' works as "bullsh%t" simply because it doesn't conform to their expectations. The teachers should note these students actually have gigs, work, and a following, where the audience certainly doesn't think the same way.

Notice that there is not a single mention of a **style** or idiom in this way of thinking.

It describes only perceptions of sound, but not style or taste or soul.

Sound doesn't care about style.... that's *our* created blessing and/or curse.

Using this chart analysis, a clear **graphic** picture will emerge when you measure the amounts and relationships of the five **elements** of music by the spectrum of the **ideas** applied to them. One can create a type of pictorial map of any song, composition or piece of music and *see* how it could be analyzed and interpreted, then utilized in a myriad of creative improvisational/compositional manners.

To give an example: If you analyze the band Meshuggah through this lens, you will quickly notice that vocalist Jens Kidman's almost inhuman screaming makes minimalist **melodies** that are highly syncopated and rhythmic, with very limited pitch variation in the traditional sense but focusing more on timbral variations in color/frequency, and delivers an incredibly powerful energy, aura, emotion and attitude to the band's sound. Very simply a *different* kind of melody.

(One could then ask: How many different types of melodies do I have in my musical vocabulary?)

The average audience member only walks away with a few things from a concert: The atmosphere, mood, or vibe of the music, and also "what happened" during the song, piece, set, or evening. This would imply that "your **story**" and what happens with **form** are the most important things to focus on first when improvising. What am I trying to say here? What kind of journey are you taking the listener on? Where did this music start and where does this music go to? The audience doesn't necessarily understand the minutia of all the intellectual musical content but it definitely emotionally recognizes what the music does, where it travels, where it goes, how it does/doesn't develop, and where it arrives and ends…and most importantly **how it makes them feel**. So, embedded in the element of form, the improviser always must be aware of this power of **transition** in their musical journey from beginning to end, idea to idea, section to section, and/or song to song. No different than piloting a boat, the improviser knows where the improvisation came from, is always aware while playing as to what the improvisation is doing and the direction it is going, and eventually steers the music to a destination whether or not it's previously decided upon.

Silence defines every idea we play; silence is your closest and most un-acknowledged and under-utilized constant companion. Silence is the most extreme example of a contrast control for our sonic ideas, which would imply a range of other ideas that maybe function as "near silence," such as quiet drones, background noise, or any extremely differentiating combination of two or more sounds in dialog.

I'm noticing, as I age in a world that becomes faster and even more dense with instrumental virtuosity, that my drumming/composing heroes like Paul Motian are more aptly defined by what they *didn't* play… and where they left space in their music for the listener to reflect or ask questions. Take for example improvisers like trumpeter Wadada Leo Smith, whose solo concerts contain almost equal parts sound and silence. I heard him say on stage after he played a solo concert recently that the spaces in his music come directly from Thelonious Monk's influence: "I never met him in person, but Monk is my mentor."

I tend to pay too much attention to creating sound instead of **creating silence** when I improvise…let alone compose. I would like to better this average before my body decides to decompose back to trace minerals and organic residue.

Sound on/sound off is such a crucial yet often overlooked action/idea. Young musicians are taught complete musical sentences within days of starting to improvise without the awareness that each word is a potential world unto itself. Try to get a drummer to play one single sound and then make them leave space to "taste" what just happened. Do they realize almost every sound the drum set inherently makes is a waveform in the shape of a literal explosion followed by some sort of fast decay? One would have to have complete awareness of musical envelopes, i.e. **ADSR** (attack, decay, sustain, release) to shape just one sound in a different way. To play a drum or cymbal in the way Billie Holiday would sing, sustain, and swell a long note takes some serious figuring out. This process is what I like to refer to as the idea of **translation**, implying that every musical idea *could* be superimposed or played on every instrument by any and all means possible, which takes great thought and work if one would like to have that kind of freedom of musical expression. Thinking out of the box and "extended" instrumental techniques go hand in hand here, which could include the implication and/or gesture of an idea to get the musical point across.

Short of writing a music book on describing every element, parameter, and idea mentioned on the chart, I will move on to what I share with my ensembles to help us make music together.

Two Powerful Lessons

It seems inescapable, but all my heroes seem to do just this:

Play what you hear. Hear what you play.
Play what you sing. Sing what you play.

On tour with Steve Coleman in Fall 2011, a student asked in a workshop at Cal Arts what was Steve's "point" when playing, or is he thinking about something while playing. Steve replied "the only thing I do, or try to do, is play exactly what I hear *the first time*....the first time, not the second time." (That same workshop Steve also told us his sense of rhythm used to be terrible when he started playing music and that he had to *work* hard for it.)

On tour with David Liebman in 2014, I asked what was the main takeaway from his book

A Chromatic Approach to Jazz Harmony and Melody. He asked me "Do you want the short or the long story?" As we were on an airplane tarmac on a bus I opted for the short one. "Basically all music is... and I mean **all** music... is... *some* sort of color... in *some* sort of rhythm..." As stupidly clear as it sounds, I have a hard time arguing that one. Sounds like making music *could* be pretty easy in that case.

With these ideas in mind, let's focus on the almost invariably most awkward moment of starting an improvisation (spontaneous composition) with a group—which typically begins with the longest amount silence measured that day with a default improvisation starting at a volume that sounds more shy than quiet.

One exercise: **Imagine** a dynamic and an intensity first, and **then play** any singular sound or idea with that character in mind...followed by another idea... the musical ball is now confidently rolling across the room for anyone else to pick-up, or ignore. Game on.

In Practice

Make exercises that explore one (or more) of the common five elements on the left side of the chart and apply one (or many) of the ideas from the right-hand column to these elements.

Examples:

> Improvise very loud rhythmic ideas using more silence than sound for 2 minutes.
>
> Improvise very quiet sonic/non-pitched ideas with a slow rhythmic flow for 3 minutes.
>
> Improvise over the shape of a form where the music starts immediately very dense, harmonically complex yet quiet, and evolves over 4 minutes to something very loud, clear, and tonal.
>
> You can perform (or practice) these solo or in a group situation. Take a moment to stop in between and reflect on what happened. Was that what I wanted to have happen? Could I execute the ideas more effectively? Did I like it... did it resonate with me? Did that improvisation unearth some other creative feelings or energies inside to explore?
>
> This is obviously limitless in terms of what one could design to improvise with.
>
> Since composition *could* be viewed as a slowed down version of improvisation, you now have potentially limitless compositional ideas available at your creative disposal.

As in the examples above, each member of the ensemble sketches out two to three improvisational scenarios for the band on paper, if only by just using words and descriptions. Subsequently gather all the scenarios together to create a long form band composition that can be immediately worked on and rehearsed for a performance, the group deciding how and what kind of transitions to make between each idea or section. If you need literal pitch, harmonic, and/or rhythmic information it can easily be sketched out on a few scraps of music paper, or infinitely better yet, the person who has the idea teaches it to the ensemble by ear via singing or playing it to the group, which demands concentration and builds invaluable ear training and memorization skills.

Everybody is now embedding the music by learning every part, they get to practice making musical transitions from idea to idea, and they get to experience long form memory and awareness of the whole composition. The musical ideas reflect each members' own vernacular and taste while having to adjust each of their vocabularies throughout the piece to accommodate and realize everybody's ideas.

These almost instant group compositions, practiced over a few days start to sound like a band... one can literally hear the students' musical minds "open."

Some Final Thoughts

Concentration and focus on the music and direction of it while playing is key. Other people's judgments on your music or your own self-loathing/insecurities/stage fright will cease to be a problem in that moment if you focus **all** of your attention and energies on the music.

Practice *playing*. I never liked to practice when I was younger and realize now it was because I was practicing *things* but not practicing the act of making music, as described in the chart.

The space between the two extremes (or poles) of an **idea** is where the "new" generally lies, an expanding black hole of hybrid musical ideas and energies that borrow varying amounts from both sides of an idea's spectrum. This is where most of the improviser's identity can be extracted from as well, and how our unique individuality can be defined and described sonically. Perhaps gone are the days of radical new musical paradigms, the last hundred years of recorded music document well the polar extremes from minimalism to maximalism. In these times the "new" tends to be more subtle, maybe less shocking, yet strong and distinctive.

Imagination versus creativity. It's easy to be **creative** when all the objects (i.e. the twelve tones of equal tempered melody, harmony, and common rhythms) are laid before you to play with—the jazz musician's specialty. It's infinitely harder to design your own unique objects to build new structures with, hence the need of **imagination**, and spending time to cultivate it.

Critical thinking is healthy for you, like eating well and exercise. In this insanely rapid existence, you literally need to make time to think deeper about things with an open creative approach, to let your instincts wander around creatively. You would need time and a safe space to explore critical *feeling* as well for that matter, taking the time to gaze into your own soul to ponder, or exercise your empathy skills.... maybe fish out what's in there and see if there's some artistic use for it.

Also worth mentioning, for anyone who says "hey man, let's not talk about it and just play, it will ruin the music..." or if thinking about music scares you, or robs the magic of it for you, please remember that talking about or thinking about music is **not** making music. It's thinking and talking about music. Studying and analyzing music is completely different from the act of actually playing music. Learning to think and talk about music can only make one a more conscientious listener and improviser.

Usage for the young and the new improvisers: This chart is one critical and clear way to think about, explore, and discover finding your sound/voice/approach in this cosmos of music. Enjoy discovering other approaches. Invent as many of your own as well. Never let others tell you "no" when it comes to creativity.

Usage for the older and the experienced improvisers: Refresh your thought patterns, reboot your creative system simply by standing outside yourself and asking the question "Is this still what I want?" If you get bored with your own traditions, habits, or run out of things to practice, look for new music inside yourself by breaking it down element by element, idea by idea.

As you get older you run the risk of becoming a cliché of yourself...going for the easy and well known/tried and true/successful or virtuosically played music....you run the risk of becoming stale, predictable, not interesting...tiresome. If this starts to ring true for oneself then simply go back to the beginning and re-examine some other ways to manipulate those five elements of music you might have overlooked, or perhaps found uninteresting in the past that would have an incredible rejuvenating effect on your improvisation/composition in the now.

After all, we are eternal students of music. This chart was a way for me to summarize some of what I have learned about improvising so far in my life's journey as a musician, and hopefully it can provide some regenerative fuel and inspiration to continue asking questions to help create more music for as long as we can. Thank you for your time and **curiosity** to read these words.

I would like to thank the writings of J. Krishnamurti and his wisdom to ask the big questions, John Zorn for writing/composing the game piece *Cobra* which inspired this way of thinking, and my band AlasNoAxis: Chris Speed, Hilmar Jensson, and Skúli Sverrisson for 20 years of conversations and every opportunity to have heard these gentleman speak about and perform music. Special thanks to Josephine Nagorsnik and Elias Stemeseder for critical dialog and proofreading.

I would like to dedicate this article to Páll Ivan Pálsson, a young Icelandic artist who wrote a colorful book entitled *Music—Thought Instigator—Volume One* which simply asks questions about music, which inspired my own journey to *attempt* to answer some of them...

CHAPTER
4

SHORT TIME, LONG TIME, SHORT TIME, LONG TIME

MARTIN BRESNICK

During a recent composition seminar Anteo Fabris, an engaged and imaginative student played a recording of his latest composition. He told us the work was influenced by a musical genre called *Vaporwave*. Since I knew nothing about *Vaporwave*, I asked him to email me an example. He sent this link *https://vektroid.bandcamp.com/track/420* and also added a comment: *Macintosh Plus (Early Vaporwave, c. 2011)—A* ***seminal work.***

I was struck by my student's close attention to the historical development of *Vaporwave*. After listening attentively to the recording he sent, I was both cheeky and superficial when I responded:

Ah, early Vaporwave! Those were the golden days...geez, what happened?

Clearly all phenomena, including musical styles such as *Vaporwave*, have a temporal history, whether ephemeral, glacial or somewhere in between. How might a creative listener or composer respond thoughtfully to things that change from moment-to-moment as well as very slow almost static transformations? Might there be a way to understand and integrate multiple temporal transformations that would permit both detached observation as well as creative participation?

Since we are all thrust willy-nilly into our historical moment and cannot choose the constraints, possibilities or objective correlatives in which we find ourselves, I wonder if someone with my essentially materialist, empirical standpoint might be able to usefully engage with such an unceasingly transforming musical environment?

By studying the insights of the French historian Fernand Braudel I have tried to find a place for myself where, as a composer and musician, I can listen, learn and act creatively.

Braudel's most important book, *The Mediterranean* (1949), is an attempt to understand that great sea and surrounding region in a temporally expansive way. Braudel considered the Mediterranean as a vast geographic, economic and cultural entity he wished to track across an immense span of time he called the *longue durée*.

Braudel's approach did not focus, as had often previously been the case, only on the relatively rapid chain of conquests and wars, or the succession of rulers or "great men" whose careers were considered to be the most significant, decisive events in the history of the Mediterranean. Rather, Braudel stressed the interactions of the people living around the Mediterranean sea with the region's often barely perceptible geological and environmental transformations beginning around the time of the Bronze Age.

Braudel's historical approach, which came to be called the *Annales School*, emphasizes how the profound continuities of the *longue durée* or "long time" affects human activity, as contrasted with the "short time", the *histoire événementielle* ("event history") or ephemeral time he considered to be the domain of the chronicler and the journalist.

Braudel thought historical time could be conceived of as a polyphonic fabric of different temporal velocities—from the rapidly changing time we experience in our daily lives to the glacial, barely perceptual transformations of geology, evolution, and the environment in general. One example might be the magnitude of change in yesterdays' weather in New York City in comparison with the change in the overall climate of North America over the past 10,000 years.

I began by imagining what the constituents of the long time (*longue durée*) of music might be. Here, I think, are two of them:

1. The capacity to hear, or what is meant by ear to brain coordination and functionality.

2. The acoustical parameters of any terrestrial sound (frequency, amplitude, duration, spatial-temporal location).

These essential features change at a glacial, evolutionary rate in comparison with any human life span. Millennia passed before the ear evolved from its earliest appearance as a spatial orientation device in early vertebrate animals to the ear in its current human form. This very slow development of the capacity to hear has likewise been affected by ongoing changes in terrestrial sounds and with the usefulness of the perception of those sounds for human survival.

There were likely immense periods of evolutionary time with almost no change at all followed by sudden significant transformations. The biologist Steven J. Gould usefully described this pattern of change as punctuated equilibrium.

The *longue durée* of music may be understood as the long history of human fascination with the manipulation of the basic acoustical parameters of sound for a variety of expressive ends. Attending to those parametric sonic changes over time will expose the simple sonic architecture of any music. Even wholly unfamiliar music, music that is remote to us in time (history) or space (geography), reveals audible traces of the alteration and refinement of those four indispensable parameters by musicians.

In the Olympian detachment of the *long durée,* that birds-eye view of a vast temporal landscape, I achieve, at times, a momentary, calming perspective of barely changing sonic continuities. Music has been, and will, in whatever new forms it takes, continue to be based on the inescapable acoustics of sound and the very slowly evolving capacities of the human ear.

Of course this view takes no notice of the varying polyphonic temporal changes of genres and styles we ordinarily understand as the history of music. In living memory many changes and alterations have occurred in concert music, jazz, folk music, popular music, non-western music, and indeed in any and every kind of music made on the planet. In my own time I have witnessed a great number of generational debates and successions of style—Stravinsky versus Schoenberg, Modernism versus Minimalism, Bebop versus Free Jazz, Punk Rock versus Disco, and apparently, recently, the ascent and decline of Vaporwave.

Turning to Braudel, I consider these contemporary musical events as part of our musical *histoire événementielle,* including:

> 1. Current or relatively temporally adjacent musical languages or dialects, performances, and musical events as well as individual compositions.
>
> 2. Evaluations and criticisms of current or relatively recent musical practices.

These dynamic, short-lived phenomena might well be termed

ephemera. Like the events in the *long durée*, they grow, recede or vanish on their own in response to natural or unnatural environmental catastrophes, or due to dire interventions such as holocausts, ethnic cleansing, or other examples of malign human behavior.

In this storm I try but mostly fail to engage with music solely from the standpoint of the *longue durée*. As a composer and teacher I inevitably respond passionately to what is close at hand, to what seems to matter most now. On local, temporal ground I am buffeted and stimulated by dynamic, uncontrolled exposure to new music, new musical languages and other traditions of music making new to me. Under such direct intimate circumstances I struggle with the limitations and constraints of my personal taste and judgment in light of my stance as a political and social actor. I think of all these considerations as part of an intense effort to come to intelligible terms with new musical experiences.

In my own now, my own time and place, I often find I cannot sustain the thoughtful detachment and contemplation required by Braudel's *long durée*.

I acknowledge sadly, ruefully, Henry David Thoreau's observation in Walden that "One generation abandons the enterprises of another like stranded vessels." Still I wonder, as a composer and teacher, considering the multiple polyphonies of the passage of musical time, whether before those ephemeral, stranded vessels sink and vanish forever, might we board them for a last time to find what could be still useful there for a creative musician? Might we find evidence of significant, still vital continuities that could connect us meaningfully to our long musical past?

Unable to resolve the dilemma, I swing back and forth between the long time (*long durée*) and the short time (*histoire événementielle)* of music. I find consolation and encouragement when Thoreau, as a farmer of his own very ephemeral bean rows near Walden Pond tells us:

> "The same sun which ripens my beans illumines at once a system of earths like ours. If I had remembered this it would have prevented some mistakes. This was not the light in which I hoed them. The stars are the apexes of what wonderful triangles!"

—November 2019

CHAPTER

5

HOW NINO ROTA SAVED ME FROM A SUBTERRANEAN FREAKOUT

CARTER BURWELL

There is no widely accepted explanation for the ubiquity of music throughout human culture. Anywhere you look, thousands of years of effort have gone into carving flutes, stretching skins, memorizing tunes and rhythms. To what end?

It's not that there is a shortage of explanations—that music cements social bonds, organizes neural development, etc.—It's just that none of them seem sufficient to explain why we've inherited genes that make us want to drum instead of collect more food.

In the 1980s I was on tour with David Hykes and the Harmonic Choir, and we had an afternoon in Paris with nothing to do. Two of us chose to visit the Catacombs of Paris, an 18th century ossuary deep below the street, filled with the skeletons of millions of people arranged in elaborate geometric patterns.

In our casual choice of the catacombs we'd done no research at all and probably imagined an elevator taking us to a vast underground tunnel, the kind used for the final chase scene in *The Third Man*. After waiting an hour for a long queue of people to make their way in, we instead found it to be a stone shaft and stairway of more than a hundred steps, just wide enough for one person, taking us 60 feet below street level.

As I descended this narrow staircase the muscles in the back of my legs started to tighten up in a way I could not control. With a long line of people in front and back of me, and no room for them to walk around me or me around them, it was impossible to stop and try to understand why my legs were starting to shake and my breath was quick and shallow. It was all I could do to keep myself from trampling the scores of people behind me. But neither could I imagine continuing through the two kilometer tunnel at the horribly relaxed pace of the crowd in front of me.

When we reached the bottom of the stairs, I told my friend Alan what I was feeling—that I could barely breath or stop my legs from running. I was apparently having the first claustrophobic panic of my life, at the age of 30 in a crypt below Paris. Fortunately, Alan, who had bipolar disorder, was very comfortable with uncontrolled anxiety. He looked at me with clear eyes and said "Well, what should we do?" This shifted my mind into problem-solving mode. Did I have anything with me that could help? Well, I had a Sony Walkman tape recorder, as I often did back then. The cassette in the tape machine held Nino Rota's music to Fellini's films—*La Strada*, *La Dolce Vita*, *8½*.

I put on my headphones, hit Play, and my state immediately changed. I was able to put one foot in front of the other in a way that resembled walking. I was able to stop worrying about breathing and simply breath. While it was no pleasure spending an hour in a subterranean tunnel, it was survivable. I didn't soil myself. I didn't trample anyone. I left the NATO alliance intact.

While in the catacombs I was too focused on survival to reflect on my experience, but I've often thought about it in the years since as an example of music serving a function much greater than entertainment. It helped me maintain my sanity, my relationship with the world around me, at a time when that world was not only foreign but terrifying.

How did music do that? And can anything about my experience be generalized to suggest music's evolutionary value?

Nino Rota's music of course took me into the world of Fellini's films, and by doing that took me out of the catacombs. When I score a film, I try to create music that is specific and unique to the world of that film, and a side-effect of this is that the music by itself can conjure up that world. That's certainly something we use music for—to transport us to other times and places and flood us with feelings from those times and places, even imaginary ones.

Also, any recording contains a virtual world of performers and spaces that inevitably cause our physical reality to slip a bit. This is quite pronounced with headphones and other immersive media. While listening to Nino Rota, part of me was in an Italian studio with an ensemble of musicians, their fingers moving bows, their lips squeezing reeds, the sound bouncing off walls and ceilings that didn't exist in my physical reality—which thus became a little less real.

But of course, Nino Rota and these particular recordings are quite specific and I can't help but feel that there is some more general explanation of how music helped me when I needed it. Something fundamental that's present in Bach chorales, Javanese gamelan, and a child humming to herself.

So I've stepped back and looked at what defines a sound as music. A fundamental aspect is the repetition of patterns. As they repeat, musical patterns organize time into units, what musicians and poets call meter. These repeated forms create anticipation of the next beat or bar, and the momentary satisfaction of its return. This is a simplification obviously, but this quality of patterns repeating—beats, bars, sequences, motifs—is one of music's defining features.

When I'm a bit anxious I've noticed myself unconsciously humming or whistling, and when I examine this activity it seems there's a reassurance in the returning melody. If I instead whistle a free, non-repeating melody, it has the opposite effect. My aesthetic preference is for music that's less predictable, less reassuring, that has higher entropy in information theory terms, but regardless of one's taste in musical form it all plays on our evolutionary need to know what's coming in the next moment.

By organizing time into patterns, music gives continuity to moments of discontinuity—such as when one walks off the scenic streets of Paris into a nightmare. It gives us reason to believe the next moment will relate to the previous one, and this connection between the past and the future makes us feel grounded in the present. I would suggest that this has evolutionary value, a value made clear to me when I was freaking out in a mega-tomb one day in Paris.

CHAPTER
6

PLACES IN MY MUSIC/ MY MUSIC IN PLACES

ANN CLEARE

The Irish writer John McGahern once wrote that "Ireland is a peculiar society in the sense that it was a 19th century society up to about 1970 and then it almost by-passed the 20th century".[1] Modernism is a peculiar topic in Ireland, and, as a young artist based in the country, I can attest that it mostly feels like it never reached these shores or emerged in a fully palpable form within the country. The majority of the Irish population seem either oblivious to this, indifferent, or relieved by its non-appearance. Beckett, Carrington, Joyce, Wilde, (this list of Irish writers could go on and on...), contributed greatly to modern literature, but on a world stage, outside of Ireland, as their work was not supported in their home country, and they perhaps also felt they could only create what they needed to create away from the conservatism of Irish Church and State. One thinks of James Joyce and how each of his works is based in Dublin, yet mainly written in exile from his home; however, within his work, he lived in Dublin, his imagination firmly rooted in the daily rituals of where is was born and raised. Known for centuries as the land of Saints and Scholars, it has taken, and continues to take, time to unravel Ireland from its political, religious, and cultural colonisers and to imagine what a modern Ireland can or should be.

1. John McGahern, *The Whole World in a Community*, Interview with Robert McCrum in the *The Guardian* newspaper, January 2002.

Why does this interest me? Well, I suppose, because I am, and always have been, intrigued by where I come from, and I know that, whether I want it to or not, it has and will continue to inform the work I make, and so it feels like something that I should attempt to understand. And I don't come from anywhere as happening (if you could call it that) as the Dublin city of Joyce's *Ulysses* or as alluring as W.B. Yeats *Wild Swans at Coole* or as troubling as Northern Ireland's political past in Marie Bennett's installation works. I come from the Midlands of Ireland, from county Offaly, which lies at the very centre of the country (see Fig. 1). Many consider the Midlands of Ireland as similar to the middle of North America: dull, flat passage between livelier, coastal parts of the country. The Midlands have always existed somewhere between land and water, as the area was once a lake that covered the central plain of the country. After the Ice Age, this lake gave way to bog, and many centuries later, in the early 20th century, any remaining water was drained away by industrial peat manufacturing, which was then used to power domestic and commercial needs within Ireland and beyond. And so, for much of the 20th century, the Irish Midlands was known for having the most advanced equipment for cultivating and transporting fossil fuels (peat/turf) from its Bog Lands, which was a great source of pride to communities who were employed by this industry for many decades. It is far from the most well-known area of Ireland, not just internationally but nationally too, as many Irish people that I meet for the first time often tell me that I am the first person they have ever encountered from Offaly. This is astounding considering the relatively small size and population of Ireland. I am often presented with the question, both in Ireland and abroad, of how does someone from where I come from end up writing the "ultra-modern" music that I do? Why would you want to live there again (which, after years of living away, I now do)? As if the area couldn't be anything but a bleak and backward wilderness from which to escape.

Figure 1. Picture of Midlands, Ireland. Lough Boora Park. ©Ann Cleare

Like many of the Irish artists mentioned above, where one is from and its influence on one's work can be difficult to process until you leave that place, until you are at a physical distance from it. As a young adult, I left my Midland's home because I was thirsty for new knowledge and adventure. Instead of dreaming and imagining new cities and cultural experiences from afar, I wanted to go and live in those places, to actively engage with them. It was a good reason to leave, and a necessary one. But no matter where I have lived or studied or travelled to, two foundational structures have remained integral to my sonic work: one is the presence of a terrain and particularly one that is similar to marshland—the ground in my pieces is, to varying degrees, dense, deep, active, and porous, as if whatever musical material that is traversing it could easily be absorbed into it, and the second is a sense of the mechanical, the kinetic, a motion which traverses the surface and depths of its sonic terrain. From *Dorchadas*,[2] what I consider to be my first well-formed piece, where the trombone dives into a dark, viscous ensemble texture to *eöl*,[3] where a newly-built percussion instrument of metallic finger and hand pieces is borne from the aeolian timbre of a surrounding chamber ensemble to *anchor me to the land*,[4] where a trio of piano, percussion, and guitar tries to "ground" to wild dreaming of its surrounding chamber groups. Analysing the presence of "terrain" and "mechanical" over many years of pieces, the connection of both the mired earth and the mechanical industry of my homeland is undeniable and constant in my work—if I remove their presences from any piece, very little other content would remain. These are not habitual working metaphors or crutches that I lean on, but are integral to how I see and interpret the world through sound: as a place/object/person of rich matter that needs to be explored and understood.

2. Ann Cleare, *Dorchadas*, further details: https://anncleareccomposer.com/listen-look/dorchadas/

3. Ann Cleare, *eöl*, further details: https://anncleareccomposer.com/eol/

4. Ann Cleare, *anchor me to the land*, further details: https://anncleareccomposer.com/anchor-me-to-the-land

Metaphors of natural elements and how humans and/or technology interact with them (and vice versa) stand at the fore of my work, in the same way that they stand at the fore of where and how I grew up in the Irish countryside. As a child, I learned to play both Western Classical Music and Traditional Irish Music, and even though I enjoyed both very much, I remember thinking they were both limited systems of information and expression, like a very simple surface of a much more complex, multidimensional system. I would sit at the piano and play D4 and then a D♯4 and would think to myself that there is such a distance between these semitones, so much information missing, and the mechanisms of the instruments I was playing (piano and woodwinds) would not allow me to bridge the distance between such semitones. Playing the common intervals of a piece in A major or E minor felt, to me, like taking giant, one-dimensional steps and leaps, and I wanted to traverse the sound in between these sounds. I would listen to the sounds of natural elements around me and to the sounds of farming and industrial machinery, and hear them mostly hovering around one main tone and that there were so many gradations to this tone. Even though I didn't know of the terms at the time, they were microtonally and timbrally complex in a way that the tonal music I was playing was completely lacking. And furthermore, they possessed their own temporal and rhythmic character, and one that was not bound by periodic pulse. Looking back, I realise that I do not seem to have ever discriminated between music and noise as very different things, either on a frequential or temporal level, in the way that most people do: to me, every and all sound is a component on a huge scale of sound, which one could compose from, and none is more valuable or worthy than the next. And this thinking is representative of the work I now make: to explore places and ideas (real and imagined) through sound, to present alternative orders of sonic being, and to do this in a way that three-dimensionalises sonic material and the spaces it inhabits.

When I describe my work as above, it often surprises general audiences that I use sound to think and create in this way—that this type of direction and subject matter could be at the heart of a musical work, that the place of my music is often rooted in rural Ireland—how can sound be an expressive medium for such a topic? And what is there to express about this landscape and its happenings? And I, more often than not, feel adrift from the world of music, because when I describe myself as a composer, working in music, what I do and create is immediately misunderstood, and I can understand why—such words as music and composer are misleading for people and, I have been increasingly feeling, that they are not terms that I should be using anymore. This is why I use the word sonic because it relates more suitably to the huge scale of sound that I mention above and create for each and every piece. And so, my role is in devising this scale and composing from it, and this process often feels both scientific and sculptural in nature—measuring a sound's frequency and volume and finding new harmonic and inharmonic relationships between different points on the sonic scale. It is composerly, in the same way someone composing within a tonal system works with consonance and dissonance, but somehow, I feel this word of composer belongs only to a Western tonal tradition. Perhaps what also creates detachment from these terms are the places within the work and how and where the work is presented in concert venues? Given that I think in such visual terms, for work that isn't always visual in its presentation, how do I create an evocative sense of place in art that is sonically driven? One future project that presents and will extend this challenge, in a variety of manners, is related to my home terrain and particularly to Lough Boora Sculpture Park.[5]

5. Lough Boora Sculpture Park: https://www.loughboora.com/sculpture/

Lough Boora is central to the history of the Midlands that I describe above. Over centuries it has transformed from lake to raised bogs to being inhabited by Mesolithic tribes to mechanised peat harvesting in the 20th century. It now serves as a sanctuary for wildlife, a place to walk and cycle, and at the core of this is a Sculpture Park, where the industrial materials of peat manufacturing are recycled into land and environmental sculptures and placed back on to the terrain that they harvested for many decades. These unusual works of art dramatically change the landscape, with varying contrast throughout the seasons. And over time, the effects of nature have altered the sculptures in colour and developed fascinating colonies of plant growth, enabling them to become a type of hybrid landscape of natural and mechanical materials (see Fig. 2).

Figure 2. Sculptures during the snow in Lough Boora Sculpture Park.

This project is fascinating to me because it allows me to make tangible the metaphors of terrain and mechanical that have stood at the heart of my pieces since I first began composing. In the following video (see Fig. 3), you can see me rummaging through the warehouses of this old machinery at Lough Boora, exploring materials for their sonic potential, carrying them home to analyse their timbral properties, taking the materials to a sculptor that I work with to weld them into instrumental forms, and then testing these prototypes with a musician who will play the sonic sculptures/instruments in a piece that I compose.[6]

6. A short *Video Documentary on Ann Cleare*'s work, directed by Johannes List, commissioned by the Ernst von Siemens Foundation, available to view here: https://vimeo.com/340163451

Figure 3. Short video documentary on Ann Cleare's work, directed by Johannes List.

I see this project taking many forms, from small to medium to large scale, both transportable and fixed on site, and most importantly for place to be firmly visible at any performance, whether that means creating site-specific sonic work at Lough Boora or bringing newly-made instruments from Lough Boora into concert spaces around the world—that people can travel to Lough Boora or Lough Boora can travel to people. I want the sound of this land and its history to drive whatever Sculptural, Land Art, Theatrical, Performance Art collaborations this work may produce, and not only the sound of its recent past but of its ancient past too.

As I mentioned earlier, the Midlands, where I come from, lies at the very heart of Ireland, but are rarely considered to be at the core of activity in the country. It is generally forgotten or unknown that at one time the Irish Midlands were "the core of all life, the multi-directional and dimensional centre... for our ancestors, there was no doubt where all life and energy radiated from".[7] Ireland is currently divided into four provinces: Connaught, Leinster, Munster, and Ulster, in the Irish language these are known as "na Ceithre Cúige". Note that the Irish for province is "Cúige", which means fifth. Therefore "Ceithre Cúige" is actually four fifiths. So what happened to the fifth fifth then? Therein lies the tale of Midhe, the Midlands. From the Iron Age onwards, the Midlands were the royal centre of governance, the centre of all life in Ireland. In Spring of each year, people would gather on the Hill of Uisneach for Beltane, at the centre of the country, for what Manchán Magan describes in his rousing article on Midhe as a "ritual of rejuvenation, sparking the land into fertility by means of sacred bonfires which then spread out from the centre to all points around Ireland... its impact on the Irish psyche was profound: the fire radiated out all in all directions, shining, warming, enlightening, and illuminating the darkness. Uisneach and other sacred sites in the Midlands were the navel of our world, the centre of our firmament."[8] This disconnection from it shows how far people have drifted from their ancient core. But how could this happen? Well, it's simple, really: those who colonised the country, from Christian missionaries to Vikings to Normans to the English Tudors made sure to disempower any vital centres and to supplant them with their own or move them to become coastal ports, where trading and consumerism flourished. Animism, the illuminating life force within all things, which the Chieftains of the Irish Midlands lived and died by, slowly disappeared into obscurity.

7. Manchán Magan, *Midhe: The Irish Midlands*, Midlands Arts and Culture Magazine, Autumn/Winter 2015.

8. Manchán Magan, *Midhe: The Irish Midlands.*

In the current climate crisis that we face, where humans have depleted natural resources in such callous and capitalist ways and where populations need to decentralise from over-crowded, buckling urban centres, how can Animism become part of my project at Lough Boora? How can I create work there that proposes a prosperous vision for Post-Industrial life? Climate Action on a site that in the last century has badly damaged the climate. Can Sound Art be a medium for reconnecting people with the Earth? A place that invites the public to engage artistically with the materials around them, without the conventions of a concert hall, envisioning a future of sustainable energy where land and non-human energy is treated with the respect it deserves. And, in doing this, can I find a way to change people's perception that Art is highbrow, deals only with unattainable goals that have nothing to do with their lives and heritage, and is only accessible to the wealthy? That work such as mine is influenced by the most earthly of materials that most people encounter and harness on a daily basis: explorations of light, darkness, electricity, water, industry, earth and how humans interact and transform these, and vice versa. I, too, know how it feels to be alienated by words—as I explained above, I don't feel like I belong to the world of music or its composer tradition. No matter how hard I try, I struggle to align myself to it and to its audiences. But I can connect to the word Art. Its boundaries, practices, and possible reaches are wider, and I believe in its ability to liberate imagination and thought. In a country that modernism bypassed and that is still rebuilding itself after centuries of colonisation and its repressive forces, perhaps these approaches might be worth exploring.

Finally, I return to the idea of place and the title of this piece of writing: *Places in my Music and My Music in Places*. My project in the Midlands of Ireland brings these situations together. The place within my concert music has always been rooted in my homeland and now it will be tangibly present on that homeland's terrain in what I hope will be a place for futuristic artworks that can acknowledge the Post-industrial world we live in and the spirituality of the ancient past of Midhe that is buried under it. A place for sonic gathering, activism, reflection, and imagining for all that lies between those two worlds and what comes next.

—Co. Offaly, *Winter 2019/2020*

CHAPTER 7

COLOUR TALK

BRAM DE LOOZE

A couple of years ago, I embarked on one of the most revelatory musical explorations in my life, as I got into the world of temperaments and tunings. At that time, it was entirely uncharted territory for me and, the first time I felt the sensation of a pure major 3rd on an 1860 Bechstein, it was a revelation that still fascinates me today as much as it did then. This was a complete departure from the equal tempered tunings I was used to.

Piano e Forte

After my time studying at the New School in New York (2012–2013), I was thinking of slowly moving back to my home country, Belgium and to settle in Brussels. I'd received the opportunity to play an increasing number of concerts in Europe. During this period of flying back and forth, I went back to visit the extensive collection of historical pianos by Chris Maene, piano manufacturer from whom my parents had bought my first piano. In his overwhelming workshop I was able to discover the countless instruments from *the* great piano builders—I played on replicas and original instruments from Erard, Pleyel, Anton Walter, Broadwood and many more.

A new chapter started for me then: the fascination for non-equal temperaments combined with the distinctive characters of these instruments. Soon I made plans to record an album with the three instruments that I was most attracted to: an 1836 Erard original, an 1843 Pleyel replica and a 1795 Anton Walter replica. I'd instantly fallen in love with the individual qualities of these instruments and this reminded me of all the situations in which pianists have to adapt to the instrument and acoustics you get in clubs or festivals, every situation is unique so always you have to go for that search inside the sound. The fascinating thing about a piano is that there is always a way to make it sound like you want it. This search is such a precious process for me, and it becomes exhilarating once you find a piano's sweet spot. It is one of the joys of performing. Because I instinctively had the habit of exploring the distinct sound of each piano I played, I was able to apply the same sense of discovery to these very specific pianofortes. What greatly challenged me were the differences between the pianofortes which were way more extreme than the differences between modern pianos.

When I started working on this project, I wanted each instrument to be tuned in a different temperament, in *Quarter-comma meantone*, *Rameau* and *Thomas Young*. While preparing the music for this project, I realized that the complexity of the tone of the piano influenced the perception of the temperament. The Erard's tone was much more complex than the other two, so a less extreme temperament suited the Erard better. The *quarter-comma meantone* is the most extreme (which means the furthest away from equal temperament) and could be paired with either the Pleyel or the Anton Walter. Since the Walter is an early fortepiano, its construction was fairly light compared to the instruments from a couple of decades later. This Walter piano had a round sound quality in the middle register which differs considerably from the other registers: the basses buzz and the highs become thinner and shorter the higher you go. With modern pianos this is not the case as there is a pretty much homogeneous sound throughout all registers. This extremely individual sound made the Walter an ideal match for the most extreme temperament of the three. My decision was soon confirmed after I became more familiar with the instrument and the tonal centers of *quarter-comma meantone* temperament. It opened up a range of a musical expression that I had never experienced before. Finally, the *Rameau* temperament was left for the Pleyel concert grand replica. After spending some days diving deeper into the sound of the Pleyel and its *Rameau* temperament, I once again began discovering an ever-expanding range of harmonic and improvisational possibilities. Especially certain major 6th intervals had a special character combined with the great sound of the low-mid register of this piano. This is for example very audible in *Aigo I*, the opening track of the album.

The whole process of this album, *Piano e Forte*, made me become aware of the power of temperaments, specifically in combination with the individual character of a given instrument.

Sensation

I remain intrigued to this day by non-equal temperaments, since I feel there's so much left to explore. It all began during that important visit to Chris Maene's collection, when I kept going back to one Bechstein from 1860 which was tuned in an 18th century temperament. The reason why I kept returning to it was because I fell in love with the sound of a pure 3rd. Hearing this interval on an acoustic piano, you feel a vibration go through your body... Its generous resonance in particular left a strong mark on me. But I continued exploring the entire collection, playing every instrument carefully and experiencing how they differed from one another, sometimes in striking ways, sometimes very subtly. Every time I started playing a new piano, however briefly, I felt an entirely different physical sensation. However, I kept going back to that one Bechstein to hear that pure 3rd again. I've never experienced such satisfaction with a simple C major triad (!), especially in "wide" position (C-G-E).

Going back home after being overexposed to all of these pianos, that pure 3rd kept ringing in my head. From that moment on, I started researching how temperaments were constructed. Yet, as I began studying this intricate subject, I felt my focus lay too much on the temperaments themselves, to the extent that it started sounding like I was making music with only that in mind. I felt as if my creative flow had been interrupted and I needed to free my mind again.

Werckmeister III/The Golden Mean

It seemed to me that the best way forward was to choose one temperament and explore it in greater depth. It had to be a temperament which contained some of those enthralling pure 3rds, while still leaving the possibility to play in every key imagineable. Crucially, I didn't want my musical flow to be interrupted whenever I felt that the music was going into a certain key where the intervals didn't sound quite as good. After experimenting with different temperaments, I settled on the *Werckmeister III* tuning. One key would sound dirtier or nastier than the other, some keys would sound warmer or purer than others. While some temperaments, such as "meantone", contain more pure intervals, this inevitably resulted in more extreme constraints on the number of usable keys. *Werckmeister III* can be considered as a golden mean between "meantone" and equal temperament. It's the temperament with which I felt the strongest connection as it included pure 3rds and it was still versatile enough to play in different keys.

The human ear is very sensitive to pitch, but when it comes to the sound of pianos, most people find it hard to pinpoint differences. This becomes even more apparent when tuning and temperaments become involved. If you listen intently, especially in direct comparisons to another temperament, the distinctiveness of each tuning system becomes evident. But aside from this conscious listening effort, to me, the temperaments also automatically impart an additional emotional layer to the music. When a certain phrase or harmony is played, it can have such a different impact on your perception and experience.

Not all music benefits from this temperament of course, but I enjoy listening to the different colors and vibrations these temperaments have to offer. The feeling of a pure 3rd becomes so satisfying on the piano, similarly to how a major 6th sounds in for example the lower register of a certain key, a sound I'm just as addicted to. Applying this to acoustic piano music opens up a new world for me to explore—it shouldn't be the main focus of the creative process, but it complements the work on composition, improvisation, flow, and sound.

In the Long Term

I've started exploring tunings and temperaments 5 years ago now and I'm convinced of the value of this endeavor. On my first solo album, *Piano e Forte*, I felt entirely immersed in a completely new realm, mostly getting by on intuition and by creating my own compass to navigate and improvise. The following two solo albums (*Switch The Stream* and *Colour Talk*) are more focused on the *Werckmeister III* temperament as a bridge between distinctive interval coloration and the flexibility to play in different keys.

At the same time I was playing in different projects where I didn't think about tunings and temperaments at all, playing all kinds of pianos in the "normal" equal-tempered tuning (although, frankly, it's difficult to talk about "normal" tunings once you start noticing the difference between good and bad tuning). I still greatly enjoy playing in equal temperament, but it just limits your possibilities to a specific set of harmonic colors, which simultaneously allows you to focus on different aspects of the music. To me there's a benefit in going back and forth between equal and non-equal tempered tunings, mainly because it prevents you from getting stuck in one way of thinking. But it also gives me a fresh outlook and excitement, going back into non-equal temperament after having done something radically different.

I strongly believe that in the long term non-equal tunings nurture a different kind of imagination. You become more sensitive to a temperament's colors as you reprogram your ears, leading to a deep, lasting impact, both consciously and subconsciously. Most people I've spoken to after a concert say they experienced an unusual feeling in the first 10 minutes of the performance, but then their ears adjust to the tuning and they start to enjoy it. While non-equal tunings are by no means inherently better than equal ones, there is something unique to be discovered in them, something to be felt, maybe something that many generations before us have felt. It makes me wonder at the complexity of this whole evolution.

CHAPTER 8

TACHITIPO—THE LIVING PASSPORT

ZOSHA DI CASTRI

Hybrid Approaches to Composing and Recording

I recently released a debut album of my music, *Tachitipo,* on New Focus Recordings, and the process of preparing, recording, editing, and mixing the album has raised several fundamental questions for me regarding the way I think about my work. Two of the main ideas I have been contending with are: what is the ideal representation of my music—the version the nearest to the way I imagine it in my head? and, why record concert music in a professional studio environment rather than relying on quality, live, archival recordings from performances? My goal with the album was to document my recent compositions, while collaborating with musicians who have been closely involved in my creative process over the past eight years. I also wanted to feature women in roles traditionally underrepresented in the field, including myself as composer, critically acclaimed classical recording engineer/producer Martha de Francisco, and internationally recognized new music conductor Lorraine Vaillancourt.

Before deciding to undertake the project, I experienced a strange period of hesitation which I am still trying to unpack. At first, the idea of recording an album seemed rather self-indulgent and expensive, though several mentors and friends encouraged me to take the leap. While I understood the potential usefulness of having a recording as a calling card and way of disseminating my music, there was something "permanent" about it that unnerved me. By issuing a professional studio recording, would I be locking the work into a single, fixed, definitive interpretation, which others would then simply replicate? Over time, I have grown to see my music as something quite flexible, in dialogue with performers, and often in a state of perpetual revision. This unease toward studio recording also related to my ongoing questioning of *what is the work itself*: is it the sound in my mind, the mockups I make, the notated score, the live performance, the recording, or the complex kaleidoscope created between these iterations?

Over the past few years, I have come to think of my compositional process as a hybrid drawing from multiple musical traditions and methods, and in examining this mixture I am slowly coming to understand my relationship towards recorded sound. On the one hand, I am writing with the intention of creating concert music, which links back to the lineage of classical music, though my sound world is of course much more experimental. Yet, even when composing instrumental music, I usually work using studio conditions by creating hyper-realistic mockups within a digital audio workspace (DAW; in my case—Logic Pro). This method is closer to how an electroacoustic composer or pop producer might work, allowing maximum control over the sound and balance, while offering immediate sonic feedback. Within this practice, there is a "closeness" to my material that I very much like and a hands-on ability to sculpt sound. Though I just recently started using high quality commercial MIDI samples (such as Spitfire Audio and Kontakt), the bulk of the pieces on the album are built from sound-files I recorded with various collaborators, which have come to form part of my personal sonic vocabulary. In this way, I combine workshops, improvisations (created by myself or performers I've worked with), and sound editing into my compositional process. It is not atypical for me to generate the complete form of a piece from beginning to end with full orchestration, extended techniques, and detailed timbral and dynamic information in Logic before beginning my notational process.

This last step is an arduous task of careful transcription. Though it often feels like an exercise in compromise with many nuanced details lost along the way, I do my best to translate as precisely as possible what I am hearing into musical notation through dictation and meticulous analysis. In my DAW, the music does not necessarily adhere to a regular metric grid. In fact, this was one of the primary reasons I was drawn to work digitally—to free my sense of timing and chronology of form (I often compose non-linearly)—so there is a constant negotiation between how to preserve the complexity and spontaneity of the imagined music, while transcribing it in a way that is idiomatic and clear for the performers. Though the final result is often remarkably close to my mockup (or so I've been told), there are nevertheless discrepancies between the controlled DAW environment and a live performance, in which many more unpredictable variables are at play. The score and parts serve as the primary way of communicating the music to the musicians; however, I sometimes also share the mockups to fill in the gaps where my transcriptions might fall short. By hearing the intended sound world, the musicians often have a better idea of how to shape their interpretation to get closer to my initial conception of the piece.

Mostly, performers have responded positively to this input, or have even requested the mockups when they know the way I work. Others however, have asked: "Is the mockup a more 'ideal' version of the piece than the live performance itself?" I am well aware of the potential murkiness at play within this methodology and by no means want to lessen the importance of the performers to the realization of my work. In fact, I am not terribly interested in writing purely electronic music without any live performance aspect. And in contrast, workshopping musical ideas with performers is the part of composing which I find to be the most gratifying. Though keeping a piece completely digital would allow me full control over the sounding result, there is a "liveness" that I would miss, and I always look forward to the perspective and suggestions that gifted musicians bring to my work. But the question remains: how is composing in studio conditions affecting the concert music I create? And by making a studio recorded album of my concert music, am I returning full-circle to the initial impulse and creative conditions the work was generated from?

For instance, let me briefly describe how the solo piano piece *Dux* was written in collaboration with Julia Den Boer while in residency at the Banff Centre. Both Julia and I had our own huts: one for composing, the other for practicing. As a trained classical pianist, I was struggling to find a new way of writing for my instrument that didn't involve falling into the traps of my muscle memory. Each day I would record myself improvising at the piano, I would then edit these recordings into small gestural blocks, which could then be rearranged or layered in my DAW. I basically treated the material as if I were composing an electroacoustic piece. This process resulted in music that was generally idiomatic, but less predictable than what I might have written sitting at the keyboard. Once I was satisfied with a chunk, I'd transcribe it and print a copy for Julia to read through and give me feedback on. And so we went, back and forth between our huts, until we had a full draft of the piece. One interesting result was the surprising physical choreography this process provided. *Dux* has a unique geography that is quite virtuosic in terms of the physical exertion and speed required to follow its spatial layout, jumping extremely quickly between registeral extremes.

A few years passed between the premiere in Banff and the studio recording of *Dux* at Oktaven Audio. What struck me when editing the recording with Martha was just how similar the process was to composing the piece, as we stitched together the modular form to get just the right rhythmic flow and pacing. Though we miss the physical choreography that is present in a live performance, the studio recording still conveys the erratic, almost belligerent energy required to execute these very quick movements.

Just as the recorded version of *Dux* differs from the concert version, I realized this would be the case for many of the pieces on the album to differing degrees. I have thus come to question the presumption within classical music that a studio recording should be an accurate *replication* of the concert experience. Some artists of course have challenged this notion, such as the Canadian pianist Glenn Gould, who gave up concert appearances entirely in favor of the studio, but it is nevertheless still a widely accepted view. In popular and improvisatory music, however, I would argue there is a much more open embrace of the album as a distinct, separate entity from the live performance. Both versions exist and are legitimate in their own right, and there is no pretense that they should be one and the same. Perhaps in circumventing the need for a score (another object of fixity), this distinction is made more easily in pop and jazz. I therefore see this album not as an attempt to recreate the concert versions of these pieces in the classical sense, but rather as a different, malleable take on the same material. They are two distinct products resulting from two discrete (though related) processes. This moldable approach is more compatible with the way I think of composition itself, and therefore feels true to me as an artist.

A critical shift in perspective came when I began re-thinking the album as a series of "snapshots"—much like a passport—gathering places and people I have interacted with. Rather than being an inward looking venture, I see it as documentation of the rich community that I am a part of, an opportunity to acknowledge and celebrate the many incredible musicians who have inspired and helped form me as an artist since moving to New York. By imagining the album as a living passport rather than a museological object in a glass (or jewel) case, I gradually became more comfortable with the idea of moving forward with the album. Like a passport, I felt that the album could stand as a testament to where I've been and who I've worked with, and I was comforted by the knowledge that these pieces could always be revisited in the future—each visit bringing its own new set of experiences, relationships, and possibilities.

Fixity and Flexibility: Concert vs. Studio Platforms

As I moved from the planning phase to the recording stage, I quickly realized that rather than being daunted by the studio and potential "fixity" it might present, I actually found it to be a very stimulating and freeing place to work as it felt like an organic extension of the way I compose. Much like the way I grew accustomed to sculpting sound in my DAW, the studio environment allowed the same level of control over detail in recording that is characteristic of the way I conceive of sound. Rather than crossing our fingers and hoping for the best as one might with a one-off concert recording (especially a world-premiere), we were able to carefully stitch together multiple takes, layer in complex lines, and map out a unique editing strategy for each piece. Some pieces were recorded in a fairly straightforward manner once we found the right sound (such as with *Quartet No. 1* and *La forma dello spazio*), whereas others, especially those involving electronics, were incredibly involved and time-consuming to put together, such as the 24-minute title track *Tachitipo*, which involved an elaborate percussion setup, many microphones, a full day of recording, layers of electronics, and 125 tracks in the final mix!

I have, therefore, flipped my perspective and come to think of concert recordings as more *fixed* objects representing how a piece is heard at a given place and time. In contrast, I believe studio recordings have the *flexibility* to allow continued shaping of each piece throughout the recording and editing process. As a result, I have tried to think creatively about what could be done <u>differently</u> in a studio environment that could not be as easily accomplished in a live setting. Some of my main objectives became:

—achieving a very clean sound without the artifacts or extraneous noises one would find in a concert recording,

—getting very "close" to the music, as if the listener were sitting within the ensemble or were "inside" the sound while maintaining a natural, unprocessed aesthetic,

—exploring the liminal spaces between classical, electroacoustic, pop, and improvisatory recording approaches to allow my music the most flexibility, and,

—actively shaping the acoustic space the sound inhabits by subtly adjusting the spatialization and reverb throughout a work, especially with the pieces involving electronics.

At the beginning of the recording and editing process, I realized that my producer Martha de Francisco and I were coming to this project with slightly differing aesthetic perspectives. While I was curious to explore a kind of hybrid, autodidactic approach, Martha was coming from a more traditional, trained background, having studied as a *Tonmeister* in Germany and having worked with many classical music greats such as Alfred Brendel, Anne-Sophie Mutter, the New York Philharmonic, Kent Nagano, as well as established composers such as Holliger, Kagel, Ligeti, and Stockhausen. I observed her spending the first hour of each session testing out the microphone choices, fine-tuning placements, and setting levels to achieve a beautiful, balanced sound for each instrument in each piece. This of course was a fantastic foundation to work from and I am extremely indebted to her vast knowledge and years of experience. Like other detail-oriented artists Martha has worked with, come editing time, I continued to search for my ideal sound, "composing" even during postproduction (not in an attempt to optimize the performance, but to find a particular sound quality). Since I have a strong enough command of studio technology and well-tuned ears, I was able to express quite specifically how I wanted the sound to be sculpted, and in some cases, like with the title track *Tachitipo*, I could do much of the editing myself. In the end, I think we were able to achieve an interesting mix of approaches blending our two perspectives. The resulting sound is clean with a wide dynamic range like most classical recordings, but also embraces the detailed micro-control of my electroacoustic training. Though several of the pieces are challenging and quite dense in activity, Martha and I worked hard to make sure each line was made audible, each composite timbre carefully balanced, so that the complex web of textures, such as in the large ensemble piece *Cortège*, could be appreciated in their detailed intricacy. I personally was drawn towards a more close, compressed, bright sound than Martha would normally go for (which is perhaps informed by listening to popular music), but after much experimentation, we found a happy middle ground.

Because improvisation is also important to the way I compose, I chose to bring an element of this into the studio. In the vocal ensemble piece, *The Animal After Whom Other Animals Are Named* (for six singers and electronics), Ekmeles and I re-recorded various passages that were originally in the electronics as "found objects". I played the singers soundfiles through their headphones and asked them to imitate what they were hearing. I then re-worked this new material into the electronics that are in the album. With the Yarn/Wire piece *Tachitipo* (for two pianists, two percussionists, and electronics), where certain passages fall into a pulsed metric grid while others are more free, we employed multiple recording strategies. The pulsed parts were recorded using click track, and for the free passages we did multiple contrasting takes (sometimes much longer than were needed) to have various iterations to choose from. Bringing in the performers' creative input, re-imagining the score, and re-injecting spontaneity into the studio helped dispel the fears I originally had that a studio recording would lead to a flat, fixed, rigid product. The flexibility we were able to find by incorporating elements of freedom in our process helped bring a "liveness" to the music, which I hope can be heard.

In editing pieces like *The Animal* and *Tachitipo*, I also worked very closely with the engineers to create multiple spatial perspectives and to move smoothly between these to give depth to the recording. I pushed this much further in the album than I have in performance because I believe there is a visual discrepancy that occurs in live settings which limits our ability to accept drastic electronic spatial shifts. Because we see and experience the space we inhabit (i.e. a concert hall, church, amphitheatre, etc.), it is more challenging for a listener to suspend their disbelief if suddenly the sound changes spaces dramatically. For example: it sounds fake to move from the acoustics of a small, dry sounding room to that of a large cathedral, when in fact we are sitting in a medium-wet hall. Our eyes don't believe our ears. Or, if a clarinettist is on stage, but we hear their sound come from a speaker at the back corner of the hall, there is a disconnect between the body of the performer and the perceived musical event. But when we listen to an album on speakers or headphones in the comfort of our homes, without the physical presence of performers or a hall, we are not confronted with these same cognitive dissonances and new creative vistas open up. It becomes difficult to perceive the divisions between what is live and what is electronic. In this fluid state, we are much more likely to go along with the journey and experience these shifts in space as yet another way of expressing musicality and contrast.

Adapting Theatre: Rethinking Movement and Visuals

Going further with this notion, I quickly realized that although I could expand the spatialization and reverb in the electronics for pieces like *The Animal*, I would need to radically rethink my strategy for a piece like *Tachitipo*. In the concert version of this work, the musicians move between stations on stage, lighting cues are used to dramatic effect, and in a rather humorously absurd postlude, the percussionists wheel the pianists off stage as they sit on small carts, clacking away hunched over typewriters and castanets. In the premiere, the musicians wore headlamps as the stage lights faded to black. The pianists perform a variety of stretches and exaggerated mechanical movements that correspond with the stopping and starting of the push-carts and electronics. These theatrical elements are of course impossible to convey in a purely recorded format, so I revised the ending for the album by re-editing the electronics to be more vibrant, active, and distorted, and intensifed the spatialization to give the illusion of a physical trajectory for the performed castanet and typewriter sounds. I also used volume and reverb curves to give the illusion of distance as the performers move (theoretically) offstage. Again, this recording is not meant to re-create the concert experience, but is rather an alternate take on the same material. Much more could be said on the subject of translating theatrical movement into recording settings, but this must be reserved for a separate essay.

Another piece that required serious rethinking was the solo percussion work, *how many bodies have we to pass through*, written in collaboration with Diego Espinosa Cruz Gonzalez and dedicated to the victims of the 2017 Mexican earthquake. The finished album contains six tracks, however, initially I had wanted to include this piece as part of the release. Due in part to the durational limitations of a physical CD (roughly 78–80 minutes), we decided the piece with Diego would best be included as a bonus video track. This was not simply an after-thought, but rather was integral to the conception, documentation, and longevity of the piece.

How many bodies was co-composed over two intensive week-long workshops held two years apart in New York and Paris, respectively. The video was recorded and filmed at Reid Hall by David Adamcyk and Antonia Fritche. Taking its beginnings from a humble suitcase packed with hand percussion from around the world, it eschews traditional notation for a quasi-improvisatory, pictorial "storyboard score", mapping physical gestures across instrumental surfaces. By modifying and combining hand percussion, we sought to create a multiplicity of simultaneous voices performable by a single musician. For instance: whereas the South Indian kanjira is traditionally played by one musician (with one hand holding the frame and bending the skin, while the other strikes), here we rigged two kanjiras to a Brazilian tamborim in a pyramid structure played on the shoulder, which is then scrubbed across a travel conga to bend its pitch. Maracas from Venezuela, Mexico, and Brazil form an inharmonic timbral scale played at times like a keyboard, or shaken in joyous polyphonic clusters. Chinese opera gongs and a Korean jing are tapped and struck with fingers and fist. Even the voice sneaks in, playing tricks on the listener's perception. Using clamps, foam, combs, and other implements to cross-connect surfaces, Diego's intimate, tactile, and highly kinetic dance invites one to peer in, as if witnessing a secret ritual. Gestures reincarnate through cycles of repetition and variation until we see and hear that the macrocosm is as the microcosm, and vice versa.

Because the visual choreography is so integral to the music and Diego brings such a unique physical presence to the stage, video seemed like the ideal format to convey our work. In fact, an audio recording would not really do this piece justice. Given the approximate nature of the storyboard score vis-à-vis the detailed work we had accomplished in our workshops, we wondered how (and if) this piece could be disseminated so that others could eventually play it. Again I returned to the question: *what is the work, where does it reside, what is its essence*? Should the next step in its evolution be a detailed transcription in musical notation of Diego's interpretation? Or would some of the expressive freedom and spontaneity be lost by abandoning the storyboard score for something more fixed? I liked the fact that Diego could play the piece from memory without the intrusive presence of music stands (the score being more of a mnemonic device than something strictly adhered to). Video thus seemed like an excellent next step in our process. Having danced quite seriously for many years, this methodology of video + oral history for passing down choreographic movement seemed very natural to me. Creating a music video allows us to show all the details that are impossible to notate, and rather than fixing the piece in a single authoritative version, we hope it will inspire future performers to understand its essence, while leaving them freedom to find their own interpretation.

The video can be seen as an extension of the studio environment, adding an extra layer of visual information that would otherwise be impossible to convey in either traditional notation or in an exclusively audio format. Lastly, in the age of social media and internet culture, having a video associated with the album release has helped to accessibly engage people who might not otherwise buy contemporary music, encouraging them to explore the rest of the album.

New Perspectives: Transience and Traceability

Now that the album has been officially released, I have been reflecting upon how this experience has changed the way I think about composing. Generally, I write quite quickly in short bursts of intense production, usually completing a piece in a week to three months. Juggling the responsibilities of teaching full-time at Columbia while raising two children, I am usually able to write three or four pieces a year. I'm always on to the next thing, barely coming up for air, often not having time to catalogue my work properly before being swept into the next project. Working on the album was perhaps the first time in my creative life where I've allowed myself the space and time to truly listen, revise, reflect, and document my work in a satisfactory and thorough way. The album *Tachitipo* has taken roughly three years to complete, from the time of applying for grants and planning the project to its full realization and release in November 2019. Whereas I often make decisions very quickly when composing, working on the album over such an extended period of time (with several fallow intervals of inactivity away from the music) has been an illuminating creative experience. It was at times difficult to keep up the momentum and motivation; however, I definitely grew to appreciate the value of considering my music through a less urgent lens. Though some composers record albums to preserve their work in an idealized form or to "fix" their legacy, at this stage in my career, my motivation was more pushing back against the transience I'd come to accept in my rhythm of production, composing works that are sometimes played just once or twice due in part to a lack of proper documentation. The album has thus been a way to leave a trace—a mark of the existence of an idea (albeit one that is flexible and open to multiple interpretations).

Another perspective this project has brought is a consideration of *when* is the best time to make a recording of a work. I've noticed that as I get farther from the point of creation of a piece, there is a threshold between the moment when I begin to forget the intentions behind it, and the moment when I have enough critical distance to be able to hear it for what it truly is. (This is the reason why I usually bury all archival recordings deep in my desk for a period of at least three months before ever taking a listen.) Too close, and one focuses on all the minute details that are not actually that important or perceivable to the outside ear. Too far, and one can no longer remember how the piece was made or what is essential to its ethos—this goes for the composer as well as the performers. So finding that sweet spot between when the ink has dried and the point when the music is forgotten is perhaps the ideal time to record.

Over the course of the recording process, especially as I became more deeply involved in the engineering side of the editing and mixing, I came to realize that I had a much more specific vision of what I wanted than I initially thought, and that I knew more than I gave myself credit for. (I wonder whether this was perhaps a gendered response toward the studio environment, having witnessed many of my female composition students also doubt their technological abilities without good reason.) Ultimately, my experience of making this album has been empowering and has given me the confidence to pick up the reins moving forward. Though I am happy with how *Tachitipo* turned out and don't regret the decisions I made, I would be curious in the future to pursue a new recording project that is more streamlined, less expensive, and less logistically involved. Relying more on my own abilities, I'd be interested in pursuing something rather centralized, perhaps a solo piano and electronics album, in which I perform and edit the recording in collaboration with a single engineer.

Finally, I have tried to bring the same level of detail to the production of the album as I would to composing my music, right down to the design of the physical object itself. Since I see *Tachitipo* as more of a "living passport" than a museological object, it didn't make sense to seal the disc away in the crisp confines of an impersonal plastic jewel case. I felt strongly that the CD should have an identity unto itself, that unwrapping it should be a memorable, tactile experience—one that would invite the listener to unveil and reveal its contents with curiosity and a sense of discovery. I thought back to my student days in Montreal attending indie shows at Casa del Popolo, and approached artist Kiva Stimac of Popolo Press to collaborate with me on the packaging design. I had always admired her bold, distinctive, hand-printed posters for shows around town (having briefly run a small handmade paper business myself as a teen), and she seemed to be someone equally invested in the detail and craft of handmade production. We bonded over our mutual love of paper, texture, and color, and worked together over several months to create the unique hand-folded box and insert that houses each CD.

Coda

This project began with reflections on how I think about my work. What is *the work* itself? What is the ideal representation of my music and how is it best documented? More than ever, I think there are no simple answers to these questions, but I do see my music being informed by the multiple manifestations and hybrid aesthetics it inhabits. It is not simply the imagined sound, the DAW mockup, the score, the performance, the recording, or the video. It is rather the complex topography created through the superimposition of these multiple iterations. And in this same way, the studio recording represents yet another angle within this complex prism, rather than an attempted replication of the concert experience. Embracing the flexibility inherent in the studio, this album explores what can be done *differently* from the archival recording, including finding creative solutions for how to incorporate freedom, and how to adapt visual or theatrical information into an audio or video format. All of these elements have been woven together to create a trace of my work, fighting the transience sometimes inherent in the making of new music. For myself, the album has been as much about the music as it has the remarkable relationships and collaborations that unfolded throughout the process of its production. Fundamentally, a hidden but invaluable mark of the work is the community of artists that came together to bring this music to life, and for these extraordinary musicians, I will be forever grateful.

CHAPTER
9

SHARDS OF ETHER

GANAVYA DORAISWAMY

A map to these shards of my ether. All paths are equally valid.

A note:

Each shard is *exactly* 100 words.
Read them by level (of indentation), randomly, from top to
bottom, in reverse; read the essays that end in your favorite number,
only read the titles. Don't read anything.
Treat the *s as a portal. You don't have to take them. You can, if you'd like.
You can ignore them.
They are just jumping pads, ready to be activated at your will.
Each of these stories relates deeply to my practice in music. The deeper
you go, the further the web reveals itself to be the same shape, birthing
and dying in itself continuously. This written work reveals to the reader
the innumerable ways in which our lives form our music.
Welcome to *harikathā*, the song of words and life.
Here, you can stay with me for as long as you need, or want.
Leave when you want, or need. Come back when you need, or want.
With sincerity, these words will always try to be here for you,
to offer company when my voice and presence cannot.

1. on *training to be water dancers*
2. on *säm әna wärq*
    3. on *breaking a word*
        4. on *breaking a number*
            5. on *breaking metaphysical rules*
        6. on *letters on nourishment*
        7. on *training to be a word-breaker*
    8. on *the invitation to the simhāsanā*
        9. on *house-holders*

10. on *breaking a fast*
11. on *breaking time: a family portrait*
12. on *making sanctuaries*
13. on *mrs. samuel holden's first name*
14. on *hanging upside down together*
15. on *amma, my throat is hearting*
16. on *ms. hardeep mann's "ashram"*
17. on *non-musician*
18. on *feeling [ar]rested*
19. on *breaking away: 588 vanderbilt ave*
20. on *finding a way*
21. on *breaking a way*
22. on *bops*
23. on *the long[ing] tones of a cherub*
24. on *the map to "success"*
25. on *having ishtyle: a map to ourselves*
26. on *what frame story as a literary technique is*
27. on *a map for a new world (2013)*
28. on *the brea[d]th of a being*
29. on *being wi[d]th*
30. on *buddhakṣetra*
31. on *the first edit*
32. on *cerberus*
33. on *co-travellers*
34. on *breaking time again*
35. on *to whom does what belong?*
36. on *inner shimmers*
37. on *who lives within*
38. on *drawing circles*
39. on *the rectangle girl*
40. on *peter*
41. on *pauline*
42. on *matcha lattes*
43. on *the sound of the dharmā*
44. on *the sounders of the dharmā*
45. on *a beckoning*
46. on *intoxication: an awakening*

47. on *witnessing how intoxicating a monk's love is*
48. on *another monk's love*
49. on *dreaming with a monk*
50. on *dreaming of mothers: for Seiyoung Jang*
51. on *singing for a monk*
52. on *a resignification*
53. on *kalākshetra*
54. on a *resign[ific]ation of habits*
55. on *drawing swirls in the ether*
56. on *embodied cognition*
57. on *64-bar solos in a jam session*
58. on an *excerpt from a class presentation; feb. 5, 2019*
59. on *the night of flights*
60. on *prayers: old and new*
61. on *books and glass*
62. on *mapping my way*
63. on *agency and abstraction*
64. on *wadada's coffee (2016) and prof. silvaticus*
65. on *tao*
66. on *reading music*
67. on *clothing music*
68. on *mapping music*
69. on *embarrassing music*
70. on *editing scripture*
71. on *unnamed music workshop, summer 2017*
72. on *improvisor's view on notated music; banff, summer 2017*
73. on *department of excellence and mastery*
74. on *an interview with the guardian of the frequently encountered*
75. on *an excerpt from a paper on mastery*
76. on *who isn't a master*
77. on *who is a master*
78. on *game time*
79. on *working to the bone*
80. on *breaking the cycle of darkness*
82. on *bringing cycles of light*
83. on *ontologies of you*

84. on *an excerpt, from an interview for Elle India*
85. on *chronicling my Deccan years*
86. on *our lives in a 100 words or less*
87. on *our lived nows in song*
88. on *the innumerable nows*
89. on *metamorphōseōn librī*
90. on *an excerpt, from an interview for Elle India, pt. 2*
91. on *rest your weary head*
92. on *the city of angels*
93. on *the village of pillars*
94. on *the hall of thousand pillars*
95. on *the map to the inner world*
96. on *surfaces and what resurfaces*
97. on *the ending of the beginning*
98. on *arriving to the start*
99. on *new york, the old ghost town*
100. on *7 deer hill lane*
101. on *live, from our living rooms*

shards of ether

0. Thereupon

1. on *training to be water-dancers*

There's the sound of people learning how to dance in water nearby. We are in a large room, one that lets the sky in. "Why don't we just read this a few times?" asked Peter.* And so we did:

> **Thereupon, a certain goddess who lived in that house, having heard this teaching of the Dharma of the great heroic bodhisattvas, and being delighted, pleased, and overjoyed, manifested herself in a material body and showered the great spiritual heroes, the bodhisattvas, and the great disciples with heavenly flowers.**

Again, again. Again. Hear the syllables teach something new every time.

> **Thereupon, a...**

—

2. on *säm əna wärq**

A certain goddess: as in, there's a certain...kind of goddess? A certain goddess: the Mahāyāna Buddhist variety. Where might you find her? Everywhere. But if you want to find a decent family portrait, you could go see the near two millennia-year-old paintings at Mogao Grottoes, Dunhuang, China—a place I went to with Peter for this story.

A certain goddess. Something like Plutarch's image of Cleopatra being carried by Apollodorus in Shakespeare? "A...certain queen in a mattress."* Okay. Certain goddess. Keep repeating.

No.

Not just any certain kind; she is *certain.* Incontrovertible.

A Goddess with certainty.

—

3. on *breaking a word*

One July, Rajna and I listed with certainty what we wanted from a new house, knowing fully well it was impossible: she wanted earth, I wanted sky, we both wanted water.* That September, the word impossible broke, and we moved in. I think she's the manifester; she thinks it's me. In a recent interview for CMA, Larry Blumenfeld wrote of our home: *the living room window grew ablaze with the sunset bursting through lifting cloud cover.** Almost every sunset we get to be home, Rajna asks I turn off the lights. We then sit in silence, and witness creation together.

—

4. on *breaking a number*

I've been telling people I haven't been in the house for a weekend in months. I don't actually know how long it's been.

I say random numbers: 12 weeks, 10; 14 weeks, 7. I don't actually know anymore. I'm afraid if I look it up, I'll feel sicker.

"Well, you're getting hired," a friend remarks, with a quickness that fails to mask a hurt.

Don't get me wrong, I understand it's a privilege to have enough work to fill days. But don't you think, it's a different kind of privilege to not feel like you *have* to fill every one?

—

5. on *breaking metaphysical rules*

How much does a musician's anxiety surrounding self-promotion weigh? *An Insta-gram.* Ha.

Each spirit world has its set of metaphysical rules. One has memories of different ways of being. One facilitates bringing those remembered-states of being into *this* world; but by existing in *this* world you acquiesce to its specific set of metaphysical rules. So, one creates ways to circumnavigate assumed limits.

One such circumnavigation of this world's limits is performance. Astral bodies may dance together with an intimacy and fluidity that gross-bodies readily cannot.

When I think about Instagram ... it is also one such magic.

—

6. on *letters on nourishment*

A little circle with the letters "l o n" rests below my name on Instagram.

It's a portal to a set of collected thoughts I once wrote, when in Lisbon, on nourishing the self when touring. The exercise compelled me to unearth images of and around me—versions of me—I cannot always remember.

> *I've known the road for 15 years now.*
> *My first international tour was when I was 12.*
> [Image: El Amir walks across our stage.]*
>
> *But these words mean different things for different people. By international, I meant I was performing in countries that weren't my home...*

—

7. on *training to be a word-breaker*

> *... it didn't mean it was a glamorous life;*
> *sometimes we had to do two performances the same day,*
> *in two different cities, to break even.*

I'm reminded of a 2-year-old conversation with my mother. *Amma*, I'd sighed. *I overbooked myself. I don't feel time. Monday, I sing in Poland. Tuesday night, sing at Roulette, New York. Wednesday morning, I have a talk in Cambridge; that evening, I sing at Rubin, New York. It's...impossible.*

*Pātti, Tukārām Māmā. Nammakku therinjavā vayasānavālām pannalayā, kanna?**

"Your elders had to do this, remember—" she said.

"—Abundance is always there. Even in scarcity."

—

8. on *the invitation to the simhāsanā*

There's an image that surfaces often in Dunhuang: innumerable chairs flying into Vimalakīrti's house.

Chairs? *Simhāsanā*-s.*

They are thrones summoned from Merupradīparāja's universe, measuring 6,800,000 leagues in height. The house magically expands to fit these cosmic chairs. Vimalakīrti proceeds to offer these seats to all.

Enlightened *bodhisattva*-s expand their bodies to become 4,200,000 leagues tall to sit comfortably. Vimalakīrti gently teaches beginner spirits how to expand themselves, so they can complement the chair.

You could describe every collaborator in terms of the size of the chair they think you warrant. For some, you must shrink. For others, you will grow.

—

9. on *house-holders*

Buddha had asked his student Śāriputra to go to Āmrapāli's house, where a merchant named Vimalakīrti lived. *But a house-holder—a materialist—can't be enlightened, why bother?* wonders Śāriputra. The answer to this is the Sutra.

Chapter 6, titled *The Inconceivable Liberation*, recounts a conversation between Śāriputra and Vimalakīrti. After arriving to the house, Śāriputra wonders to himself if he might have a chair to sit on.

Didja come for the Dharma, or for a chair? teases Vimalakīrti, who hears Śāriputra's thoughts. *Dharma,* sheepishly responds Śāriputra.

He who has understood the Dharma is not interested in sense-media, begins Vimalakīrti.

—

10. on *breaking a fast*

My father is antimaterialist.*

In one way, he is an antimaterialist because he speaks with Spirit. There are days he meditates more than he speaks to us.

But he is also an antimaterialist in that he understands, deeply, that material things do not control your state of mind.

As a child, my father had an Aunt named Poverty. They kept each other company. Together, they raised her son Hunger. I don't know when, but one day, her husband Resentment passed away in sleep.

But I think, of them all, it was her son that taught my father what antimaterialism is.

—

11. on *breaking time: a family portrait*

My parents have to come to visit my Cambridge apartment.

A few weeks ago, a friend visited. He was a monk-in-training, but now travels a different—yet equally beautiful—life-path. He sat down on the meditation chair, and closed his eyes. "Thank you… for inviting me into your temple," he smiled.

So: *my parents have come to visit a temple.*

My father is looking at an old, torn studio picture; a life before my birth. *Look*, he says. *Everyone's looking around the camera. But your mother, our house-holder…*

She looks forward. With certainty. Straight into our futures.

—

12. on *making sanctuaries*

This sky-filled room, our rehearsal space, is in the "Glorya Kaufman" building. A friend once said the building reminded them of a mausoleum. So be it! Cold marble does not tightly grasp onto even the gentlest of sounds.

Give a whisper, it gives back many. Your voice is not alone with marble.

The "house" we draw was donated by Āmrapālī* (this reminds me of Ajātashatru c. 460 BCE—Oedipus premiered c. 400 CE—a strangely royally patricidal time?)—*

Sorry. I'm wandering again.

What I mean is: we should study these women, who are behind all these sanctuaries…

—

13. on *mrs. samuel holden's first name*

How often have you wondered: what is the story behind this particular place?

There's a building called Holden Chapel, in Harvard Yard. I think the story goes something like this: a Mr. Holden—who I presume, for whatever reason, is a banker—passes away, leaving the Mrs. Holden with his power (read: money).*

Upon learning that there was no place for the young men of Harvard to pray, aghast, she builds the chapel (as one does). The chapel has since witnessed many violent operations in its story.

But today, it is where many ensembles—such as Claire Chase's* classes—meet.

—

14. on *hanging upside down together*

Claire's* given us all these… clickers. What else do I call this? It's literally a…clicker. It is plastic, in purple, with a parrot-green button. You could wear it like a ring. If you press the green button, it…well, clicks. Rather loudly.

"Go on," she says. "Close your eyes, walk around. Use your ears as your eyes. This is echolocation." I want to say this to bandmates. "Look to X for cue?" *Nah. Let's close our eyes, let's see with our ears...*

...echolocation.

Wherever you are in the world, when you say something, it will always whisper back.

—

15. on *amma, my throat is hearting (excerpt from essay)**

Alaín Perez,* a warm Cuban bassist I knew when living in Spain, once characterized my musicality to someone after a show: "*la mujer cuyo corazón se queda en la garganta*," as he traced fingers from a heart to a throat. Perhaps it is the closest someone has come to describing the sensation that overcomes me when I sing: the weight of my being, with the innumerable transtemporal networks that shape/d it, travel through my throat into manifested, sounded breath. I may travel within the ether, through this projected sound. It awakens a capacity for echolocation that otherwise stays dormant.

—

16. on *ms. hardeep mann's "ashram"*

Every Wednesday, for about 27 years, at 7:00 PM a group of people have been gathering near Central at 885 Massachusetts Avenue, Apartment #9.*

Well, there's that uncle who'd come early and dry his socks on the heater, but typically people came at 7:00 PM. I lived there for about a year. Rent was unbelievably cheap.

This was because we all had to pretend to be somehow related to a Hardeep Mann, who'd signed the original lease about 28 years ago. She came back every Wednesday.

Everyone was welcome. Often, we played music together. Always, we ate together.

—

17. on *non-musician**

A long time ago, a friend retorted that my music-making practices made light of the path we were walking. I had emailed a listserv in the community about a small, sudden gig; I'd asked if they might consider playing with me.

Now that I let myself think about it, he'd suggested that emailing a group of "non-musicians...trivialize[d]" my work. I knew this friend to be a deeply caring, gentle person. Even so, a sternness escaped me, in my grandmother's voice:

"There is nothing internal that trivializes, and I don't need to concern myself with the externals that choose to."

—

18. on *feeling [ar]rested*

I counted the holes in the walls of my room, in this apartment that many lovingly called "The Ashram." I patched about forty. I painted it in Benjamin Moore's #143. My hands learnt the grips of sandpaper, drywall knives, spackle. I resuscitated sockets. A found piece of wood became my desk. My cherished haven.

Still, Rajna asked:

What would life [read: music] *be, if you didn't have to spend so much time making the foundational structure functional?*

A good question to ask ourselves in any collaborative relationship, even among friends.

Does something house you as much as you house it?

—

19. on *breaking away: 588 vanderbilt ave*

After the ashram at 885,* I moved into the home that was at once earth and sky.* Soon, the time would come for something else.

4 years ago, when in Brooklyn, Rajna pointed to Zaytoons: "this is my favorite restaurant. There used to be this venue called Seeds over…there. Liked it. It shut down. If I move back, this area would be good."

A few months ago, a friend was looking for someone to take over her apartment: *comes with a piano, rehearsal space downstairs.* Area? *Next door to Zaytoons…opposite to a venue called Seeds that just reopened.*

—

20. on *finding a way*

We read the paragraph a few times. I look to Peter, then to Michael.* *What now?* "Well, now, the house, of course!" Peter says. *Of course,* I smile.

Michael, master shapeshifter, becomes the hard lines of the walls; he becomes ornate arches, the tea whisker. I stare, until I remember I have a job.

My wrists are rusty, but I recall near-forgotten symbols with my fingers and throw them into the air with my voice. It is a deeply personal, sacred, private practice. My stomach folds into itself as I remember the teachers I've abandoned in my way-finding.

—

21. on *breaking a way*

My singing can involve confronting a particular tension around the presence of *karnātik* stylings in my vocality. *Karnātik* practice hasn't been the center of my vocal world for a while. Yet, as my first learnt musical grammar, it will forever inform my utterances.

When tired, my mind has conversations with the memory of long-lost teachers on my choice to live in liminality. *You want the benefits of appearing to belong, without actually doing the labor of belonging*, they'd say. I'd say: *if musical belonging didn't have to come with so much extramusical disciplining, I could belong to more people.*

—

22. on *bops*

I think this gig was in 2017...somewhere near Central.* Four of us: a throat-player, skin-player, string-player, wind-player.

The song we're about to rehearse was written by the skin-player, right after their mother had died. They must have been 17 years old. It spoke of an ancient story, of longing and belonging.

Wind-player snorts: "this is like a ... *pop* song!"

Skin-player, pained, immediately withdraws it from the setlist. *I will sing it*, I ask. *It tells a story we need.* "Only if you don't tell them I wrote it," skin-player says, resigned.

—

23. on *the long*[*ing*] *tones of a cherub*

I agreed to sing on *Of Agency and Abstraction* on one condition: I would sing on her album if she would sing on it, too. She sang. (Hear: Track 12: *Yathi*).*

Rajna is a powerful, gentle, seraphic percussionist. I knew her first as a vocalist.

About 10 years ago, in an unreleased album titled *Liminal Spaces*, she recorded a composition titled *Vagabonds*, where she sang lyrics she'd written, interwoven with a Śyāma Śāstri* composition titled *Marivérégathi:*

Everyday, I wanna go
somewhere that's new—
but some day, I wanna belong

Maybe, somewhere along the way,
in disarray—
we'll discover, we're vagabonds

—

24. on *the map to "success"*

I'm reminded of when a student asked a half-circle of musicians on a stage how they got to be as successful as they were. It felt like... asking the crescent if she was waxing or waning. It doesn't matter. The moon is always full.

That depends on what you mean by successful, Vijay said.* *Every night I'm not at home with my daughter...*

Listen, cut in Wadada.* *What is meant for you, will come to you. Even if you try to get in the way. What isn't meant for you, won't come for you.*

So, just make your music.

—

25. on *having ishtyle: a map to ourselves*

"Oh, she has style," my mom said once, looking at the *kathākālakshepam* performer on stage.*

What...? "She knows how to dress." *Amma, we aren't naked.*

Clearly everyone knows how to. "No, Kannamma, she knows how to dress well." *How can you tell?* "Look at her. Everyone wants her to belong to them. They want to belong to her." *Above all, she looks like… she belongs to herself.*

She was certainly a confident guide. We trusted her that evening. If I am to create ease when performing, tuning between various compulsions of being, may I remember:

We always belong to ourselves.

—

26. on *what frame story as a literary technique is*

Kathākālakshepam. How do I describe this? I don't think I can, my friend.

We dissolved time. The guide would take one story, one song, and spin out a million.

Earth: intercalation is the insertion of stone into stone. In timekeeping, intercalation is inserting something into the time-archive-mechanism, showing something is never complete. Grandmother Latin tells us, *inter* is "between, among;" *calare* is to "proclaim," or to "call." We claimed each other as we called out to each other. Yes.

Layers. Time into time. Stories into stories. *Mise en abyme.* You into me into you.

Come. Let's sing together.*

—

27. on *a map for a new world (2013)*

A student in Vijay Iyer's musicality seminar, Anna Wang, explained she felt *guided* in this particularly effective performance. *Guided.*

There's this one picture in which I sit with unrestrained hair. Smiling, my hands are on a *veena*. I look like a person claimed. In it, I'm sound-checking a piece. The drummer-composer who made this piece called himself *one with the plan.**

He took this responsibility of guiding very seriously. He'd walk as if the future was relentlessly sucking him into itself.

The name of his piece sat atop the score, declaring boldly:

A MAP FOR A NEW WORLD

—

28. on *the brea[d]th of a being*

I felt a relief whenever he snorted. He's so often serious.

I should have clarified: when I said I loved this man, it didn't mean I was *in love* with this man.

When you make music with someone, your spirit-body joins theirs in a dance of creation that can never be undone. You forever become a part of them, and they become a part of you.

If you ever discover someone's innermost rhythm, for however brief a moment, you can never completely forget them. In that moment, they are our lover-child-parent-sibling-friend.

A most powerful love.

—

29. on *being wi[d]th*

Paatu Class. Krishna Anna* sits in front of me, on his iPad. I'm trying to sing something I knew how to sing 10 years ago. The child in me is sneering, the adult is ignoring her. The student is focusing, as to not waste more of his time. There's a me observing all of this, detached. I sing, he makes a sound. I sit, corrected. I sing again, he makes a sound. I sit, corrected.

> *Ganavya*, he says. *Kélu. There are like six versions of you I am teaching. You have to consolidate. I can't teach all six. Just you.*

—

30. on *buddhakṣetra**

Who lived in that house?

She floats in clean lines. Not that there is linearity in non-linearity; perhaps it's just the creation of a slit, to travel in-between worlds. She floats with the ease that bodies emanate when in the pure lands. Do you remember these worlds?

Where intuition was the first sense organ?

Where we saw each other through an ocean of light-filled symmetry? Where all paths led to pleasure? This is the ease I speak of, with no concept of struggle, or defense. Fear whet nothing. Ease warmed us into a graceful fluidity.

She floats in such easy, clean lines.

—

31. on *the first edit*

The Goddess, I knew how to draw with my voice.

This house? I had no idea. But we did, over and over again. The tea kettle, the whisk. The stove, the bed. The arch, the throw, the pots, the gold. We kept drawing the same house: over and over and over again.

> **Thereupon, a certain Goddess, who lived in that house...**

Peter keeps reminding us: "the house is here. Show us, *this* house," *Well, should we start saying who lived in* this *house?* "Yes." We edit scripture:

Thereupon, a certain Goddess, who lived in *this* house, having heard the teaching...

—

32. on *cerberus**

There is something curious about the *Vimalakīrti Sutrā*, reader. Well, there are innumerable curiosities in it. But, there's one thing in particular I wish to tell you.

But first, I want you to meet Robert Thurman.* He translated the *sutrā* to English.

Bob came to visit. To Peter's 300 person seminar, he says: *we need a woman president! But the country isn't ready. So! We need three presidents, one a woman. She'll fix everything, and the men won't be too freaked out.* So on, so forth.

At first, the students laughed. By the end, they had stars in their eyes.

—

33. on *co-travellers*

Bob Thurman. He is Uma Thurman's father.* He tells us a story: he was this mendicant, disheveled clothes; she is the "Baroness Birgitte Caroline von Schlebrügge." He left the Order to be with her.

The Dalai Lama* and him—they were trainees together—have promised each other they will leave this world together.

Our friends voted us least likely to stay together, he says to the class, chuckling. *Well, I'm about to have my 30th anniversary dinner. We'll probably see some of my friends... now divorced,* he laughs.

It's his seminal 1976 English translation of the *sūtra* we're working with.

—

34. on *breaking time again*

There's something curious I'd like for you to know about this *sutrā*. English, a young language, was considered the most recent translation. That's about...two millennia between Thurman's translation and its source.

The Sanskrit version was written about two millennia ago, but was lost for centuries. Thurman was working with Tibetan, which had been translated from Sanskrit.

But then, recently, a Sanskrit manuscript was found buried in Potala Palace.* In 2006, *Āryavimalakīrtinirdeśo Nāma Mahāyānasūtram* was published.

This makes the Sanskrit version *simultaneously the oldest and the newest version* of the *sutrā*. And I'm holding one in my hands right now.*

—

35. on *to whom does what belong?*

Being sprayed by what the adults were angrily chewing and spitting, *what is culture appropriate-ton?* asked the child whose kindly presence was warming my lap.

Something about this moment pierced my heart so deeply, my breath froze. In my memory, most of her head fits in my right palm. I hold it against my chest, praying she isn't ingesting too much.

I'm not sure, I whisper to her, weakly. *It's... like when Natalie had her own toys, but she took yours.* "And didn't share *my toys* with *me*! As if!" she yells. The adults look at us with raised eyebrows.

—

36. on *inner shimmers*

"Having heard this teaching of the Dharma of the great heroic bodhisattvas,"

What is the teaching? How to describe it? I feel it in my bones.

I'm reminded of Wadada's Ankhrasmation.* Did you know where the *ankh* got its shape from? It is a cross section of a thoracic vertebrae of a bull. In Egypt, it was once believed that if you cut open a spine, you would find the masculine liquid of life force.

There are days that flowers unfurl on my skull. Those days, you could cut my spine open, and you would see the Dharmā. It shimmers.

—

37. on *who lives within*

It is *varalakshmi nōmbu.** My father sits front of the altar, smoke billowing. "Time to sing," my mother prompts.

I can't remember what I might have sung back then. If my mother asked me today, I might sing a Dīkśitar* composition called *Śri varalakśmi namastubhyam*, in *Śri rāgam.* I must have sung *Saraswatī vidiyuvatī* in *Hindōlam?*

"Time to bow down," my mother then says. *I will not,* I respond. I am…7 years old. Chaos erupts. *We and she are one,* I say. *I cannot pretend to submit to something I already am.* My father opens his eyes. He smiles.

—

38. on *drawing circles*

I cannot always speak of the Dharmā. I am not such a master of life. But ha! Somewhere between Plato's essentialism and Descartes's duality, we live with Nietzsche in metaphor.* I cannot speak the Dharmā, *but I can sing the Dharmā.*

It is the sound of everything in its right place.

Soon, we arrive to the moment where the Goddess

> **heard this teaching of the Dharma.**

Michael, I ponder, sharply inhaling. *How might I sing the sound of hearing?*

"Hmmm," he says jovially, drawing circles on the floor with his limbs. I recall an old *mudrā*,* and together, we listen.

—

39. on *the rectangle girl*

We'd stand there, frozen in whatever position we were in after having heard the sung Dharmā. I remember: *chathurō*, the 21st *asamyukta* (singlehanded) *hastā*.*

For a moment, look at your palm now. Bend your pinky away. Do you see three fingers, each with three boxes each? You see, this makes three rows and three columns. My limbs were always too long to be the sightly dancer I had hoped to be, but perhaps your boxes are more square-like than my rectangles. 3x3: this is *chathurō.*

Place it to your ears, and you become the image of a still listener.

—

40. on *peter*

But there is a danger to having this kind of language. I do not want to be the *image* of a listener. I want to be *the listener*. How do I do that? Without any prompting, Peter says:

> "Listen to the sound of the trees. This is the Dharma.
>
> The sound of the water splashing. This is the Dharma.
>
> The sound of that swimming coach who is definitely yelling at his student! That is also the Dharma.
>
> The sound of *gandharvā-s** singing, this is the Dharma."
>
> The sound of air as it brushes your nose. This is all the Dharmā.

—

41. on *pauline*

The sound of each cell singing, this is the Dharmā. I think Pauline Oliveros* asks us to make the "sound of a flea circling a singular hair of a polar bear" in *13 Changes*. This is also the Dharma. The sound of lullabies from the future; this is the Dharmā. The sound of your fears, of whether or not you are a good enough artist—this too, is the Dharmā. The sound of you being recognized as an artist, this is the Dharmā. The sound of you no longer caring; this is the Dharmā. Everything, my friend, is the Dharmā.

—

42. on *matcha lattes*

The sound of hopes dying. This, too, is the Dharma. The awards you didn't get, the grants you didn't win—my cherished one, this too is Dharma. The sound of hearts breaking, letting go; this is the Dharma. The sound of the spirit swimming backstrokes in the ether with ease—this, too, is the Dharma. The sound of love being made, this is the Dharma. The look of assurances we give each other, as strangers—this is the Dharma. The million sharp edges on a blade of grass is the Dharma. The Starbucks latte it becomes, too, is the Dharma.

—

43. on *the sound of the dharmā*

Time has travelled since I began this article. It has seen three homes, with an eye on the fourth. In this particular essay, I write to you from a period of great illness and stillness. The pandemic has begun.

We have begun a second production.

In a production meeting, Craig* remembers singing in a cave in Dunhuang. "The paintings began to move," he says, in his deliberate, pensive way. "Her voice activated the work... *It became so clear to me right then...that sound was always meant to accompany us."* I want to reach into the screen and hug him.

—

44. on *the sounders of the dharmā*

Peter says the *karmā* of this—the Vimalakīrti productions—might be a particularly... expeditious one. Michael's father passed during one of the rehearsals. He came back and gave an indescribably transcendental performance. I cannot begin to imagine, but I understand. My first trip to Dunhuang, in a moment of unlistening, my wrist and trust were injured. It still clicks, as I write to you now.

But when we were in the caves, nothing mattered. Everything dissolved. Gently, I hummed in them, comforted by the echoes.

One cave, everyone began singing with me.

This is how they fixed my broken heart.

—

45. on *a beckoning**

I'm reminded of a particular cave in Dunhuang, where the Buddha's heart had been punched into by thieves looking for relics. From a dark, private corner, reaching out to him, I started whisper-singing a song I'd written for a grieving friend:

if I could I would
draw something beautiful
into the holes that were
punched into your heart

if I could I would
lie and tell my mother
father, brother, and my lovers

we'd never be apart

but I'd really rather die
die, if I knew that the
life once in me would fill
the holes in your heart

—

46. on *intoxication*: *an awakening*

I used to drink something to open my heart before shows. When performing, we feel the spirits of all those who have come before us. We become them, they become me, we become we.

But two weeks into driving across the country with little sleep, your heart doesn't have the wherewithal to keep getting out of bed to open the door. Caffeine would wake it up. A dirty martini could shake it up.

Then I'm reminded of what my father said: "go to gym daily, you won't need—*or want*—steroids. The strength of your mind-heart works the same way."*

—

47. on *witnessing how intoxicating a monk's love is*

A brother named Witness sits next to me in this seminar.* When we start talking about Thelonious Monk,* he raises his hand a few times, but the professor isn't facing him.

I reach into his keyboard and petition: "Brother. We want to hear you. Maybe...don't wait to be called. The others didn't wait." He nods.

I just want to take a moment to speak about Monk's love, Witness exhales, steadily.

Witness tells us a story: Bud Powell* and Monk get arrested

for drug possession. Despite the drugs not being his, *Monk claimed responsibility to protect Powell.*

My eyes close.

—

48. on *another monk's love*

A young pianist arrived about 20 minutes late to our rehearsal. Gingerly, the young one tiptoes up to Prof. Newton.*

"I'm sorry," he whisper-speaks. "The bus… it never came. So I took a cab." For a moment, Prof. Newton's face is unreadable. Everyone stiffens.

And how much was this "cab?" he quizzes. "Uh, about $45, sir."

Prof. Newton pulls about fifty from his wallet and hands it to him. "Oh, no, sir." *Yes*, Prof. Newton smiles. *This isn't just for you. We fight for love. This is how we should* always *treat each other.*

We all close our eyes.

—

49. on *dreaming with a monk*

The night after that class, I dreamt of Thelonious Monk. At first, his face was unreadable. We sat in silence for what felt like an eternity; the kind of silence that is almost unbearably loud.

He cleared his throat, and cracked a somehow deeply familiar smile.

Well? this spirit said.

Yes. It's hard for me to usually remember things, let alone in a dream realm. It comes: *Um. Is the story real? Did you regret it?**

We do exactly what we're meant to do, he smiled. *In that moment, I knew I would've regretted not doing it. You get me? That's love.*

—

50. on *dreaming of mothers: for Seiyoung Jang**

We were tasked to write a composition together. *Remember,* our gentle but firm teacher had said. *You are responsible for the music, but also how we will experience it. Frame it accordingly.*

The night before our performance, I dreamt of mothers who raised me. My body was once again small, their warm figures towering around. I sat, cross-legged, eyes closed. It was the most intimate of rituals between women: the braiding of hair.

The next day, while we sang our composition together, my co-performer's experienced hands gently and deftly braided my hair. I knew then: this was a sister.

—

51. on *singing for a monk*

All composed things are like a dream, a phantom, a drop of dew, a flash of lightning. That is how to meditate on them. (Thích Nhất Hạnh,* *The Diamond Sutra*).

I struggled for a while with the descriptor "composer." No two utterances are the same; anything I sing is in forever dialogue with the changing nature of each moment and space. Agency nurtures every choice. Who is not a composer?

But in Meredith Monk's* presence, all these things float away. When she asks us to *compose*, I *want* to. She makes "composer" sound like it is *one who manifests love.*

—

52. on *a resignification*

There are multiple Buddhas? "There are multiple *bodhisattva*-s. You have known *bodhisattva*-s. Remember?" *Well...* I sit with the image.

Spiritual heroes.

How can the spirit be violent? And is that not who a hero is: one who *fights*?

But fighting for good is a necessary fight. In this way, there are spiritual warriors. Once, after returning from a most difficult performance, a friend looked at another and said: "oh, you're exhausted; this is why they call it *spiritual warrior.*"

I repeat the word to myself, letting go of my fear of the word's shape.

Hero. *Let it signify love.*

—

53. on *kalākshetra*

Similar to the Persian suffix *-stan*, in Sanskrit *-kshetra* means "a place."

Kurukshetra, for instance, is the place where King Kuru lived. Kurukshetra is synonymous with war: it is where the epic Mahābhārata war took place.

Kalai is art. Kalākshetra, then, is "the place of art." And indeed it was.*

Moonlight that beamed through tree canopies. Vines, slowly clothing everything from their toes. Dancing...the sound of feet slapping so hard into unforgiving red clay, somedays it felt like the ground was punching our bones back into our knees.

A child, my tongue kept confusing the two: *Kalākshetra. Kurukshetra. Kalākshetra.*

—

54. on a *resign[ific]ation of habits*

...and being delighted, pleased, and overjoyed, manifested herself in a material body.

"Talk to each other," says Peter. "Show us, in *this* house—she is de*light*ed, pleased, OVERJOYED." Every time we arrive to this set of words: *delighted, pleased, and overjoyed,* my body mass becomes a little lighter. Old practices of *bhāva* threaten to surface, *hāsya rasa* waiting to bubble up into my face.*

Then, uttering the words can become a show. It is difficult to walk that line between *feeling* a truth when remembering a memory, versus *telling* of someone's truth when storytelling.

Remember *feeling* the truth.

Then tell.

—

55. on *drawing swirls in the ether*

Delighted, pleased, and overjoyed. My shoulders draw swirls, eddying the spirits and airs around me as I sing—drawing shapes that trace ghosts of graceful movements past. The more I give myself to them, the spirits and airs move me *for me*, slowly buoying my spine as it arches away from pain, shame, and the shrinkage that comes with it; giving wind to my arms, life drawing itself into my fingers through the body's spirit-xylem. With a body already in such movement, the notes that arise from it sit in the nexus of indescribable pleasure, lightness, trust, dissolution, wordlessness.

—

56. on *embodied cognition*

Thus so, **she manifested herself in a material body.** Material body. Gross body. As in: causal, subtle, and gross body*—not as in, "ew, you're gross" body. Strange that these two resonances could live in the same utterance, but our discomforts with the gross body after having known astral bodies could very well reveal itself in, well, gross ways.

And so I must sing a manifestation into a material body. How?

I sing a perfect storm. A note so powerful, I must reckon with the power of my body—*a power that can come only from this kind of body.*

—

57. on *64-bar solos in a jam session*

I mean, this is a long run-on sentence. We could give Jonathan Franzen a run for his money. Typically, by the time we get to the end of "**and being delighted, pleased, and overjoyed, manifested herself in a material body,**" I've found the full-stop.*

But Michael will remind me, there is more: **and showered the great spiritual heroes** (look at each other, remind each other of) **the bodhisattvas, and the great disciples with heavenly flowers.**

The great disciples? Dear Peter, who are they? "Well, we're about to find out!" he laughs.

The so-called "great" disciples. Oh, Sāriputrā.

—

> 58. on an *excerpt from a class presentation; feb. 5, 2019*
>
> "...Auditory Scene Analysis, according to Prof. Trainor, is still unable to provide an explanation for the fact that music induces emotional responses in people, and that music is an intensely social activity. There is scientific proof, she offers, that after '*people move together in synchrony, they rate each other as more likeable, trust each other more.*'
>
> The Darwinist explanation, framing music as an exhibition, an indicator of fitness, lends itself well to the ongoing discussion in music studies on the role of exhibiting virtuosity in music. Um...
>
> It also helps me better understand many an insufferable jam session I've attended." [laughter]

—

59. on *the night of flights*

I'm exhausted. I haven't slept in 50+ hours. I tried to work, but my mind is so tired, I can't write a sentence without it being mangled.

"These people are gonna lose their minds when they hear you," he says. *I just want to pray*, I confess, almost in tears.

He slows.

"That's okay," he says, assuringly. "Just...pray by my side."

Jam sessions can be strange, I say. *Lotta unlistening. My bassist...he likes to call it jazzturbation.* "Oh my God. That's brilliant!" he laughs. "*Jazzturbation*. Text that to my manager right now. Copyright that shit. I'm stealing that!"

—

60. on *prayers: old and new*

We are performing the seventh chapter from the *Vimalakīrti Sutrā*, called *The Goddess*. According to Peter, this is the first feminist text. And perhaps if time was true, so could this assertion be.

The *Vimalakīrti Sutrā* has been around for about two millennia, as have our vehement circumventions of what it speaks of: the simple truths, loves, and pleasures that we were born with, and for. A review of a recent performance called a song I wrote an "ancient Indian spiritual." It was a lullaby for my—and I suppose every—mother.

What does the ancient sound like to you?

—

61. on *books and glass*

I remember the first time I went to Peter's home in Culver City.

As a child, I had two aspects in a dream home: the walls that separated the home from the outside world were to be made of glass, and the walls inside the house were lined with books. My therapist has a thing or two to say about an aching for windows instead of walls, but having a home lined with books… this is a more simple yearning.

As I change, so do the books in this dream home.

And Peter Sellars' home…had all the right books.

—

62. on *mapping my way*

I can't remember where exactly in Detroit we were.

I remember drinking some version of Earl Grey—was it Lady Grey? Something about a dignified taste?—from a place like Panera. We had just spent the afternoon going around Detroit in a service called "Very Special Van Service" to sites like Dr. Ossian Sweet's home,* and meeting Tyree Guyton at the Heidelberg Project.*

Standing in the sun, the master we had all come to work with—Carrie Mae Weems*—asked me:

> "So what is it
> that someone like you
> is doing in school?"

Finding my books, I wanted to say.

—

63. on *agency and abstraction*

I want to ask you, reader, what education means to you.

Particularly, if you are a musician, what does the term "music school" mean to you?

A few of us were having tea in Samita's house.* The walls were a kind of yellow. We were talking about what it means to *create* work.

In my experience of it, you must learn not only *how to read* the symbols of the world (abstraction), but you must also learn that you can *effectively interpret* them (agency).

The currency for this exchange is metaphor. Could school teach the art of trading in this?

—

64. on *wadada's coffee (2016) and prof. silvaticus*

"Over the past year or so, I've become familiar with Smith's coffee-drinking practices.*

The sugar must be brown—sourced from raw sugar cane, if possible. The cream must be thick, and the beans freshly (often manually) grounded. If time permits, steaming water must be poured carefully over the special filter paper, spoon by spoon."

"Okay…?" Prof. Silvaticus says, after reading. "What's the point? He drinks coffee? You know your subject?" *No*, I wince, grabbing the essay back. *Don't ever call him that again.*

This… isn't radical to you because you've always known you can get exactly *what you want.*

—

65. on *tao**

Abstraction—the art of living in metaphor—is the only way to begin describing the indescribable. Folklore and music are but two beloved cities in the land of enlightenment. I have visited a few other cities: dance, writing…

But still, a symbol is a symbol is still a symbol.

Andromeda can only be seen when the eye is not directly looking at it.* Similarly, we may only see the true reality that lives past this particular world when we let it live peacefully in the peripheries of our symbols.

But there is still yet immeasurable pleasure in describing the indescribable.

—

66. on *reading music*

When I told Esperanza* I couldn't yet "read" music, she responded, without missing a beat: "Um. Yeah, you can." *No...I mean, like, Western music. Staff notation. You know.* "You don't have to." *But I want to.* "Why?" *I've had the privilege of studying this much. I have to read what people write for me.* "Why? Clearly, a part of you is resisting." *Yeah, part of it feels violent. But can't keep avoiding everything that feels wrong.* "Mmmmmm. We need people to hold it down, you know? You don't need to believe in someone else's cosmology. Time is being colonized..."

—

67. on *clothing music*

"I've edited the older version...this is what I have now," says Rajna's note. I think of the name of the older song from 10 years ago. Is that perhaps the younger song?

I hear the recording, and begin measuring the sound-body she has sent me. I hastily scribble out *swaram*-s:*

M G S S	G S P N P M
M R N N	R N P N P G
M R N N	M G S N S G
M G S S	R N D N S R

Then, I begin stitching its words-clothes.*

—

68. on *mapping music*

If I were to write a score for this Vimalakīrtī piece, it might just be text from the chapter. It would say: *read the chapter.*

What is a musical score to you? Is it a map that reveals the path to the piece? What is a map to you? Is it what reveals the path to you? I am retracing my steps in this essay, exactly one hundred words at a time. Can this essay be the score for the piece, then?

Instrumentation: How many ever performers. One master portalmaker.

Go, now. *Begin making the house* as only you *could.*

—

69. on *embarrassing music*

I've been asked a few times why I don't reveal or revel in more new material. I want to. But—not to give myself a poetic pass for laziness—all things are both new and old.

For as long as a song has something to teach me, I wish to keep singing with it.

I could sing the same songs for the rest of my life, but I suppose those by my side have the right to ask me not to bore them. Or is it embarrass? I can't always tell.

When did humility and humiliation become such close neighbors?

—

70. on *editing scripture*

> **...and showered the great spiritual heroes, the bodhisattvas, and the great disciples with heavenly flowers.**

Indeed, this is a run-on sentence. "Manifested herself in a material body" would be me feeling the end of a 32-bar solo; hearing "and showered" would be me realizing they're not done yet, arriving to "heavenly flowers" would be me knowing, with certainty, it was time to sing the head.

Scripture and tradition might be holy, but in performance, getting the message across is of paramount sacredness. Peter offers edits:

> **... and showered the great spiritual heroes, and Buddha's "great" disciples with heavenly flowers.**

—

71. on *unnamed music workshop, summer 2017*

"Oh my god, you're like...a goddess," says a *vellakkāri* French participant, after a session in this residency. Something about how she says it feels like she is taking me away from myself. Everything in this place feels virtual.

"And your throat singing! You were doing that, right?" I want to say: *I'm fairly certain nobody was throat singing.* Instead, caught in the space between impulse and execution,* I say nothing. I wonder if it is crueler to go along, or if it is possible to gently burn something. I turn away.

Tell me, are "goddesses" allowed to get annoyed?

—

72. on *improvisor's view on notated music; banff, summer 2017*

One of the powerful lessons I've had was from an Inuk

throat-singer.* She was a holder of space. It is not *space* she held, it was me. A *holder of people.*

She tied a scarf around my waist, restraining me. She wanted me to fight: to repeat the song's story, louder and louder, while I dragged her. It was not easy. She had the strength of a thousand elephants.

Louder. Who sang the song?
*Kanhopatra.**
Louder.
Kanhopatra.
LOUDER.
KANHOPATRA.

NOW! SING!

I sang so loudly, I lost consciousness.

When I regained it, she was right there, by my side.

—

73. on *department of excellence and mastery*

I once understood deeply, that virtuosity could be used as a violent magic.

"Be excellent enough to pull their uneducated spirits out of the mundane," a teacher once said to me before we ascended the stage. "Understand?"

In the past few decades, I have gained language to better pull my fully extended spirit into the mundane. If I had then what I have now, I might have responded:

*Listen carefully, confused one: just as one cannot leave one's mortality, you can never fully leave the mundane. Your—*all*—messiahs are already in the mundane. Fear shrouds their excellence from you.*

—

74. on *an interview with the guardian of the frequently encountered**

"Toumani* also wanted to bring the instrument 'back home,' to reassert its musical soul. He feels that the kora—much like the guitar in the wake of Jimi Hendrix*—has become a vehicle for finger gymnastics and empty displays of virtuosity."

"*People today think that the kora is all about speed,* Toumani says.

Like a Kalashnikov firing off rounds... rat-tat-tat-a-tat-a-tat!

But our forefathers, may they rest in peace, were great players and very fast too. But they preserved the melody. We can all do brrrrrrr ...

But it's not just about improvisation. Where's the melody?"

—

75. on *an excerpt from a paper on mastery*

"'We music scholars, masters of the obvious' says Dr. Vijay Iyer, in a syllabus.

All scholars are masters of the obvious, really. Is that not what scholarship is? A mastering of the obvious?

What exactly is the obvious to you? *Ob viam*; late 16th century Latin for 'frequently encountered'—what is that which is most frequently encountered? To me, it is experiential data; it is life.

By this virtue, every single being is a master of the obvious—a master of life—simply by virtue of living. Every single one of us has access to the canvas of the obvious..."

—

76. on *who isn't a master*

Some strange things music teachers have said to people I love:

"You will never be as good as me. Never. When you become better, remember, I become thousand times better."

(Madras, c. 2005; a 70-year-old master to a 16-year-old soon-to-be teacher)

"You call yourself a musician?"

(Banff, c. 2015; a 60-year-old master to a 25-year-old soon-to-be teacher)

"The only reason we keep you around is for your looks." (California, c. 2016; a 65-year-old master to a 23-year-old soon-to-be teacher)

—

77. on *who is a master*

"Are *you* calling *me* for one of *your* gigs?"

(Boston, c. 2019; a 40-year-old master to a 27-year-old soon-to-be teacher)

"Wait, that's how much they gave me. They're giving *you* the same?"

(New York, c. 2019; a 50-year-old master to a 30-year-old soon-to-be teacher)

"You can't play." "He can't play." "She can't play." "They can't play."

Rarely, have I heard the simplest truths of them all: *we were all meant to play together.*

A true teacher embodies virtuosity without ego.

Come.

Let's go out and play.*

—

78. on *game time*

I was a composer* at The Banff Centre's Creative Gestures residency. We worked with dancers, choreographers. This is where I first worked with Michael.*

During a 7-hour game-ritual where we decided we would do nothing but stay in state of creation, in a sustained state of bliss, I wrote out our war-cry song. We sang:

I asked my ____ to play;
I asked my ____ to play
And this they said to me:
I love you, but not today.

I asked myself to play;
I asked the Spirit to play
That's how it came to be.
We went out and played.

—

79. on *working to the bone*

I tried to flow like water
instead I fell like the rain—

Lyrics, from an old song.*

Michael* guided our daily movement sessions in this residency. "Generous eyes! Don't look in straight lines. Look with the entire eye," he said one morning. Twenty-four bodies released tension being held unbeknownst to themselves.

That evening, a young dancer was crying by the river, drowning in doubt. "Help," she asked. I try to set aside anger that someone chose competition with her, instead of community.

We are the river/
we are the rain—

I sang, holding her, as our tears joined Makhabn river.*

—

80. on *breaking the cycle of darkness*

I want to ask them all: do you not remember the moments of grace that fortified your spirit-body? Do you think not kindness to be a virtue? Did someone tell you that the Manual of Successful Being says you must continue a cycle of pain, and give exactly what you received? My friend, abundance exists right outside of the purview of insecurity.

An invitation for the artist reading this. Write the following sentence in your inner heart-notebook, slowly.

I can yield and bring unspeakable powers into this field without drawing it from another. My practice can give without taking.

—

81. on *a reckoning**

but instead I must
reckon with the fact that I
have nothing
nothing
in this world

that would let me even

draw something beautiful
beautiful, beautiful
into the holes that I've
punched into your heart

draw something beautiful
beautiful, beautiful
into the holes that I've
punched into your heart

Stone sings with you, as marble does. The caves, witnesses of innumerable temporalities, beckon a remembrance of the sound of love, of trees, of dust, of forests. The words morph.

but instead I must
reckon with the fact that I
have something
something
in this world
that would let me even

—

82. on *bringing cycles of light*

We all have musical, artistic, and literal ancestors who lived a life that drew at times from another person's life force to sustain themselves. They did so either from fear or necessity. Although it is a separate work for us to ask ourselves why one does this, that is a separate thought-stream. For now, it is enough to commit to not keep repeating the same violences.

To those ancestors who drew from another's life: *ask for their blessing to live a different way.*

To those ancestors who already found the path to the unlimited source: *ask for their guidance.*

—

83. on *ontologies of you*

I was born in Flushing, New York, on the 10,043rd day of my mother's life. She was far away from her colorful, warm motherland…it was a sacrifice. We spoke about it once. A calculated decision, she wanted me to be able to travel as a musician. She named me *Gānavyā.*

"Your grandfather named you. One who was born to spread music." Two roots: *gānam*, music. This I knew early on. *Vyāpithal*—to pervade? This was not a word I heard used often. I wondered if she made the conjugation up.

I wondered if we all need a creation myth.

—

84. on *an excerpt, from an interview for Elle India:**

"My dad used to play this trick on younger cousins. First, in an unassuming voice he'd ask: '*oru rua venuma?*' Then, with wide-eyes, he'd say: '*pathu paisa venuma*?'* The kid would always pick the exaggerated option. 10p over Rs 1.00.

I have this hazy memory of my mother asking me: *do you want to stay in this strange country, or do you want to go to India, and learn the ways and music of our people?* I must've been four. I went for the one that sounded like *pathu paisa…*"

—

85. on *chronicling my Deccan years*

Interviews are strange in the same way making sound-installations are strange.* You're asking me to have a conversation with many people, without me being present to read their spirits first. It's a different kind of mastery.

But interviews can be nice. They invite us to reveal previously unspoken truths to ourselves.

15 years ago, an interviewer for *Deccan Chronicle* asked me: "M'am, what's your life outside of performance like?"

It feels like a commercial break. Everything is loud, competing to be heard. Lot of bad acting.

But...it helps pay for the show. You learn to sit through it.

—

86. on *our lives in a 100 words or less*

A beloved master biographer once told me: *the secret to writing about others is to listen to their highest self.*

The art of writing a 100-word bio, taking press pictures, chronicling our journey on social media—why do we keep telling our stories? Is it all in service of convincing a listener that we are competent guides?* That we deserve to be heard, attended to? How honest can a story be, if needs to serve a purpose?

I think the highest self does not judge any other self. It allows for the kind of honesty that gently changes histories.

—

87. on *our lived nows in song*

What to say of Mû, the griot?*

Mû and I would sing at Guzzo, a small Barcelonian pub on Plaça Comercial. The money was little. Mû filled my heart. It was enough. Once, I took a 6-hour bus twice to see him for 4 hours. We sang for three.

In an old language, I sang a song about walking together in life. He responded, somehow knowing, with words I recognized: "*com-partim... caminho...* Ganavya." Names followed: of the production assistant, engineer, cameraman.

Someone told me later: "he was singing into history, how we are all are sharing the way together."

—

88. on *the innumerable nows*

When Mike Wallace* told journalist Oriana Fallaci* she's "not a historian," she bit back, literal smoke coming out of her: "*Listen.* A journalist is a historian who writes history in the same moment history happens...*and it is the best damn way to write history.*"

I wonder, are musicians the same? In 1965, John Coltrane* said: "I want to get to a point where I can feel the vibrations of a particular place, at a particular moment and compose a song right there, on the spot."*

Every time, we step into the now, grasping at the future, carrying the past.

—

89. on *metamorphōseōn librī**

Recounting the Rig Veda (c. 1200–900 BCE), an author writes on what is *The Role of A Poet*:

> Varunā confided in me, the wise one:
> *who knows the trail*
> should whisper them like secrets, if he is to speak to future generations as an inspired poet."*

It goes on: "only after the intervention of [the Vedic God] Varuna does the poet—who is the *wise* one (*medhira*)—become the *inspired* one (*vipra*)."

This metamorphosis comes with a responsibility: you simultaneously "become both the keeper and the transmitter" of a tradition, where *performance is a way of knowledge.*

—

90. on *an excerpt, from an interview for Elle India, pt. 2:**

"...but ultimately, here's the truth: just as all money is constructed value, all notions of cultural belonging or purity are constructed.

There is beauty in knowing the way home home, learning to ask my tongue to dance in the same shapes of my foremothers'... but *sanctuary is a state of mind,** and I think learning this is what my growing years was about.

For as long as I remember, my mother had a deep aching to return home. I think she wanted me to know what it was she was aching for. Or perhaps she didn't want an American daughter..."

—

91. on *rest your weary head*

My first home in India was *Sengottai*, the "red fort"—a village near *Kuttrālam* waterfalls. Every home had a *thinnai*: an *-anai* (sleeping place) with certainty (*thin-*). It's an open part of the house where weary travelers, perhaps a traveling musician, could always come rest.

It was a permanent platform bed, attached to the front of the house like the ever-welcoming ear of an elder. We had seven streets in the *agrahāram*. I lived on *Amman sannidhi theru*, or the "street that stretched out from the inside of the Goddess's temple."

From every *thinnai*, you'd see the sanctum sanctorum.

—

92. on *the city of angels*

James and Jo Ann Newton:* this is who I thought of when I wrote *like the ever-welcoming ear of elders*.

Following the premiere of *Goddess*, Esperanza* met them briefly. "They look like...benevolent angels," she said. Indeed they are, and there are days I wonder what I've done to deserve such immense love.

"Your happiness is our happiness. Do you understand?" they'd said, a week ago. *Yes, I am happy*, I'd said. But some days, I don't understand.

Years ago, when sitting in his LA studio, I took a rare picture of him. There was a halo around his head.

—

93. on *the village of pillars*

Women have gathered in Bāmā Māmi's house. She lives in *Mel theru*: three streets and an entire world away. I am seven. I hide behind the pillars in her Senkottai garden. She teaches them a song that would plant itself deeply in me:

Āyirangāl mandappathil annai Meenakshi,
alankāra ponnoonjalil ādum kankākshi
Meenakshi ādum kankākshi

in the thousand-legged hall, Mother Meenakshi,
sways in an ornate golden swing, what a sight for the eyes
Meenakshi, what a swaying sight

The thousand-pillared hall is real. Every time I whisper-sing this to myself, it carries the weight of a thousand echoes.

—

94. on *the hall of thousand pillars*

The thousand-pillared hall is real. It exists in my mother's beloved Madurai Meenakshi Amman temple. Mother saw her Meenakshi Amman everywhere. She saw her in me, in the music I tried to play, in the games the neighbor's child made up, in a bride's shyness, in stone, in sky.

Meenakshi ādum kankākshi,
aval ādum kankākshi.
Navamani magutam ...

I notice that this chorus of elder women sing "*aval.*" They use the informal. Meenakshi—the one wearing a nine-jeweled crown—is still somehow their *little one*. Peering from behind this pillar caked in cracked *sunnāmbu*,* I join in the chorus.

—

95. on *the map to the inner world*

A single tear falls. It is close to 7AM, snowing in Cambridge. Gently, but surely, I am mourning. I am mourning my thousand-pillared hall. When will I sing again with the family that swims on its ceilings? For a moment, I don't want to live here anymore.

This thousand-pillared hall is real. It's so real Google tells me it has 4/5 stars and twenty-two reviews. We have a *phone number* now, for this ancient hall? "Suggest an edit. Own this business?"

Breathe.

I walk into the temple inside myself. There, I whisper-sing:

Āyirangāl mandappathil …

—

96. on *surfaces and what resurfaces*

I remember the first time I looked back at the video of our opening. I hadn't seen myself move in a while. Although the room in Kaufman* had a mirror-wall, Peter and Michael were my trusted mirrors. I faced them.

The auditorium was not marble, nor stone. The seats, and the bodies that soon came to fill them, absorbed what little resonance the hall had. This was okay. Their presences gave us something else.

A minute into the drawing of the house, I quoted a song from my childhood. Something about a Goddess swaying in a thousand-legged hall…

—

97. on *the ending of the beginning*

with heavenly flowers.

We began the piece by reading this paragraph together, to the audience. We perform the paragraph in song and dance, and then we utter the entire paragraph one more time, together, a little out of breath.

After having rehearsed it in Glorya Kaufman's building, we created Āmrapālī's house,—both women who understood what dance does for the human spirit. A certain Goddess floated, in such clear lines, slits between worlds, before becoming still to listen to the everything-nothing Dharma.

Overjoyed, the Goddess manifested herself into a tangible body. She rains divine flowers. Here, the prologue ends.

—

98. on *arriving to the start*

Except the text *still* isn't revealing itself. The day before the performance, Peter closed his eyes tightly, exhales, and returns.

> **"The great heroic bodhisattvas."**

Let's just say awakened beings, he says.

Yeah. Let's just say awakened beings.

This is how we arrive to the prologue text as it stands today:

> **Thereupon, a certain Goddess who lived in this house, having heard the teaching of the Dharma of the great heroic awakened beings, and being delighted, pleased, and overjoyed, manifested herself in a material body; and showered the great spiritual heroes, the awakened beings, and Buddha's "great" disciples with heavenly flowers.**

—

99. on *new york, the old ghost town*

The pandemic has struck. Life has changed, for everyone.

Live performers understand how close livelihood and liveliness have been all along. An exodus forms from the city.

For many, it is unprecedented terror. It has mobilized others. The line between public and community fades. There is no time for incoherence.*

For some, the state of ar/rest is a relief. We have not allowed ourselves the opportunity to stay at home, confront our familiar fears for more than a few days at a time,* eat food that has been made by familial hands. A time of great illness, and stillness.

—

100. on *7 deer hill lane*

After quarantining alone for months, Adobuere* wonders if we could visit expanse together.* We find Bear Mountain, by Seven Lakes.

She sighs: *sorbet?* Everything's closed.

It'll work, we bet. And...it does.

The woman hands us a bag with "JOY" scribbled. It's the best ice cream I've ever had.

While driving back, Rajna points to a deeply familiar house. We pull in.

We could open a residency, we quietly think. *It'll take all of our savings. And then some.*

But...artists will need homes and food soon. We shudder.

She thinks I'm the manifester; I think it's her.*

—

101. on *live, from our living rooms*

Every time we do an online show during this pandemic, I remember Vimalakīrtī. "836 people are viewing right now."

In these strange times, like his *simhāsanā*-s,* through the magic of these devices,* my living room expands to fit 836 guests—and it can expand to fit a thousand more. But I am not Vimalakīrtī; I am struggling to sense everyone with the ease I am used to.*

Next week, we begin *Ch. 2: Inconceivable Skill in Liberative Technique.* Master Wang Dongling will beam in from China; Peter from LA, Michael from Amsterdam.* It reads:

The body is egoless, like ether...

Footnotes

By special request of the author all footnotes have been placed at the end of the essay instead of within the body of text. —Editor

1. Peter Sellars (b. 1957) is a theatre director. He doesn't like the word director. Peter is a studier, lover, and maker of worlds. Perhaps in that order.

Once, I told my father that I was working with Peter. He was impressed. This surprised me—father tends to inhabit a different set of worlds than my own—only for him to put his book down, take his glasses off, and clarify: "I'm impressed because Peter *Sellers* died many years ago."

So I opened the computer and would show my father our Peter Sellars: hair, bejeweled eyes, patterned shirt, *māla*, and all.

2a. Qene (ቅኔ), also referred to as *säm əna wärq*, is a style of Ethiopian poetry where words are composed with two layers of meaning. The *säm* ("wax"—the apparent meaning) and *wärq* ("gold"—the less apparent meaning). Through my friend and curator Anita N. Bateman's work, I found this writing by Emanuel Admassu from *Age of Anxiety* Double Take for *Manual 14: Shadow* (published in conjunction with *Defying the Shadow* exhibition, RISD Museum) that is useful here:

> Quene, or sem ena worq (wax and gold) is an Ethiopian linguistic strategy used in poetry, music, and daily language to share a hidden message. A word or phrase can have multiple meanings, depending on varied enunciations of different sections. The *sem* (wax) provides the first layer, while the *worq* (gold) represents the deeper, hidden meaning ... the goldsmithing analogy refers to the subordinate role of the wax in the process of shaping gold jewelry. The phonetic system of Ge'ez alphabet also permits another level of flexibility, allowing the speaker to loosen or tighten the pronunciation to achieve different meanings.

2b. The quote is from Act II, Scene 6 in Shakespeare's *Antony and Cleopatra.*

Common belief is that much of Shakespeare's insight into Cleopatra came from Plutarch's *Lives.* About 200 years after the death of Cleopatra and Antony, Plutarch writes the account of how she managed to travel to the inner chambers of Caesar by rolling herself within a mattress and ordering Apollodorus the Sicilian to clandestinely carry her in. (I would try and be more specific, but when I tried to look up "Cleopatra mattress," I'm met with a wall of adverts for a memory foam bed, and I'm already a month late in sending this piece in. So I trust you will be able to sort the rest out, if curiosity persists. The mattress seems to have good enough reviews, though.)

I invoke this line in particular for a reason. Cleopatra is not often remembered as the brilliant politician she was: a queen who barely needed a translator despite being at the nexus of innumerable worlds. Perhaps Shakespeare saw her more clearly than Plutarch did.

Cleopatra VII was quite the *certain* queen, often reduced in our collective stories as "a certain queen."

3. You'll notice that in this collection, I will cite my sources as I would speak them. This is intentional. It is more for my mother and daughter to understand what I write (if they choose to read this one day), than to irritate the academic. I trust that I may depend on you, my dear academic, to find ways to be irritated regardless of what I do. Cheers. Right. So—

The article I refer to that was written by Larry, was published in the 2019 Winter edition of the *Chamber Music* magazine. It was called "Changing Courses," and can be found in pp. 20–23.

6. Amir John Haddad (b. 1975) known popularly in the flamenco community as "El Amir," is a beloved spirit and guitarist. During this particular memory, we were working together in Lisbon, answering a call that flautist Jorge Pardo (b. 1956) had put out to about ten of us, all from different corners of the world.

7. Tamil: "Grandmother, Tukaram Uncle. Aren't elders known to (literally: seen by) us doing this, my child?" *Kanna* is a word we use in Tamil to describe Lord Krishna as a baby; it is also a common term of endearment used among Tamil speakers.

"Grandmother" refers to Seetha Doraiswamy (b. 1926), a Tamil musician primarily known as a *jalatharangam* artiste. Tukaram Ganapathy, born Ganapathy Moorthy (1956) is a *harikathā* exponent of Tamil origin.

8. Most commonly, in Sanskrit, *"Simha"* is understood to refer to a lion, but it may refer to "powerful one," a kind of temple, a mythical animal, or a kind of melody. *"Asanā"* refers to a seat, or throne. Lion-throne. A melody that holds you. In the sūtra, the seat of a powerful one.

10. Materialism is defined as the belief that everything—even intangible things, like states of mind—is born from the interaction with tangible, material things. For instance, the belief: "if I don't eat food, I will starve."

12a. Āmrapālī was a court dancer in Vaishāli, ca. 500 BC. I suppose saying she was a court dancer doesn't do her story justice.

A story goes that she was so beautiful, men in the country began fighting over her; the only way the country could find peace was to force her to become a *nagarvadhu*, the wife (*vadhu*) of the city (*nagaram*). In return for this "service," she was given a home and a grove.

In some stories, when she first approached the Buddha to become his student, he is said to have gently told her that a woman could not join, for it may confuse the men.

She is said to ask: *are your students so easily distracted? Is the dharma so fragile?* And so, Āmrapālī would become the first *bhikṣuṇī*, or ordained female Buddhist monk.

12b. Somewhere, amidst all this, King Bimbisāra—ruler of the neighboring kingdom of Magadha—would hear of Āmrapālī's beauty, eventually falling hopelessly in love with her. The years would reveal that his son Ajātashatru would fall in love with Āmrapālī as well, and would later imprison and eventually kill his own father.

In the Dunhuang caves, you'll find images from this story. One in particular stuck in my heart: the image of Bimbisara licking his wife while in prison. When we first saw it, somebody in the group made a strange joke. Peter laughed, and clarified: "no, what's actually happening is, his son was starving him... so the Queen covered herself in an edible paste, so she could feed him."

If memory serves me right, Ajātashatru's mother sensed during her pregnancy that her son might prove to be a greatly violent force, and had him tossed from the balcony soon after being born. He survived, and eventually realized the Queen's fears. Similarly, in Oedipus—which written around the same time—Queen Jacosta hears of a prophecy that states that her son will kill her husband and pursue her. She tries to have him killed as an infant. This child, too, survives, and realizes the prophecy. A royally patricidal time.

13a. For so long, while looking in the archives for primary sources, I had no idea what his first wife's name is—the one who made Holden Chapel possible. Eventually, I learnt that his mother's name is Priscilla Watt. I can tell you when Samuel Holden's father died, how much money he left behind (£60,000 in the mid-1700s: is that close to £4,000,000 today?); I can even tell you what Priscilla Watt's father's name was. I can tell you every job her father had. With very little effort, I can tell you all of these things. But what I couldn't tell you with certainty, was what Samuel Holden's first wife's name was.

13b. Claire Chase (b. 1978) is a flautist; a soloist, collaborative artist, and cultural activist. See essay (8): on *the invitation to the simhāsanā.*

Hers is a liberative pedagogy; the most generous and generative of presences. She is an activist and an activator; she fights for the *dharmā* like lives depend on it—*because they do.* As an educator, she is unparalleled in her enthusiasm and belief in students. Also, sometimes she'll wear incredibly shiny golden shoes, and her big flute is lovingly named Big Bertha. BB, as it were.

15a. This is an excerpt from an essay I had written in 2019 titled *Tilakāśtamahiśabandanam: The Deconstruction of Reality in the Child* for Profs. Vijay Iyer and Chris Hasty's seminar on musicality. See essay (27): on *a map for a new world (2013).*

15b. Alaín Perez (b. 1977) is a Cuban bassist, composer, singer, and educator. He bursts to the seams with love and radiance. I studied with him when I became one of the first graduate students to be accepted into Berklee College's newly minted graduate program in Contemporary Performance.

A particular evening comes to mind. Following the passing of his mentor, friend, and bandleader, the legendary flamenco guitarist Paco de Lucía (b. 1947), we played together. It was the first concert with Paco's band after his death. The grief was palpable. Prof. Danilo Pérez (b. 1965) guided the evening's performance. We sang Paco's songs, in the Palau de les Arts Renia Sofia in Valencia, Spain. It began a heavy evening, but the music slowly lightened the weight in their hearts, by cracking open the cage that held the rivers threatening to overflow in them. It was an intergenerational exercise in healing.

16. Central is a red-line subway station in Cambridge, Massachusetts, one stop away from Harvard.

17. To those who subscribe to a particular kind of world view, non-musician refers to an individual who is not a musician. When read in Tamil, the phrase curiously becomes *nān musician*: "I am a musician." This kind of humorous inter-linguistic wordplay is typical of my grandmother.

When writing this, I am reminded of my grandmother's infamous "kitchen orchestra," where she would make instruments from what grains, pots, and pans were in the house. Many a woman found reprieve in this orchestra, including myself. It formed a network of trust; it subverted a meme women were expected to submit themselves to. It allowed for a moving together. For further study on advantages of making music together, see footnote (58). "Remember," grandmother would tell the women, while carrying and dropping a million things. "Just use your ears, don't think too much. You will see you already have the music."

19a. See essay (16): on *hardeep mann's "ashram".*

19b. See essay (3): on *breaking a word.*

20. Michael Schumacher (b. 1962) is an American born dancer-choreographer. He has taught many of us how to move our bodies and voices with more freedom, and less fear.

22. See footnote (16).

23a. The album *Of Agency and Abstraction* was released on Biophilia Records in 2019. Jez Collins wrote of this particular track on *Pop Matters*:

"Yathi" opens with the deep, husky tone of Rajna's own voice, a perfect accompaniment to the sax, mridangam [sic] and violin instruments, before unexpectedly, and rather wonderfully, merging with Ganavya's voice.

23b. Śyāma Śāstri (b. 1762) is a *karnātik* composer.

24a. Vijay Iyer (b. 1971) is an American pianist, composer, scholar. He is the Franklin D. and Florence Rosenblatt Professor of the Arts at Harvard University, where he founded a doctoral program in music called Creative Practice and Critical Inquiry.

It was with his presence that I began writing short essays, exactly 100 words each. (The alternative was a constant barrage of tiny thoughts, or sporadic long—and I mean, truly, long—essays. This helped.) During a formative period at Harvard, as I was finding the path back to myself, his light was always to be found, somewhere nearby. His is a remarkable—and sometimes intimidating—focus. But in the quiet in-betweens, his is a *sātvik* gentleness and awareness that keeps its ears wide open, even when eyes are closed.

24b. Ishmael Wadada Leo Smith (b. 1941) is an American composer, trumpeter, author, and creator of musical language-system Ankhrasmation. My thesis at UCLA focused on his way of life, and Ankhrasmation. Once, in Banff, a promise was made to always be friends. I hope to honorably fulfill the promise in our lifetimes.

25. *Kathākālakshepam* is a ritual performance. See essay (26): on *what frame story as a literary technique is.* The performer on the stage was Smt. Vishākā Hari (b. 1981), a *kathākālakshepam* artist.

26. See essay (77): on *who is a master.*

27. José Andrés Cid de León Márquez, (b. 1986) is a Mexican drummer and composer. His pseudonym is "one with the plan." Hear: Track 2 "Homage to Fear" from *Rise* (2015).

29. T. M Krishna (b. 1976) is a Karnātik vocalist, author, activist. Anna is a Tamil word that translates to "older brother."

30. *Buddhakṣetra* translates to "place of Buddha." See essay (53): on *kalākshetra.*

32a. Cerberus is a member of a multi-headed animal family in Greek mythology, and is most commonly depicted as a three-headed hound charged with having to guard the passage between earth and the underworld.

32b. Robert Thurman (b. 1941) is an American Buddhist author, scholar, and educator.

33a. Uma Karuna Thurman (b. 1970) is an American-born actress. "*Karunā*" in Sanskrit and Pāli translates to "compassion."

33b. Here, I refer to his Holiness the 14th Dalai Lama, Tenzin Gyatso (b. 1935).

The reader may know that the Panchen Lama is a reincarnated figure who will help find the next Dalai Lama. The Panchen Lama was identified as Gedhun Choekyi Nyima (b. 1989). Shortly after being identified, both he and his family disappeared into what the People's Republic of China refers to as "protective custody," to receive a "free compulsory education." They have not been seen since 1995. Instead, the People's Republic of China "chose" their own Panchen Lama. For this reason and others, the 14th Dalai Lama may not choose to return to this earth hereafter.

34. Potala Palace was once the Dalai Lama's winter abode, many years ago. It has now been rendered a non-viable option to live, after recurring military attacks. It has held innumerable scrolls and artifacts.

I think Craig made this observation while we were at U.B.C. Coffee in the Xi'an Xianyang International Airport. To know who Craig is, see footnote (43).

36. Ankhrasmation is the music language system developed by Wadada Leo Smith. See footnote (24b).

37. *Varalakshmi nōmbu* is a day of rituals dedicated to the goddess/es. The ritual is said to have been born in the ancient land of Magadha. See footnote (12b).

38a See essays; (63): on *agency and abstraction* and (64): on *wadada's coffee (2016) and prof. silvaticus.*

38b. The *hastā*-s, or *mudrā*-s, form the dactylological language that *bharatanātyam* dancers use. It's worth saying the history of *bharatanātyam* is fraught with inaccuracies; it is worth reading Prof. Davesh Soneji's book published in 2012 titled *Unfinished Gestures: Devadasis, Memory, and Modernity in South India.*

39. See footnote (38b).

40. The *gandharvā*-s are heavenly musical beings in Hindu, Buddhist, and Jain mythology. Highly revered musicians are also referred to as *gandharvā*-s. See footnote (53b) for *gāndharva veda.*

41. Pauline Oliveros (b. 1932) was an American composer, accordionist, and founder of the "deep listening"

improvisatory school of thought. She was Claire's mentor. [See essay (14): on *hanging upside down together*]. Pauline's was a philosophy of love, freedom from systems, and freedom to reimagine and create new systems through co-being.

43. Craig L. Yee (b. 1966) is an author and the founding director of Ink Studio, a Beijing-based experimental art studio. He is also a student of master calligrapher Wang Dongling (b. 1945), with whom we are working for this second production. His is a knowledgeable, assured, and assuring presence. As I write this, I see a copy of *Tao Te Ching* he sent me, which keeps me company on late nights such as this one. The second production I refer to here is with Michael [see footnote (20)], myself, and master Wang Dongling. It is a performance of the second chapter in the *sūtra*, and addresses the body.

45. See essay (81): on *a reckoning*.

46. See father's antimaterialism as discussed in essay (10): on *breaking a fast*.

47a. Witness Fireboy Matlou (b. "I'm the mystery man") is a South African pianist, composer, and scholar.

47b. Thelonious Sphere Monk (b. 1917) was an American composer and pianist who is deeply loved and revered.

47c. Earl Rudolph "Bud" Powell (b. 1924) was an American composer and pianist considered a genius by many.

48. James Newton (b. 1953), is an American composer, flutist, and educator. He was my thesis advisor during my graduate studies at UCLA, and has since been a father; his wife, Jo Ann Newton, a mother. Words cannot describe the generosity of their spirit, and the strength of their ethical compass. Every step I have taken since meeting them has been supported by their belief in me.

49. p.143 in Robin Kelly's 2009 publication titled *Thelonious Monk: The Life and Times of an American Original* has more to say on the arrest referred to in the story. See essay (46): on *witnessing how intoxicating a monk's love is.*

50. Seiyoung Jang (b. 1993) is a composer, improviser, and scholar. She knows how to fix broken lights.

51a. Thích Nhất Hạnh (b. 1926) is a Vietnamese Buddhist monk, and the founder of the Plum Village Tradition.

51b. Meredith Jane Monk (b. 1942) is an American composer, performer, director, vocalist, filmmaker, and choreographer. Hers is a nurturing, loving, wise, ageless, and steady presence. Also, we think her pet turtle might be enlightened?

53a. See essay (30): on *buddhakṣetra*.

53b. Kalakshetra is a fine arts academy, now university, founded in 1936 in Chennai, Tamil Nadu. It was founded to study "*bharatanātyam* and the *gāndharva veda*" musics as discussed in the *nātyashāstra*. An *upaveda* is considered an applied knowledge derived from a scripture; *gāndharva veda* is the study of sound in healing and being, derived from Sāma veda. See footnote (40) for *gāndharvā*-s. See footnote (38b) on casteism and the history of *bharatanātyam* and other "classical" Indian arts.

54. Although *bhāva* in Buddhism refers to compulsive emotive patterns, here, I refer to *bhāva* as discussed in the *nātyashāstra* and rasa theory: it is the art of expression in theatre. *Hāsya rasa* is joy.

56. A being has three bodies and five sheaths, according to the Doctrine of the Three Bodies. Translated to English, they are: the causal, subtle, and gross bodies.

57. Indian English for the punctuation mark known as "period" in the U.S.

58. The article I refer to was written by Laurel J. Trainor in 2015, and is called "The origins of music in auditory scene analysis and the roles of evolution and culture in musical creation." It was published in *Philosophical transactions of the Royal Society of London. Series B, Biological sciences*, issue 370.

62a. Although they had enough capital, Dr. Ossian Sweet and his family were unable to buy a home due to American racism. They would eventually find a home and pay more than it was worth—still yet, they were constantly attacked in their home by violently racist mobs. Dr. Sweet's case became a landmark trial in the ongoing struggle for equity in the United States.

62b. Tyree Guyton (b. 1955) is an American neo-expressionist artist who is a proponent of Graffiti art and Urban Environmental art. He transformed his entire childhood neighborhood into a living indoor/outdoor art museum, known as the Heidelberg Project.

62c. Carrie Mae Weems (b. 1953) is an influential contemporary American artist, who developed a complex body of art employing photographs, text, fabric, audio, digital images, installation, and video. Hers is a royal, stunning, careful, deliberate, and elegant presence.

Under her care, as a member of the inaugural cohort of fellows at Detroit's The Carr Center, we would participate in the 13th Havana Biennial, where I would premiere my first sound installation titled *Daughter of a Temple*, which drew from Alice Coltrane-Turiyasangītānandā's 1977 self-published manifesto *Monument Eternal*.

Alice Coltrane-Turiyasangītānandā (née McLeod; b. 1937) is an American vocalist, harpist, multi-instrumentalist, and spiritual figure.

63. Samita Sinha is an American artist, vocalist and composer who combines experiment and tradition to create new forms of performance using voice, body, sound, and space.

64. See footnote (24b).

65. Read: Laozi's *Tao Te Ching*, alternatively spelt *Daodejing*. The *tao* is a path, a way, a belief system, an unnamable but ever-present force. See footnote (43) to learn how I got a copy of this book.

Janani Balasubramanian (b. 1991), a gentle and powerful artist, pointed this out one day in conversation. Theirs is an astronomically beautiful mind.

66. Esperanza Spalding (b. 1984) is a vocalist, bassist, healer, composer, librettist, scholar, and shunner of such bios, so I think I will leave the rest of the sentence be. Hers is a presence with remarkable integrity, intention, and unparalleled commitment to the betterment of this world. See essay (86): on our lives in a 100 words or less. Instead, I offer this space in printed ether to house her spirit in these various books when she so desires: [ ]. (Drawing plants, flowers, and water nearby may encourage a visit to your particular book. Just sayin'.)

67a. *Swarā*-s are pitches. *Shadjam, rishabam, gāndharam, madhyamam, panchamam, dhaivatham, nishadham* make seven. Each note in-between has a name as well. In short, we write them as: S R G M P D N. A comma denotes a space. Some use capitalization to denote length as well. Happy birthday, then, might be: S S R , S , M , G , , , , , . Our notation system is fairly simple: I'm yet to see a system that handle what and how we sing. I suspect the system will remain a largely oral tradition.

67b. Hear: "Vagabonds" by Rajna Swaminathan featuring lyrics in Tamil by Ganavya Doraiswamy. Available on *Of Agency and Abstraction*, released on Biophilia Records in 2019.

71. The "space between impulse and execution" is a phrase that Michael helps me explore; this particular English phrase, although written a long time ago, I now deeply associate with him. A beautiful excerpt from a letter where he comforts me:

> You will know when the time is right. And when you know, you will act. And when you act, you will bring with you all of the experiences you have gathered while learning to be gentle enough to survive in this world. At first, you might be extra loud and rough just to create a balance within yourself. The gestures you made while being submerged might suddenly seem jerky and out of control. But eventually, after your truths are told, those jerky gestures and snapping emotions dissipate and disappear. Eventually, all gestures become the dance between impulse and character. Luckily, it is a fluid process! Nothing needs to be fixed or set. So, as you strive to find gesture while being submerged in waters heavy with worry... remember to consider all movement as dance, all sound as music, all words as poetry, all emotions as soul. Don't be afraid.

72a. Here, I am referring to Tiffany Kuliktana Ayalik (b. 1988)—a vocalist, composer, actress, songwriter, and educator of Inuit ancestry from Yellowknife, Northwest Territories, Canada.

72b. Kānhōpātrā is a 15th century saint in the *vārakari* tradition. Hers is a beautiful, heart wrenching story. One version is told this way: born into a community of entertainers and dancers, a young Kanhōpātra follows the sound of a drum into the temple of Pandharpur. Upon realizing her caste, the priests and holy men attempt to throw her out of Pandharpur. As soon as her body crosses the perimeter, it loses life. Stunned, they bring it back in, only for her life to re-enter. She challenges the men, claiming her ancestry is ones of saints who understand the human condition to be past structures of inequity—she names her chosen family as venerated saints and artists of the past. The men understand, and ask her to become their guide in life, and live in the temple. (Hear: "Ripple Effect," 2:57 onwards from *Of Agency and Abstraction*, released on Biophilia Records in 2019. An *abhang* by Kanhōpatrā is heard on *Indo Blue*, on the album *Aikyam: Onnu*, released in 2018 on Yāttirai Records; the Tamil translation of the Mongo Santamaria's standard *Afro Blue* alludes to Kanhopātrā's story).

74a. The following is from an excerpt from an interview published in *The Guardian* by Andy Morgan in 2014 titled "*Toumani and Sidiki Diabaté: It's like an entire music industry in one family.*" On the term "frequently encountered," see essay (75): on *an excerpt from a paper on mastery*.

74b. Toumani Diabaté (b. 1965) is a master griot and Malian *kora* player. For years, his song "Warbé" with Ali Ibrahim "Ali Farka" Touré (b. 1939, Malian guitarist) was my medicine for motion sickness when on tour.

74c. James Marshall "Jimi" Hendrix (b. 1942) was an American rock guitarist, singer, songwriter, and composer.

77. See essay (26): on *what frame story as a literary technique is.*

78a. See essay (51): on *singing for a monk.*

78b. See footnote (20).

79a. Lyrics are from a song of mine called "work to the bone", that which created from a monologue called *Rainbows on the Floor* by playwright Anu Yadav (b. 1977).

79b. See footnote (20).

79c. The Makhabn river near The Banff Center is also known as Bow river, in Banff, Alberta, Canada.

81. See essay (45): on *a beckoning.*

84a. The *Elle* article I'm referring to can be found on p. 77 of the February 2020 issue, titled "Vocalist Ganavya Doraiswamy's new album merges prose with genre-bending music," written by Akhila Krishnamurthy.

84b. Tamil, "do you want one rupee, or 10 *paise*?" 100 *paise*, 100p, makes 1 rupee, or Rs. 1.00.

85. See footnote (62c), on my first sound installation.

Similar to this written piece, *Daughter of a Temple* (2019) borrows from *harikathā* structure, where many interrelated theories, themes, and thoughts are organized by one primary skeletal narrative. Instead of centering what are typically male *sant* ("saint") narratives from a conveniently untraceable past, I use the tools and technologies that this old story-telling and musicking ritual offers, but center voices in the now. I do this because divinity is not a thing of the past. The gods are with us, and speak to us, now. Our lived nows in sound. See essay (87).

In *Daughter*, I use Alice-Coltrane Turiyasangītānandā's self-published manifesto, *Monument Eternal* as the *santacharitram*, or narrative of the *sant* that is used as the primary text. Here, in this collection of essays, my work with Peter becomes the largest container, within which innumerable threads are held.

Daughter was a pre-recorded performance that played continuously for a month alongside the work of a brilliant cohort at The Carr Center in Carrie Mae Weems's *The Spirit That Resides*, in Havana, Cuba. My piece was routed through two megaphones: this was in part to invoke the image of a loudspeaker, a meme that is commonly associated with the broadcasting of various religious and divine messages in South Asia. It also was a nod to Detroit's turf wars on religious sounds, between the Muslims and Christians. In the end, neither party won; both lost. Similarly, if both megaphones in *Daughter* are activated at the same time, it would render neither megaphone useful. Instead, the resulting feedback may cost you your longterm hearing.

86. On guides: see essay (27) on *a map for a new world (2013)*; see essay (25) on *having ishtyle: a map to ourselves*; and essay (26) on *what frame story as a literary technique is.*

87. Mû Mbana is a griot; a singer, poet, composer, and multi-instrumentalist from Guinea-Bissau, currently living with his family in Spain. A griot is a West African tradition of historians, where they maintain and record history through the art of song.

88a. Mike Wallace (b. 1918) was an American journalist and media personality.

88b. Oriana Fallaci (b. 1929) was an Italian journalist, author, and interviewer. The interaction I'm referring to here can be seen in the documentary film *Mike Wallace Is Here*, directed by Avi Belkin, released in 2019.

88c. John William Coltrane (b. 1926), husband of Alice Coltrane-Turiyasangītānandā [see footnote (62c)], was an American saxophonist and composer.

88d. Also said Coltrane, as described in Kareem Abdul-Jabbar's 2007 publication *On the Shoulders of Giants: My Journey Through the Harlem Renaissance*, p. 249:

> I would like to bring to people something like happiness. I would like to discover a method so that if I want it to rain, it will start right away to rain. If one of my friends is ill, I'd like to play a certain song and he will be cured; when he'd be broke, I'd bring out a different song and immediately he'd receive all the money he needed.

89a. This is the original Latin title for poet Ovid's (b. 43 BC) *Books of Transformations*, a narrative epic poem that delves deeply into mythology.

89b. Published in 2017 by R. Parthasarathy, the title of the book is *Erotic Poems from the Sanskrit: An Anthology*; this same text is also found in p. 316 in *The Tale of an Anklet: An Epic of South India*, by Iḷaṅkōvaṭikaḷ, as translated by R. Parthasarathy, published in 1995.

90a. See footnote (84a).

90b. I'm only doing this for one topic. See selected essays on sanctuary: (3) on *breaking a word*; (11) on *breaking time: a family portrait*; (12) on *making sanctuaries*; (13) on *mrs. samuel holden's first name*; (16) on *ms. hardeep mann's "ashram"*; (18) on *feeling [ar]rested*; (19) on *breaking away: 588 vanderbilt ave*; (91) on *rest your weary head*; (92) on *the city of angels;* (95) on *the map to the inner world*; (100) on *7 deer hill lane*.

92a. See footnote (48).
92b. See footnote (66). Footnote (66) can be a spring home, and this a summer one: [ ].

94. Tamil: slaked lime, used to coat buildings.

96. See essay (12): on *making sanctuaries*.

99. Says Wadada [footnote (24b)] in his artist statement, available on his website as of 2020:

> What defines all of us as human beings is the inspiration and knowledge to *make coherent choices, informed through science, art, and authentic spiritual practice* to develop a genuine care for others and the world we live in (emphasis added).

100a. Adobuere Ebiama (b. 1987) is an American author, playwright, and actor. Soon after we were both initiated into Reiki together, I decided that I won't move into the next level until she is the one who will bring me into it.

100b. See essay (8): on *the invitation to the simhāsanā*.

100c. See essay (5): on *breaking metaphysical rules*.

101a. See essay (8): on *the invitation to the simhāsanā*.

101b. See essay (5): on *breaking metaphysical rules*.

101c. See essay "a different kind of mastery," essay (85): on *chronicling my Deccan years*.

101d. Craig just beamed in a beautiful peony from his garden into my hand. The future of sense-media is here. What we do with it is in our hands.

It is time to take *responsibility for all living beings. Holy liberation is the equality of all things. Evil spirits have power over fearful men, but cannot disturb the fearless.* When my father had to be tested for COVID, he gently reminded us: the body is like an echo, dependent on the source of sound; do not feel passion around my possible illness, he says, calmly. Instead, study the structure that made the sound. We are just the echoes. The streets and hearts are burning. Vimalakīrtī is asked: after having mastered all the superknowledges, why do you choose to be sick? You could easily heal yourself as you heal others. Vimalakīrtī responds: when you truly love all beings, you feel their hurts. You can never be free of pain for as long as there is pain in this world. I wonder, of the uprising happening now: *why now?* Why not a hundred years ago? Or fifty years ago? Is it that the virus revealed discomfort to all living beings, reminding us to no longer accept it as a condition for the self or another? Did the compassion come from self-experience?

Who will you hold with your music? For that is the body that is *born of love, compassion, joy, patience, gentleness, concentrations, liberations, meditations, absorptions, learning wisdom, liberative technique*. And with such a body, my dear reader, our music can hold the entire world. Even when it's drowning in fire.

24. on *the map to "success"*

If I was where I would be
Then I'd be where I am not
Here I am, where I must be
Where I would be, I can not

—"Katie Cruel,"
as sung by Karen Dalton (b. 1937),
on *In My Own Time* (1971)

At dawn, sit at the Feet of Action.
At noon, be at the Hand of Might.
At eventide, be so big, that sky
will learn Sky.

—[So the Lord said to]
Alice Coltrane-Turiyasangitānandā,
[as told to us in] *Monument Eternal* (1977)

7.

scar

scarcity

s c a r c i t y

s c a r c i t y

s   c   a   r   c   i   t   y

s   c   a   r   c   i   t   y

s   c   a   r   c   i   t   y

s   c   a   r   a   b   u   n   d   a   n   c   i   t   y

67. on *clothing music*

அ	ன்பை	தே	டி
an	bai	thé	di
M	G	S	S
ஓர்	நா	டோ	டி
M	R	N	N
or	nā	dō	di
உந்	தன்	வீ	ட்டு
M	R	N	N
un	than	vī	ttu
வா	சப்	ப	டி
M	G	S	S
vā	sap-	pa	di

முன்	னே	வ	ந்து	நின்	றாள்			
mun-	*ne*	*van-*	*thu*	*nin-*	*drāl*			
G	S	P	N	P	M			
	உன்	கண்	ணுக்	குள்	பார்த்	தாள்		
	un	kan-	nu-	kkul	pār	-thāl		
	R	N	P	N	P	G		
		உன்	ம	ன	சில்	என்	ன	
		M	G	S	N	S	G	
		un	ma	-na-	sil	en-	na	
			தா	-ன்	தோ	ணும்	சொல்	லு?
			R	N	D	N	S	R
			-thā-n	-n	tho-	num	sol-	lu?

The love that is truly a refuge for all living beings,
The love that is peaceful because free of grasping,

The love that is without conflict because it is free of the violence of the passions
The love that is enlightenment because it is unity of experience
The love that understands reality,
The love that is even, its aspirations being equal,

A love that is never exhausted because it acknowledges voidness and selflessness,
A love that is giving because it bestows the gift of Dharma free of the tight fist of a bad teacher;
A love that is tolerance because it protects both the self and others,

The love that is without formality because it is pure in motivation,
The love that is without deviation because it acts from decisive motivation
The love that is without deceit because it is not artificial,
The love that is liberative technique because it shows the way everywhere

The love that is effort
Because it takes responsibility for all living things.

Chapter 7, The Goddess
Vimalakīrti Sutrā

Sung epilogue
Words translated by Robert Thurman
Music composed and sung by Ganavya Doraiswamy

CHAPTER
10

ANATOMY OF A BIG BAND

Splintered Stories

SAM EASTMOND

Clock Duck Strings

There is a short scene in *Duck Soup* where Harpo and Chico as secret agents are breaking into Margaret Dumont's mansion to steal Freedonia's secret war plans. Raquel Torres impresses the need for absolute silence on pain of court-martial and death.

Stealthily moving through the mansion Harpo, the seemingly accidental anarchist spots a grandfather clock, checks his pocket alarm clock and resets it, pleased at having corrected an existential problem he was obsessively unable to ignore. The clock instantly starts chiming and a horrified Harpo swiftly distances himself from it, shushing the inanimate object. As he scurries away he spots a porcelain duck.

Enamoured, he picks it up to plant a kiss on it and it starts playing a tinkling musical box melody, perfectly synced with the heavy chimes of the clock.

Horrified by the volume and proliferation of noise he panics, and then, the music hits him and transports him. His joyful smile emerges as he sinks into the sound, doing a little dance. Lost in the moment he sways, halfheartedly shushing his mechanical ensemble again before gliding to a nearby piano. He reaches into the open body and starts plucking the strings.

Compelled to music born spontaneously in the most inappropriate circumstances he has surrendered, joyfully vamping amongst the chaos.

Joyful cacophony echoes through the halls of the sleeping mansion, Harpo immersed at the centre.

Chico—the pragmatic, simpler realist—is horrified and hurries down the staircase, a struggle ensues and the piano lid smashes down, its thunderous landing silencing the music.

Harpo is brought down to earth, pulled from the moment of nirvana by a violent interjection. Hurt, he brings his bruised fingers to his mouth acknowledging the pain and loss of a single instantaneous moment of beauty.

I don't think of the Marx brother as comedians, or actors, or vaudevillian slapstick, wisecracking one-liner merchants or clowns. Though they undoubtedly inhabit those roles.

I experience them as musicians and anarchists, devoted to challenging the established order, subverting norms and creating beautiful havoc. They pull back the curtain from the absurdities of life, seeing it not through a lens of societal acceptability warped and framed by convention but with a simple honesty, discarding the warped layers of artificial double-think.

This tiny episode feels like the most apposite explanation of my mental approach to arrangement and composition.

Or:

Build something beautiful then smash it up and build something else beautiful out of the rubble.

Jigsaw Guerrilla Golem

The people make the music.

The music comes from the people.

I need to hear the voices in my head.

The first act of composition is phone calls. Booking musicians. Creating a mosaic of individual voices to form an ensemble. A group able to all operate and switch between guerrilla units inside the larger organisation, soloists, or one unstoppable insurgent force.

There is no anonymity in numbers, no faceless side-musicians, no easily interchangeable cogs in a machine. They are a coalition of dedicated peaceful warriors, of dangerous sonic experimenters, saboteuse's and agent provocateurs. The Spike Orchestra is an organism, not a machine. Their presence provides a canvas of infinite creative possibilities.

The first act of composition is to shape clay, to build a creature that sparks into life with truth.

Then set it in motion, red eyes ablaze, staggering towards the village.

Paper Possibilities Pencil

The head, a twisting sephardi melody full of flat 2s and odd time signatures. An irrepressible urge I've been scribbling variations of on thousands of scraps of paper for a decade. Working, reworking and never quite getting right. Is this its moment? If it is then the list of names down the side of the page. Excitement, inspiration, instantly possibilities present themselves; what if Josephine Davies and Yazz Ahmed play the first iteration? How can this start any other way than with a solo from Will Glaser? How beautiful is Harry Brown's Ellingtonesque rasp: where can I fit that in? What if we used hammers to play the piano? Where can I unleash the untameable chaos of Otto Willberg? Where can I make Moss Freed play that filthy, noir ostinato? George Hogg as "stunt trumpeter" no stratosphere too high. Mike Wilkins weeping on clarinet. Jeff Miller has a sousaphone, womp womp howl. I need Gemma Moore's baritone honk. Feverish possibilities clamour for attention, disparate ideas crowding the brain. At which point the score is pushed away and the notebook is reached for. Shapes, blocks, swirls, graphic structural representations, a linear construct to hang abstract emotional narratives from. A swirling vortex of thunder, a visceral assault on the ears, juxtaposed with soft winds, the two bleeding into each other, contrast of extremes, pinning back the listener then making them lean in, straining to hear the intricacies and subtleties.

Paul Booth's flute swirling delicately in counterpoint with Tim Smart pouring rage into trombone pedal tones. How do I get to the drunken waltz, crunching offbeats acting like a punches in the face, fractured melodies limping over it like broken teeth? When I get there Elliot Galvin needs to *wreck* that piano. Where can I build the brass chorale? Are all ominous, imperialistic quarter tones hitting hard and repetitively driving a violent urgency *too* Rite of Spring? How can I balance the written material with a compulsion to bring more freedom and hand signal conduction moments into this piece? To take all those unifying divisions and build something that feels like one piece?

All of this happens in a flash.

Every variation of the theme just presents itself to me, all the options just seem obvious.

Soon it is clear that this is more than one piece.

The work exists though. Live and vibrant in my head. All those competing, contradictory ideas beginning to coalesce. All I need to do is just write it down.

Rehearsals Subs Espresso

Two 8-hour rehearsals. 4 pieces. 60 minutes of music.

The piece is finished. The piece is written. The piece is a paper construct. The piece is not real yet. The piece is an idea, on paper, in a language. The piece is beginning,

The moment where I hand out paper and musicians play it is here though. It is an ending and a beginning.

Now it gets real, ideas scribbled down, refined, moments that arrived with clarity, sections which were balanced and reworked.

This is the moment I live for. The point at which those solitary days and nights playing chess with imaginary constructs of *my* musicians stops being imagination and starts being *us*.

I need to remember I sent this out to the band a month ago. I know it intimately. They don't, yet. I know the shape, weft and weave of this tapestry, but no one else does. No one else sees the whole picture yet.

I know which musicians have studied their parts, spent that month practising, annotating, exploring individual lines, worked out where which fingers go in what order, where to cheat a sneaky breath to get that climax point screaming.

I know which musicians flip it open, scan their eyes down the page for the first time today, seeing it fresh, nonchalantly tap out a passage look up and say "hey Sam you know this is hard right?" Then nail it first time in the moment.

Booking a band is always about this as well, balancing these approaches. Getting the mixture just right.

This is a process, I am here to guide, to direct, to take raw sound and channel it, to balance, to push, to point out where to blend and where to crunch. I have an idea of a piece in my mind. Our job today is to move through that until it is our piece. Something that can only exist in this moment with these people, and to understand how to replicate that in performance as a start point, so that each time it is its own unique thing. Existing, fleetingly in the room, some magic for the people who were there, until it disappears and becomes a fragment of memory, the beginning of the next story.

But first. We got to get those notes in that order. To understand the shape before we smash it up.

I am relaxed, I don't stop it, I offer fragments of advice, count it in sit back and let my eyebrows do the talking. They need to come to me. Work out their frustrations with the complexity of the mechanics, get it under their fingers and in their hearts.

Then we talk about what is impossible and how we are going to do it.

We take short breaks, more than I would like but less than are necessary. Noel Langley and Moss Freed are the Spike Orchestra union, they are there also to caution me about rest, pacing, avoiding burning the band out. I am obsessive. I stand and pace, I am on my feet for 8 hours, no break, no food, when they take lunch I schlepp round checking in with everyone, making sure they are happy, looked after, suggesting rugelach instead of cookies. Directing lunch.

The rugelach unites the band. The sugar hit is on. We go back and do it all over again.

And again.

And again.

Each time it grows, it lives.

We go home exhausted.

I travel for an hour on the tube, reliving every note. I get home. Open the suitcase of charts and go through every single part making a note of every pencil annotation. Every comment, every moment where they felt they need to add to the information on the page, judging every nuance of how I can better explain my intention to them.

Rehearsal Rehearsal Rehearsals

Jewish holiday. So the arts centre commissioning us is closed. We are in the Vortex. A less imposing edifice but a place of worship.

Smaller, confined, in each others faces.

8 more hours.

Noel asks how a passage should be played.

I launch into a soliloquy unable to stop. Minutes explaining the piece is about conspiracy fantasy, how it warps and twists truth, how words matter, how words kill, they are like shrapnel, that in a world where each opinion is equal how can we quantify objective truth and whose voice is drowned out? What human casualties are there? How do we tolerate and equate giving equal weight to discredited and disproved fantasy that shooters use as justification for killing in synagogues and mosques.

Noel says "so mezzo piano then?"

We laugh, but the next time round he plays that passage with an intensity and fire that raises the hairs on my arms.

I take no credit for that. That is his work. I just gave him a way to think about it.

Whatever he put into it is his.

Mics Amps Soundcheck

I try to only ever have one conversation about this.

I spend a week emailing with the Hall manager.

We turn up. Wrong guitar amp. No drum kit. The sound engineer asks what Noel means when he points a mic and gestures up to with his finger.

The band is ready. Tight, tense, energy tangible.

Sold out Purcell Room, Royal Festival Hall.

It doesn't matter. The space matters. The music matters. But the rest is garnish. Nice for the commissioners meaningless to me. Any space we play this music is holy.

Music.

Bouncing on my sneakers, tzitzit flying. Every single one of those beautiful people putting everything into the music.

Magic floods the hall and disappears, leaving me drained. Empty.

The next week we play it again.

On the road. Up North.

The soundcheck goes like a dream.

I stand outside, depressed, my only thought, we played this already. Why not play something else?

We do.

We find new ways to reimagine. New ways to travel the same path and arrive at our destination changed.

Familiarity breeds exploration.

Surf Skronk Sticks

The perfect Spike Orchestra appositeness of Moss Freed.

Able to inhabit any role. Improvisor, reader, confidante, conscience, collaborator, friend.

A telepathy exists.

Words on a page are understood. Deeply. Beyond what is explainable.

A journey over years, each individually reaching into new ideas and approaches that coalesce when we convene.

We play in each others bands. Our roles flip and exchange.

In search of a drummer

Will Glaser.

Search over.

When they first arrived they changed everything. They got the way I wanted music to sound from the page. They made it live. They started the alchemy.

Recording Lepidoptery Intensity

Ben Greenslade-Stanton recorded the first three Spike Orchestra albums. They would not exist without him. Then he moved to Australia. Gone from my process was my best friend, my emotional crutch, and my mechanism.

Three stories about Marc Urselli:

> 2018, the morning of the Gulgoleth, Moss Freed, Elliot Galvin, Otto Willberg, Will Glaser, recording. We meet in north London for a coffee before we walk to the studio. We talk about the impossibility of good coffee in London.
>
> On the walk he gently says something along the lines of so long as you're all well rehearsed we should get what you want (There's only one recording day, there's only every one recording day) I tell him we ran ALL the pieces with everyone except Will in Moss's kitchen last week so I was feeling more rehearsed than usual. This is not the answer he's looking for.
>
> In the studio, the band setting up. Moss cautioning me to not be disappointed if we don't start recording for a couple of hours, setting up levels takes hours, at that point Urselli comes over the headphones and tells us he's ready, all set up, let's go! We record all

eight pieces, twice. It sounds AMAZING.

I don't tell them about the two new ones I have in my bag. (bonus story; whilst mixing it Marc tells me he knows exactly where in the session the track comes from due to the degradation and wreckage of the piano. This makes me smile.)

2019 the Spike Orchestra session. Fourteen other musicians in the studio. Easily a 14-hour day, only Marc and me don't take a break. Every second is music. Everything is recorded. Afterwards editing just Mike Wilkins, Marc and me. We order food, inexplicably Marc's Lassi arrives in a tub and is mouldy. I don't know that this means anything.

Marc makes the impossible possible.

Zorn

Jair and Naked City changed my life.

The way John Zorn kicked down the door and threw in the hand grenade that exploded Jewish music. Made it mine not my Grandfathers. I obsessively bought every CD. Inhaled them, revelled in them. The way Naked City moved, stretched, dug deep and spat out. Here were all the things I wanted, even if I didn't know I wanted them.

The period I went through first experiencing this music, reaching out and back through the Tzadik catalogue is the single most formative experience of my existence.

The Spike Orchestra was born because of this. An experiment in trying to do the things I'd heard talked about conceptually, and pumped into my ears sonically.

A path I couldn't quite imagine but felt should exist.

His torch leading the way.

It all starts with Zorn.

Rules Spike Beginning

No swing 8ths

No Lyrics

No covers

Everything else.

Bereshit

Lunch with Jacqueline Nicholls. Golders Green.

A grey, miserable, North London winter day.

One of those grey, miserable, North London winter days where even the rain seems unable to muster the enthusiasm to fall with any conviction. A fine drizzle coating my glasses and frosting my beard as I move through it.

Headroom. A small warm, vibrant, charity cafe, bright and vibrant in stark contrast to the outside world of dull trudging figures. Shakshouka and borekas exploding with a loudness matched only by the clamouring clientele, oblivious to one another and at times seemingly their companions. Loud incessant chattering layering up to the ceiling like smoke, so thick you instinctively duck under it and lean in to talk. Condensation on the windows obscuring the grey reality outside and cocooning us in a temporary lagoon of warmth and life.

Jacqueline is the brilliant radical artist whose work was the conceptual start point and visual identity of my Gulgoleth project. A London friend I know through my New York friend Jon Madof. She's also the arts programmer for a large arts centre. I'm here to listen to an idea.

There is a one of those arts orgs funding opportunities, the kind of thing I hear about and I know exist but that float past me like obsolete Soviet space junk as I dysfunctionally plough my lone idiosyncratic orbit.

What if we put together a project, on an impossible deadline for the submission, a sonic representation of Radical Jewish Culture through a British lens?

(most of my life or at least the interesting parts, feels like it starts either with Jews talking over food or impossible deadlines. If I'm lucky I get lunch before I exist solely on coffee, anxiety and obsessive commitment until the deadline passes.)

How do I feel about this? Right there, in that moment, I'm not sure I have anything left to say on the subject. I made two Masada albums in 3 years. I'm right off the back of a beautiful but intense period of making *Binah* for the *Book Beri'ah*, I threw *everything* I felt into that, and was sure I knew what the next album was going to be. And it wasn't going to be Jewish.

I don't even want to get into why RJC is NYC.

But something about the idea sparks and tugs.

I hear the possibilities of the band. What is yet to explore, what is unsaid, concepts that could work with this that I want to try out. People I want to write for.

But, we'll never get funding.

This will be just the latest of the "lost Spike Orchestra albums." Moments in time that passed and the projects that died as the apposite moment passed. Unrealised sparks of being that never quite caught.

We got funding.

Subs Heartbreak Reality

Nothing I do is music until people play it.

Before that it's piles of paper, me alone with my madness talking to a plastic skull on my desk.

I write for people.

Reality hits, not everyone makes it to the rehearsal, the gig, the recording.

Life intervenes, lucrative tours, health issues, the unknowable and surprising distance between Moscow and London. Big band logistics and economics are leviathan and draining.

Every replacement a bittersweet heartbreak of lost opportunities and joyful discovery of a new collaborator.

2019 3 concerts 5 rehearsals 1 recording 3 piano players.

Since 2016 everything has been written for Elliot Galvin. He is extraordinary.

Elliot can't make every date.

Since 2014 I've been trying to get Alexander Hawkins on something. The timing has never worked. This time it does. Magic.

He inhabits the music, reaching inside, turning it on its head and devastating us.

1 night.

Highlights from *Binah,* Highlights from *Gulgoleth,—intermission—*all of *Splintered Stories.*

Three insane sets that deserve a night each. I promise the venue I will try to fit it into 2 hours. But it will probably be 2 and a ½.

Olly Chalk turns up to rehearsal looking like a quiet unassuming young punk. He destroys the piano, the band relax. We reconfigure music to give him space. He says hardly a word through the recording. Just lives inside the piano.

We add one moment to bridge between sections, I tell him to get inside the piano.

Strings amongst the chaos.

It all comes back to Harpo.

CHAPTER
11

RANTING AND RUMINATING ON RHYTHM

And the Sweet Mysteries of it All

DANNY ELFMAN

NOTE TO READER: *I am in NO way, shape or form a musicologist, ethno-musicologist, musical historian or theoretician. When it comes to serious musical history and theory; I don't know shit from Shinola. These are simply my own thoughts, from my own experiences, in my own life, (the only one, at this moment, that I know).*

I was writing a letter home. The temperature in Bamako, Mali where I'd somehow ended up was well over 100° and the mid-day comatose spell was coming on fast. That's the special time of day when the temperature lands somewhere between 110° or 115° and time stands still. I remember sitting cross-legged on the floor scribbling away on a low table, staring blankly, watching drops of sweat hit the paper and smudge the ink: a clear sign that the mid-day coma had arrived. I slouched down onto the floor and started to drift off. However, something caught my attention and wouldn't let me go: it was the music playing in the street outside below my room.

I was staying in a small room on the second floor of a colonial-era stucco building that had a small balcony. The surrounding neighborhood was mostly residential compounds, simple structures constructed around communal courtyards. To say music was coming from everywhere is an understatement. When I think of Bamako now that's what I remember most: the sound of music coming from every direction playing well into the night. Melodic music from multi-stringed koras and hunter's guitars, polyrhythmic music from balafons (like small marimbas) and drums—an amazing sonic collage that was intoxicating. Of course, that was a long time ago. I was only 18 years old, fresh out of high school with wanderlust in my blood... but I digress. The thing that caught my attention about this particular music on that hot sweltering afternoon was that it didn't seem to be played on traditional instruments at all. It sounded metallic and funky, but at the same time captivating.

I was too tired to move but unable to fall asleep, hypnotized by what I was hearing, so I began to deconstruct it (or try to). I attempted to isolate the downbeats and find the meter. It was so complicated. Free and obviously improvised but still tight and unified. No matter how hard I tried I just couldn't find the count in the recurring pattern.

Eventually I gave up; but at least I could discover the virtuosos who were conjuring these extraordinary sounds. I dragged myself out to the balcony and like some exhausted sea creature, hoisted myself up to the edge and looked down. Astonishment! Below me were four little kids. Three boys were playing on some kind of trashy metal cans and maybe an oil drum while a little girl danced between them. I was stunned. Such an exquisite sense of time and rhythm coming out of these little kids! And that got me thinking—where does our rhythmic sense come from?

Fast-forward about 40 years: I am a father with a young son (around 4 years old) wanting to impart a bit of musical influence into his life. We're in our home screening room, which has a pretty good sound system. We'd watched some old Max Fleisher cartoons, which he enjoyed, though my real, hidden, insidious intent was to sneak in some great 1930s jazz into his world. When we were done I opted for something a bit more challenging: I put on a DVD of the San Francisco Symphony (led by Michael Tilson Thomas) performing Stravinsky's *The Rite of Spring*. I figured my son would listen to a few minutes tops and start complaining, but something strange and unexpected happened: He sat with his eyes wide open, barely moving at all, totally enraptured, and listened from start to finish, almost in a trance. He never made a sound. I was more than surprised. It was such a cool thing to witness.

For the next few months he asked me almost every day to put on *The White of Spwing*, (which is what he called it). Stravinsky's primitively-inspired music is unquestionably complicated; how then could it connect so easily with a very young child? What is that thing that can reach a place we don't even know we have?

Soon after hearing *The White of Spwing*, he began picking up sticks and playing some big Indian drums I had lying around the house. On Sundays my brother, who is a talented percussionist, along with myself and a few friends, would start a "drum circle." My son would really wail on those drums and we'd get into some pretty complicated stuff. He also seemed to have that thing. Suddenly he was doing this amazing shit. I couldn't believe it. This continued for several years until he reached the wise old age of 7 whereupon he abruptly stopped and declared himself retired. That said, I remain convinced that he still has something that may re-emerge again in his later years. I can't un-hear what he so beautifully allowed me to hear when he was so young. But watching him play really brought me back full circle to those little kids in Mali.

During those many years between my African travels and my son's strange discovery, I found that I could hear and play pretty complex stuff. I began a lifelong infatuation with percussion and rhythm. I leaned how many different cultures around the world adapted and developed so many variations of rhythmic syncopation and polyrhythms and the use of interlocking patterns. I also became keenly aware of how absent any of this was in my own upbringing. More and more I found myself musing on where these things come from in us, and how they interconnect around the world.

I came to believe that the ability to create syncopation and complex rhythms is something that can sit dormant in individuals and in entire cultures for a long time, but under the right conditions, it might suddenly re-emerge. It's a seed. I call it The Rhythm Seed. I truly believe it resides somewhere in our DNA. Those fortunate enough to grow up in a place where polyrhythmic music is part of their daily lives are more likely to activate that rhythm seed, whether that exposure comes from their culture (like those kids in Bamako), or opportunities provided to them (like my son), or pure chance (as with me), that seed may or may not ever get a chance to germinate... but it's still there and has been for tens of thousands of years. It's something that probably comes from the same deep-rooted place in our subconscious brains that creates the fight-or-flight reflex or creates he need to form communities, to communicate with each other or to find higher altitude for our souls. We're born with these things... in the blood, in our bones.... And somewhere buried in that crazy ancient mess of built-in human software is a connection between rhythm and our bodies (although it frequently becomes forgotten).

There is no question that polyrhythmic, interlocking rhythmic and complexly syncopated music has found its way into many cultures. Whether in Africa, the Middle East, Indonesia, Latin America or India to mention a few, you can hear many extremely diverse ways complex rhythms have evolved and express themselves. Western culture was not so fortunate in that department. It seems they dropped the ball somewhere down the line. Of course they came up with a LOT of amazing music, and I don't want to trivialize that in any way, but that's another story completely. What I'm talking about is how they dropped the rhythm-ball. Why? Was it happenstance? Random? Was it considered contrary to their desire to create some form of order in their universe? If someone knows, great, but my point is that it doesn't seem to matter. Rhythm doesn't die. It may burrow down and hibernate for centuries but it doesn't die. It simply takes a little nourishment to revive.

Music behaves very much like cells do in an organic living system. Cells split, duplicate themselves, mutate and evolve. Music is exactly the same and the relative lapse of syncopation and rhythm in Western music came to a dramatic end with the arrival of the 20th century, when a musical phenomenon burst out of America and into the world's collective consciousness in a way that had never been seen (or heard) before.

Early America's enslaved African population brought their ancestral music with them.

The music slowly evolved and transformed for several hundred years, brewing in an increasingly fertile environment. Primed for change, many regional styles mixed and merged and evolved and the brew got richer yet. Suddenly around the time of WWI, with Europe in the throes of chaos, back at home something amazing happens. That brew explodes!

Jazz is born. Syncopated rhythm-based mania spreads fast. Simultaneously rhythm and blues, which had certainly been around for a long time, begins to expand and evolve as well. Jazz and R&B begin to mutate radically. Of course this eventually morphs into rock, hip-hop, electronic dance and hundreds of sub-genres—it gets under the skin… in the bones. It spreads like wildfire to Europe and around the world and returns again transformed, with each culture putting their own twist on it. Rhythm, polyrhythm, multi-rhythm and trance rhythm were back with a vengeance imprinting entire generations to identify themselves with it, even to define themselves with it while they continue to transform it.

What I felt swaying to the music in drum and bass clubs in

New York during the '90s was remarkably similar to the feeling I had swaying to the music of the Gnawa musicians playing though the nights in the Sahara desert. It was transformative in the extreme and was simply impossible not to move to. Whether it be the hypnotic, elevating euphoria I felt during funeral celebrations I attended in Senegal and Ghana, or the adrenalin-pumped feeling of sitting in the middle of a large group of intense, highly revved-up vocal chanters performing a Kecak, or "monkey chant" from Bali, it created intense mind and body experiences.

Even classical music was not immune. In the second half of the 20th century composers—like Harry Partch, Lou Harrison, Terry Riley, Steve Reich (writing specifically for percussion ensembles) and Philip Glass and John Adams (devising orchestral works) and many more—all wrote music pulsing with wonderful hypnotic energy. Music that took me straight back to Mali. To the kids in the street. To the sounds that filled the night air from every direction.

What does this all mean? I have no idea—but I continue to feel it very clearly—that pulsing dynamic syncopation has managed to find its way into practically every culture's collective musical consciousness on the planet. No matter how old or young we are. It remains a wonderful mystery because it taps into a primal part of our selves—into that great feeling of falling into a trance when certain rhythms are put together in certain ways and the mind and body react in a way our ancestors likely did eons ago when we were just becoming "human."

Rhythm is thriving! Bodies are moving! Brains are pumping out endorphins! Humans moving together—even when alone.

In my youth nothing made me happier than when I was sitting and playing tight, fast interlocking, completely hypnotic music in the middle of an Indonesian gamelan orchestra. Then I heard Steve Reich's music and saw he was in fact doing the same thing uniquely in his own way on marimbas and Western percussion. Then I heard the complex rhythms of jazz, and the sensual magic of rhythm and blues working their way into orchestral music. One culture inspiring another, which takes that inspiration and transforms it into something completely new, which in turn inspires more in an endless wonderful transformative cycle that all ties back to some ancient—but never completely forgotten part of ourselves—in our bodies, our bones, our blood, the very fabric of our

DNA. An unbreakable thread that runs through our humanity and continues to lead us on in this strange journey to discover not only who we are—but who we have yet to become.

And that is a very beautiful thing.

CHAPTER
12

A FLICKERING AND THICKENING

Aspects of Recorded Music Released Between 2010 and 2019

SASHA FRERE-JONES

The waves come every decade or so, sometimes returning later. The syncopation and beat emphasis of James Brown's band flowed under jazz and pop in the late '60s and early '70s. Twenty years later, samples of those same records found their way to the same genres, plus a few others. In the 21st century, concrete technical changes have summoned a new old wave with echoes in the visual and plastic arts both. The flickering and thickening of the new century are a known pair, found in the layers of quiet howling in Jamaican dub of the '70s. They burn in the folds of a voice that sounds like a piano that sounds like the reflection of a bell on James Blake's *Klavierwerke* EP. They surge through the hi-hats of Zaytoven's productions for Migos and run through the floodwaters of Oneohtrix Point Never's *Andro*. They skate around the edges of Future's flaking paint voice, and settle into the dominant practice of dissolve on Frank Ocean's *Blonde*. They boil down to a luminous paste in James Blake's *If The Car Beside You Moves Ahead*. These waves are the cracking blossom of music finding its digital center in a new time.

There is room, in this tessellated diary, for a story of these tendencies. Flickering and thickening are not genre labels but processes, and their rate of use can increase or decrease in any particular piece of music. Digital tools have allowed these procesess to be newly instantiated and this has transformed pop music and adjacent non-popular electronic musics, forms that are naturally heliotropic towards the sun of pointless change.

The introduction of the pianoforte in 1702 gave Western music a dose of thickening, the less unruly of the two processes. Flickering, on the other hand, can happen almost anywhere—to the element or a sequencing thereof, in a point or its reflection. Composed music of the '60s and '70s saw little flickering in element but presented great flickering in sequence and pressed layering. Julius Eastman brought flicker of both element and sequence to American minimalism, destabilizing the attack and decay of the pianoforte and settling the compositional point in the flicker rather than the pitch or bar line.

Flickering is the moment when a sound stutters but remains clear, claiming one and indicating two. Thickening is music no taller but bigger, bleeding to the edge of a frame that refuses to be strengthened, so the music must strengthen itself.

Flickering is a process carried out by the doubling and fracturing of events, pitch, segment length, and texture. It can happen at the level of the musical material and in the machine process of listening. In 1974, Roland Barthes described listening as an active process, where what is listened to is "the very dispersion, the shimmering of signifers, ceaselessly restored to a listening which ceaselessly produces new ones from them without ever arresting their meaning." This is multiplying while staying in place.

Thickening is analogous to, say, stereophonic sound or any other technical innovation that makes it seem as if a signal is more itself, more alive as an event reproduced through recordings. If people are used to mechanical reproduction of sound, they can still be sold on the anxiety that they are still somehow not hearing something, that there is an aspect of a sound experience that is somehow beyond the moment of their apprehension. The constant shifting in consumer electronic reproductions of sound are keyed to commodity obsolescence demands but also to the infinitely plausible story that *our senses never really get to the endpoint of sensation.*

How do we hear shifting in music while we are also shifting? What are the legible elements and what is our frame? If we are moving quickly, how would we know if our music was moving as quickly?

Where can we most easily hear flickering? In pop music of the 21st century, it's not a bad idea to start with AutoTune, which embodies our process without finishing it. You can also follow hi-hats, which begin to double and treble into an ornamental blur as the century finds its feet. This flickering of a rhythmic element demonstrated that time-keeping needn't be kept by the music on your behalf but can nest within the song and show its heat. These hi-hat patterns start up inside the variant of hip-hop known as trap and spread like leads through ice floes.

Where can we hear thickening? It's a separate but related distention, less complex because it's more formal than psychological. Thickening, in this century, is a response to mobile audio and digital audio, which both demand and enable greater bass response. This development is both a scam and totally reasonable.

For example, a group of untagged musicians who are lumped with ambient music, a grouping few of them endorse, are making their music flicker and thicken by adding detail and bass response, which distances their work from the anodyne and utilitarian music fed into streaming ambient playlists. This swollen music is something I call murder spa, a grouping none of them endorse. This music is slightly harder to read to any productive end, in that ten clouds and three clouds are roughly equally detailed.

The flickering and twinning of pop songs in AutoTune allows speaking and singing to be the same, to be either, and to be neither. Here, we find the psychological sweep of the flicker, as it echoes the mind of the online person, moving between tabs and platforms, remaining one while thinking in multiples. Thickening is an aspect of sound and sound alone—flickering is the bridge between a production tendency and the world that created it, the world it reflects, the worlds it echoes within.

Flickering is life, and has been. The in-person hug, followed by the merciless subtweet, from the same person. Hardly new in intent, simply faster in coincidence. The quality of flux is there in modern rap—the microscopic differences that repay attention, the ad libs, the sighs, the laughs. Flicker is a figure and a reaction, an element and its echo, the analogous sound relation of a mind looking at two screens. The ad lib in rap is the flickering of the point of origin, two voices in a competitive pattern in a non-competitive space. They're both in the song and they can't lose. They also can't leave. The flicker is motion without release, the bigger struggle in the smaller box. Taste values change as people started making fun of each other more than they made fun of each other's taste. Once you're fighting face-to-face and box-to-box, a new space needs to be cleared, to get on with life.

AutoTune allies any two users, the way an *Ashley's Pinchback* sample created a cohort in 1990, the way fuzz grouped garage bands in the '60s. Cohort and genre have attachments to technique and can be sliced horizontally. Genre flickers, too.

Flickering is the glint of the encrusted; the refraction rather than the light; the deviation from the pattern that illuminates the pattern; the seam that fills with gasoline; the reef that highlights the shore.

Vinyl wraps make a car less a car. In this way, cars flicker.

Flickering is a failed pact, a bargain between silence and noise that accepts all signatures, leaving no sovereign.

In *Sonic Technologies* (2018), Robert Strachan writes this about the voice and AutoTune's effect on it: "As well as being made up of a fundamental pitch, the voice also produces overtones, that is, secondary pitches or formants which correspond to multiples of the fundamental frequency. It is the fact that the fundamental is not heard in isolation that contributes to our understanding of a voice as 'rich' or 'full.'" AutoTune produceds a "'stable central [harmonic] frequency with minimal variation', a dynamic flatness in which 'the voice's energy remains constant' and a level of 'formant variation' in which partial harmonics are lost."

AutoTune's elimination of the portamento (sliding from one pitch to another) and partial harmonics native to the human voice creates a self-similar, coherent tone, as far as the value of pitch is concerned. But this also creates inverted mayhem—when a singer sings casually and with a conversationally wandering sense of pitch, a smooth if misshapen unity exists, which AutoTune then discards in favor of the flickering hail of notes that may be in tune but create, in their cascade, a true madness of pitch. With AutoTune's pitch selection and harmonic elimination, a slow and shallow stretch of hill becomes a set of tiny stairs that crest and fall with a dizzying lack of proportion. Serialism—who knew?—came back in the human voice, defeating the known and clichéd with controlled randomization.

Each individual pitch may be more purely calibrated as a result of AutoTune but the rapid onslaught of notes, concatenated as the software "chooses" notes from the sung input, is not simple or coherent. A singing voice fed into AutoTune keyed to a fast response spits out a wild and uncommon flapping. Beyoncé uses it for the flicker in "Apeshit"—she can hit the notes easily. She sings low and soft, where pitch varies most, bringing out the correction impulse of the software. Flicker!

Multitasking leads to the flicker of multi-level listening, the receptive aspect of flickering, which feed back into formal arrangement. In hip-hop, raps and ad-libs combine to make a two-tab reality, the center and the orbit folded together. Pop music is approaching improvisation, through flicker.

In improvised music, recording preserves the quarrelsome crack of the nervous system run into hands and feet. The most papery improv, the most stringy strings, the most throaty throats: this is the music given to us by microphones. Recordings have such exaggerated textures that we don't know what we are loving when we love it. Is it the song or the sound of two guitar strings out of six?

"The problem with written music," Cecil Taylor explained in the 1968 film *Les Grandes Répétitions*, "is that it divides the energies of creativity. While my mind may be divided looking at a note, my mind is instead involved with hearing and playing that note, making one thing of an action. Hearing is playing. Music does not exist on paper."

Flicker is neither form nor formlessness but the gap between that clears enough common space to afford a view of the opposite shore. Thickness is a demand of the sense, neither good nor bad, simply the outcome of a the reach of the body and the machine to accommodate each other. The flickering and thickening can happen independently, and the flicker is more easily found throughout the landscape: Bob Dylan's slipped hymns, Delacroix's vortical horses, Nina Simone drowning and resuscitating someone's else song in the space of 5 minutes, Mark Hollis peeling his own song, Mica Levi's strings in *Under The Skin*, Jon Hassell dissolving his trumpet, Tauba Auerbach candling the alphabet.

2010: James Blake, *Klavierwerke* EP
2011: The Weeknd, *House of Balloons*
2011: Oneohtrix Point Never, *Replica*
2012: Vybez Kartel, *Money*
2012: Future, *Pluto 3D*
2013: Young Thug, *Stoner*
2013: Autechre, *Exai*
2014: Michael Gordon, *Rushes*
2015: Future, *56 Nights*
2015: Arca, *Mutant*
2016: Frank Ocean, *Blonde*
2017: Kara-Lis Coverdale, *Grafts*
2018: James Blake, *If The Car Beside You Moves Ahead*
2018: Eli Keszler, *Stadium*
2018: The Carters, *Apeshit*
2019: Bon Iver, *i, i*

CHAPTER 13

THE SCHOOL OF THE ROAD

LEO GENOVESE

The road is endless, just like life. 20 years ago I left my hometown, Venado Tuerto in Argentina, to move to Boston.

On the road everything and everybody could be a teacher. It's important to be aware and listen as much as possible.

You can forget a tune, some changes, a melody, a name, but most likely the things you learned while traveling will live within you forever. They become you, or a part of you, and a fraction of your soul also stays in those places you visited—forever. Even if you don't like it. Spending three days in Morocco a few years back changed my life forever.

The road is no joke. It's not easy. It's not just flowers. We all know that. It could be funny, hard, tragic, positive—all things and emotions visit us when we are "out there." And the lessons that come to us are also like that.

Lessons come in different packages. My lessons come from listening to my elders, my sisters and brothers.

I think the players I hear the most are the ones who hover between the study of this music's history and the pursuit of this art form's potential future, which may completely ignore all referents and models—anything and all things that have been done before.

We've all heard a million times that in order to break the rules you must know the rules first.

But why bothering breaking the rules when there are no rules? Music has no laws. We are all free to create our own rules.

Why not do it?

I lived in Boston for 8 years. There I met a drummer named Nat Mugavero. Back in the day he had the chance to play with the touring master musicians as they came through Beantown. People like Sonny Stitt and Coleman Hawkings, and many others of that heavyweight league. Around

2007 he called me up. "Leo, I have a gig for our band, the Sewer Ratz. We'll play trio with Lockwood [bassist John Lockwood] at the Beverly School for the Deaf." Yes, that's right, a school for Deaf Children was inviting us to perform, to talk, to share the sound with the kids at the school.

We showed up, set up, and played some music for them. Every kid had a big balloon that they rested their ears against, and through the balloon's contact with the ground, they could feel all the vibrations happening, and so listen, imagine, create, fly, and finally disappear with us in this magic ceremony we call playing music. After a couple of Improvised pieces, we invited some kids to sit in with us, on any instrument they may have with them.

The first one was a beautiful young musician, maybe 5 years old. He stood on the bandstand with us, with a clarinet with no reed. He taught us the first lesson: Music is there no matter what. It's not up to us to make it, but to try to connect with whatever is already happening in the sonic universe that surrounds us at all times. The big lesson of Acceptance and Joy was clear in our faces. He blew hard, he Heard it, he Felt it, and he made us feel it too.

After that, all the kids left their balloons and came to the bandstand. Nat had six kids banging on the drum set with him. John had two young fellows jamming on the bass, and I had a couple with me hitting the ivory keys.

Music was in the room. That day the lesson of "Not Listening" was clear.

After that day we started to play from a different place; A place that has no name, still. A place of "not listening" helps us arrive at the place of "Not Playing."

The question is still loud. What else can we do with our instruments that is not music?

Can we play in a way that is musically Not musical?

That is still our challenge and maybe our goal, or one of them.

To Not listen. Not react. Keep playing. Good ideas may visit you. Let them go. Do not develop them. Do not repeat yourself. Do not listen to what you play, nor what anyone in the room is playing. Do not get caught in the music. Fly away. Be everywhere. Keep going. Don't look back. And feel what that feels like. No fear, so far.

What does that do for us, and perhaps for music?

Maybe it helps us accept everything at all times in all forms. To be more open, to be able to listen more deeply, and to let go completely of our own selves.

A few years later we played in New York with Nat, John, and saxophonist Dan Blake. After the barely attended concert, a woman from the audience who was visiting from Australia came up and told us: "It's good to see men playing, looking, and sounding so vulnerable." We felt so good being vulnerable. The band was happening. The music: who knows? who cares? We had a feeling in our guts and that was all we could remember.

The main thing was and still is: To stay in the "I don't Know."

Nat told me, don't get caught, "Keep Looking for something else, when you are in the something else."

After a gig with Tony Malaby's Quartet, in a place in Brooklyn called Korzo, a no-longer-living space for music, we were at the bar with the band. Billy Mintz on drums and William Parker on bass, Tony, and me.

We were talking with William about a Moroccan bass used in Gnawa music, an instrument that both of us play and love.

He was telling me about the day he met and played with master Mahmoud Guinea from Essaouira. William, one of the most original forces out there, didn't play the instrument in a traditional fashion. He played it with only two strings instead of three. But Malem Mahmoud Guinea told him it was ok to find your own way of playing the *sintir*.

After that William went ahead and dropped some ideas on me that I still think of every day, about tradition and about finding the voice of your own soul.

He said: "A new tradition is born with a new life. Each being emerging is born with a new tradition."

"Each life is a different musical D.N.A."

My friend and Guru composer from Misiones, Argentina, Marcelo Toledo wrote a book about Harmony. The book is one page long and it contains more information than any of the best-selling long-form books of Harmony. The book says, "Harmony is the acceptance of everything at any given moment."

Once we were in my apartment and Marcelo was playing my piano. He was playing the most original and strange chords I'd ever heard. I couldn't understand what they were, or where they were coming from. I asked him to tell me how he was coming out with these sounds. He told me to choose a couple of white keys, a couple of black keys, and play them together. Keep doing it, and keep finding.

The first time I had the chance to perform with Mr. Wayne Shorter (in 2013 in a quartet format with Esperanza Spalding and Terri Lyne Carrington), right before going on stage Mr. Shorter told the band: "Let's play about Education. Let's play about Culture. Let's play about Equality. And let's give them a Sound they've never heard before."

After these words we went on to the music. The fearless experience of jumping into the Unknown.

He gave us the power to "go for it." Through the power of his speech he encouraged us to play our best. He made us all chefs in the kitchen.

On another occasion, in 2016, we were rehearsing before our gig at the Detroit Jazz Festival with the same quartet.

We were playing a Geri Allen song, a twenty-bar blues form song that was getting me lost.

After a couple of attempts to improvise together on this particular song form and not really making it, because we were landing in four different places, he told us: "It's OK. We're playing four-dimensional music."

He said, "It should be about fun instead of technique. We have the intellectual part of music—the technique—and we have to make fun out of it."

At all times he is a fountain of deep matter. Life Lessons, Music Philosophies, History, Alien Worlds, Imagination, Movies, Books. A true Sage. If you just listen, he will talk concepts that will shake up your musical world.

Once he shared an idea he learned from Miles Davis about playing form, changes, and melody. It went like this:

> "...play something on top of the melody, so the melody becomes the changes—that will make the changes sound hipper..."

In another opportunity Mr. Shorter said: "...the challenge is to sound original to the point where you don't know what sounding original sounds like..."

Another time we were in Gdansk, Poland, with the same band plus the giant Herbie Hancock. After our rehearsal, Herbie was playing the piano, just by himself, very slow and soft, chords I couldn't recognize at all. In that moment Mr. Shorter came close to the piano and told Herbie: "That's it! ... I'm not looking for the right notes, neither the wrong ones..."

I had the blessing of being on tour with a Great jazz quartet called the

Spring Quartet, with Joe Lovano, Esperanza Spalding, and Jack DeJohnette.

Having the opportunity to stand next to Mr. DeJohnette while he was sound checking his Drum set was a big lesson. He was playing so relaxed, in an absolutely perfect position, and getting the biggest sound out of the set.

I asked him how he did it. And he told me: "Gravity does it for me. Gravity makes the sound. Just stay relaxed."

Once we were Somewhere in Germany and we went for a walk. I asked him how it was that he never ran out of ideas or material to play? He told me that whenever he needs to access information, he goes to the "Library of Cosmic Ideas."

I believe it's an open cosmic space, no need to sign in or be a member. We can all access it. No monthly payment. It's free. It belongs to us.

So when we feel stuck in our own little world, let's meet up there in the Library of Cosmic Ideas and play all night with an infinite amount of creativity.

A few years ago we visited the Peruvian Rain Forest with our friend and Activist Sara Dupont. Along with the fantastic musicians Leni Stern and Esperanza Spalding, we traveled for two weeks through the most beautiful landscapes of colors, shapes, lifeforms, and sounds.

We also traveled with Equipment and a crew to document our trip visually and sonically.

One afternoon, after we climbed a big old tree equivalent to a five-story building, we went to the river to listen to the sounds of the forest at sunset.

The flies, birds, otters, monkeys, leaves, all the insects, the whole forest was singing, shouting, grooving, and happening.

But our ears were only able to listen to certain sounds. Not the full spectrum. Not the full picture. Our auditory system automatically turns off—shuts down—some frequencies so that we can hear the most important ones. After a while contemplating the most unforgettable musical experience off my life—the most original, unique, and wild improvised concert—just with my bare ears, I tried putting on the headphones of the sound engineer who was documenting the voyage. That's when I realized how much more there is to hear, how much closer to the truth can we get through the listening experience when we are able to hear those frequencies that our system turns down. The governments turn down certain frequencies. So does the television. And the press. And our own system does it too.

How can we destroy every wall so that all sounds can be heard?

How can we open our listening capacity so that all voices can be admired?

How can we organize ourselves to feel all the silences?

What does Equality sound like?

What does Justice sound like?

What does Real Freedom feel like?

The answers may be the questions themselves. It's important to keep looking around, to keep traveling, to stay awake and close to whatever has the potential to help us grow, expand, and be one with all. Musicians are agents of positivity with an exceptionally strong weapon of love that can heal the world, save the planet, and teach us how to live together.

We arrived in Pireos, the port of Athens, where we heard a party was going on. Panaiotis, Apostolos, and the whole Greek gang was there.

A traditional celebration of an island called Ikaria was happening. Maybe eight thousand people dancing in circles, holding arms.

Very cheap and good wine, food, smoke. All the philosophers of the night were present. I was invited to dance, so I went.

I found myself in the middle of circles formed by thousands, following the music, the rhythm, and the choreography to perfection.

I didn't know anything about the steps. So I couldn't catch the moves. I tried to copy them, I tried to hang, but it was so hard. I wasn't following at all. So the two people next to me in the circle left. It was up to me to reincorporate myself into another circle, so I did.

But the same thing happened. So I went back to drinking wine with the brothers. I couldn't catch the moves.

The music was in all kinds of rhythmic meters. Everyone knew them. Everybody danced together. Age, sex, didn't matter. The dance floor was one living, moving organism. I couldn't understand the step that everyone knew, and I still felt like dancing—definitely possession power music.

Today we write lots of complicated music, rhythmically and harmonically and melodically. Some or most of it with no dance steps, some or most of it without any invitation to dance in any way at all. So my question is, are we missing something important, by not dancing all together in circles? That was unity, that was community, that was music, and it was hard to do it. I couldn't do it. It's still my goal to pick up that step, learn it, own it, and go back to that magical night, into the dancing circle, and try again. I believe I deserve another shot. Everybody does.

We were in Mar del Plata, Argentina, with the group the Nomads, with Justin Purtill, Brahim Fribgane, and Farol Ibarguen. After our last concert of the tour, we were invited to a reception by Jose, a Wine poet. It was around three or four in the morning when he told us something that still sings in my mind. He said that wine and men need three elements in order to achieve greatness: Time, Silence, and obscurity. Does music, or a musician, need these elements in order to become great as well?

In January of 2019 I had the chance to meet Orlando Vera Cruz, a poet, singer, and historian of my land. He lives in Sauce Viejo, Santa Fe, and we went for a walk on his beautiful ranch. He stopped by a Eucalyptus tree. He looked up and said that Eucalyptus trees aren't indigenous to this land, and that our native birds won't nest in imported trees.

We have so much to learn from the birds and their world. They've been on this planet longer than us, and from the branches they sing us messages that we still can't fully decipher. Maybe they've been giving us the secret of flying without the need of burning fuel. But we can't understand them, and so our reality is still ruled by the law of gravity.

If one day we can learn to fly, perhaps we will be able to explode, expand, and reach new territories. Perhaps we will be able to write the unwritable, to play the unplayable, to think the unthinkable, to listen to the unlistenable, and to love the unlovable.

CHAPTER 14

PERIPHERAL DROMES

Unfamiliar Earworms

KATE GENTILE

I'm a drummer and composer who writes and plays a lot of music influenced by the jazz tradition. I say "influenced by" because the only real remaining connections with traditional jazz in my work are the ideas of improvisation based on composed material, as well as interaction, democracy, and a love of syncopation and polyrhythm. Notions of swing have morphed into stranger feelings of time and grooves generated by more complex rhythms. Harmony has become more expanded, though still retaining a sense of voice leading, even if leaning slightly more towards atonality along the tonal spectrum.

There is a band that I co-lead with pianist and composer Matt Mitchell called Snark Horse. We each write half the music, and all the compositions are very, very short.

Sometime around the end of 2012, Matt lamented that despite a great amount of people composing music, some of the most interesting musicians did not compose at all. I suggested various reasons why people might not, or might find it difficult, and Matt said, "but anyone can do it… even if you just write one bar a day, write something." I already composed regularly, but I liked the idea of writing one measure of music a day. I recalled an étude Matt had started writing for himself titled *slarm biffle*. It was one bar long and he later developed and finished it, but it was so challenging and amusing as it was that it remained one bar a long time.

I began writing one bar a day for a while at the beginning of 2013. At first I imagined each bar would be part of a bigger piece. Some of the early bars became part of *Otto, on alien shoulders* on my first record, *Mannequins*. It soon became more fun to see how complete a measure could sound on its own, rather than like a fragment of something. Matt and I would email bars back and forth, and the bars got sillier and more clever and creative as we tried to one-up and outsmart each other.

As we began to actually play the bars, we decided to dedicate a band to playing them. Different formal and improvisational ideas emerged. My initial idea was that additional musicians were not required to learn the bars, and could improvise as free agents or wildcards while Matt and I played the material. However, every single person we played the bars with enthusiastically wanted to learn them.

Jon Irabagon and Ben Gerstein were the first to play the bars. In addition to playing tenor and alto saxophones, Jon's sopranino added an exciting color, and his ability to thread interesting ideas through picking out inner voices added clarity to the harmonic movements. It was a good reminder that on certain kinds of material, an "inside" approach of "playing the changes" of our unusual voicings of large pitch collections sounded pretty wild and "out" in its own way. Ben's entire way of experiencing music and his imaginative approach added another dimension to the music. Sometimes this included playing a bassoon reed or tape recorder through a trombone leadpipe, which are normal sounds in Ben's panoramic sonic conception. Kim Cass was next to join, freeing Matt from bass role responsibilities. Kim is a brilliant bassist and composer who Matt and I each already played with in our own bands.

Our basic approach was jazz: play the tune and improvise on it. We looped a bar, playing with the orchestration and improvising with the material, both freely and strictly on the form of the bar. Very often we would connect bars, improvising from one into the next. For some bars, we made internal forms, like playing the first beat, then the first two beats, then first three, and cycling that as a form. Some segments of bars became mini-vamps as a means of transitioning into playing the full bar, which is a somewhat amusing approach as all the bars could be considered vamps anyway. Sometimes we made forms alternating between bars, with specific numbers of repetitions or tempo modulations between them. Two bars could happen at the same time. Some sounded like they were parallel universes, and some felt like one bar was comping for the other. Matt made electronic versions of some of the bars, and we played a gig improvising with the electronic versions, adding guitarist Ava Mendoza.

What about the absurdity of performing a short set where we played every bar once, as written: sixty-five consecutive pieces that were each 2 to 6 seconds long, grindcore style, like Agoraphobic Nosebleed's *Altered States of America*? Or, we could improvise an entire set based on one bar.

The bars could function as a way to test drive material before committing to a longer piece. I'll often imagine a sound or feeling but have only a rough idea of the kind of rhythmic and harmonic material necessary to achieve it. I might write a bar trying to capture it, and see, "is this it?" After playing it and becoming familiar with it, I can decide if I want to create a whole world of a bigger composition based on that bar.

We had a rule that if we developed a bar into a bigger composition that contained the original bar, it was taken out of the Snark Horse book. *Micronesia parakeet* and *wrack* from *Mannequins* both began as Snark Horse bars. Matt developed one of his bars, *a pouting grimace*, into the entire album *A Pouting Grimace* (Pi Recordings, 2017).

By the time I had written around twenty of these one-measure pieces, I decided it was far more than enough to generate an infinite amount of material. I began breeding bars together. I'd take two or three bars and manipulate rhythmic material from one and harmonic material from another, or other combinations of elements from each. I even used the titles from each bar to come up with new titles. *peripheral drome* and *spinal thought* became *feral pineals* (feral from peripheral, pineals from spinal) [Figs. 1–3].

Figure 1. *peripheral drome.*

Figure 2. *spinal thought.*

Figure 3. *feral pineals.*

spinal thought and *mind goggle* became *ought gobs*. I wrote multiple bars entirely based on manipulating material from Matt's bar *dogmacile* [Fig. 4] including one called *adrenal halos* [Fig. 5].

Figure 4. *dogmacile*.

Figure 5. *adrenal halos*.

The ways of manipulating existing material to create new material are infinite: Repeat something. Repeat with variation. Transpose. Retrograde. Invert or flip on an axis. Rhythmic displacement. Filters (everything above or below a value x becomes y, etc.) Mapping (all notes of x value become y, etc.) Harmonic augmentation and diminution. Rhythmic augmentation and diminution. Stretch everything and add in new material in the spaces. Write a contrasting or opposite type of phrase. Divide into pitch collections and write more based on those. Derive rhythms from pitches or vice versa. Derive a larger form from a small phrase structure. Shuffle the smaller parts. Reduction. Remove and rewrite rhythms while retaining pitches, and vice versa. Add pitches or chords in unison or contrapuntally. It is endless. Even partial versions of the first handful of operations, like short chunks of retrograde interspersed with transpositions, could yield infinite results.

We experimented with the shortest bars we could write, and the longest phrases that could still arguably be considered only one bar. We experimented with the fewest and most notes per bar, and with extreme registers. We wrote bars with one or two staves and then many staves, especially when the number of additional musicians involved in Snark Horse began to increase. Guitarist/banjo-ist Brandon Seabrook, saxophonist Matt

Nelson, violist Mat Maneri, and trumpet player Davy Lazar all joined the fold. We performed in various configurations ranging from trio to sextet. The full version of the band with all ten of us would be called Snark Horsekestra, of course.

In most areas of life, people love familiarity. The "mere exposure effect" means that simply being familiar with something makes people like it more. Writers of money-making pop songs exploit this phenomenon, and it is pervasive in other aspects of life as well. Advertisers exploit it. It is a factor in racism and all kinds of biases.

During one of my music education classes in college, I learned a small lesson that has stuck with me, probably because it is actually a big lesson about a deeper truth. I was taught that with children, it was good to refer to things that would take practice to learn as "unfamiliar," rather than warn them something would be "difficult". The latter would make them feel unnecessarily intimidated, but "unfamiliar" meant one only had to become familiar with the material.

We make the unfamiliar familiar through repetition. As musicians, when we do this in our practicing, it rewires our brain. It happens the same way listening to challenging records; it changes the way we hear them. Through years of working to make the unfamiliar familiar and feeling the rewards in how we hear and perceive music, our ears can even learn to crave the unfamiliar.

In my own music, the pieces are much longer than Snark Horse bars and have far less repetition. The music is often challenging enough that it's common in rehearsal to loop one bar at a time to learn and internalize it better. When a musician internalizes a piece, it frees the brain to be available for more artful or improvisational aspects of the music. This is a similar process a listener goes through when becoming familiar with music. The brain is eventually able to predict or remember what comes next, rather than constantly processing information as it's happening. This frees the brain to notice and enjoy other rewarding aspects of the music.

I began to realize that when Snark Horse performed, we were taking the audience along in this process. Even with improvising and variations, they were hearing the material repeated enough that they too were beginning to internalize the mini compositions. This meant we could write literally ANYTHING, and because we repeated it enough, it would become familiar. The weirdest possibilities would eventually sound normal or even become earworms. Snark Horse could be an entry point to longer compositions of ours; a friendly introduction to the kinds of less conventional rhythms and harmonies we each liked to use.

The effects of repeating the Snark Horse material in performance seemed to conjure notions of hypnotism, chants, ritualistic dance, meditation, transcendent music, and chaos, although the raw elements in the compositions don't resemble the rhythms or pitch material typically associated with those qualities and musics.

In Snark Horse, compositional fun and experimentation has yielded effective results, and has proven to be its own worthy goal and reward. For me, however, the more important intention behind Snark Horse is to make a highly improvisational and expansive environment using compressed versions of the kinds of material we like in our longer pieces. We want to allow for anything to happen while putting forth only the smallest amount of our material as a catalyst, enough to create a unique universe to play in that is distinct from open improvisation. We want to allow the energy and spirit from the amazing musicians with whom we play this music to exist in that space.

At the time of this writing, we are scheduled to record Snark Horse in less than a week, with a projected early 2021 release.

CHAPTER
15

SUITE #7

A Conversation between Johnny Gandelsman and Osvaldo Golijov at the End of Osvaldo's "Falling Out of Time Silkroad" Tour and Just Before Johnny's Tour of the Violin Transcription of Bach's "Six Cello Suites"
Edited by Leah Hager Cohen

OSVALDO GOLIJOV

I. The Long Threads of Bach

O: "Nature," said physicist Richard Feynman, "uses only the longest threads to weave her patterns, so that each small piece of her fabric reveals the organization of the entire tapestry."

To me, that's Bach. His music manifests laws, or at least principles, that are true in any place in the universe, right? That is Bach's secret. He knows the fundamental laws of the universe. He can start anywhere along one of those long threads, unfold it and weave it into ever new patterns, so that each of his works "reveals the organization of the entire tapestry." The funny thing for me is that in his music, it's almost as if humans could have not existed. And I don't think any other music is like that. For instance, Beethoven's threads are long, but are dependent on humans' perception of the universe and our not just inhabiting it but being protagonists. Whereas Bach... a different planet would understand him, regardless of humans having ever existed or not. All that was just a long way to ask: how do you feel when you play the violin *Sonatas* and *Partitas* and your violin version of the *Cello Suites*?

J: The long thread of Bach feels that way when I'm playing all of them next to each other, and you see how the pieces change, one from the other. But when I'm in it, it feels more like a scientist's lab. Because from one piece to the next he keeps expanding the possibilities. The counterpoint becomes more complex, three-part fugues become four-part. In the *3rd Sonata (C Major, BWV1005)* the last 3rd of the fugue is built by inverting its theme. The whole thing radiates with the joy of continuously finding new ways to expand the technical and emotional possibilities of the violin, through the simple act of imagining the impossible, and then putting it down on paper.

O: I love that... "simple act of imagining the impossible, and then putting it down on paper". It's like when Messiaen spoke of the "charm of impossibilities"...... "certain mathematical impossibilities, certain closed circuits, possess a strength of bewitchment, a magic strength, a charm."

What you say of Bach's expansion of the technical and emotional possibilities of the violin wakes me up to the fact that I wasn't even thinking of the violin as an instrument, which is another thing...this incredible *filtering* of abstract thinking through wood, and string, and muscle, and fingers, and bow.

And when you say "expanding the possibilities" Are you implying he wrote them in order? Like he was first like Newton and he was under the tree and the apple fell, and he was like, oh! And then he went from apples to solar systems?

J: It does feel like that when I'm working on it. Because they just—it does feel like there's a very purposeful pushing, not just of technique but of form. The 1st *Partita (B minor, BWV1002)* has a standard form of four dances (Allemande, Courante, Sarabande, Bouree), but each dance is followed with a Double, which is basically a written-out variation/improvisation on the preceding dance. The 2nd *Partita (D minor, BWV1004)* follows the same basic form of four dances, but instead of following each one with a Double, Bach finishes the suite with the Chaconne, which is a set of variations built on a simple dance theme. Of course he weaves it into an incredible and astonishing tapestry, transforming even the basic idea of what a variation is, or could be. The first part of the Chaconne develops a string of notes, from 8ths to 16th to 32nds, creating one of the most incredible sweeps in all of music. It feels like a complete journey, and when the opening theme returns, the listener might feel like the thing is coming to a close. Not so fast! A whole new set of variations follows, now in D major! Warmth, hope, light, humor are introduced for the very first time in the *Partita*. We follow as the variations develop, gradually building to an incredible climax of positive energy—it could easily end there, but instead he leads us to the last 3rd of the piece, back to D minor, back to the deep sense of solitude permeating throughout the *Partita*; but this time more unsettled, more questions than answers, starting out without a forward drive so present in the first two parts. Finally, the last spin of variations brings us back to the opening theme, but now we are transformed, having experienced so many of life's emotions in the span of 12 or so minutes.

O: A progression of innocence to experience?

J: Perhaps. So going back to the overall set, the things that one goes through, from G minor to B minor to A minor to D minor to C major, which is the biggest and most complex...

O: And also, the opening of that C major is, even if it's C major, it's heartbreaking, the dotted rhythms, the insistent double stops in seconds, it's as painful as the Chorus of the Hebrew Slaves in Verdi's *Nabucco (Nebuchadnetzar)*.

J: Right! And then, after playing for almost 2 hours, and experiencing all the highs and lows of the first pieces in the set, getting to the *E Major Partita* (*BWV1006*) feels like a complete release. There's no darkness left in that piece, only light and air and innocence.

O: It is like the lightness of people that got old well, right? They understood that life is not so, so, you know. That after all there is just breath, or laughter, which is also mostly air, like in Verdi's *Falstaff*.

To me it's interesting that the last one, the lighthearted one, was the one they sent in the Voyager. A message in a bottle to the universe.

There is also something I love that Yo-Yo (Ma) said about the *Cello Suites*. The idea that, strictly speaking, in chronological time, it's for the most part one note at a time. But what Bach discovered is that music reveals that linear time is an illusion, or, at least, only one manifestation of time among many. In Bach's music, those one-at-a-time notes imply a harmony that *we* are completing. We are playing with him, right? If you're attentive, you are completing all those harmonic progressions going on. Yo-Yo brought this idea to say that we, as listeners, are engaged in an active dialogue with Bach, and even beyond Bach, with those long threads.

J: I feel like that when I listen to Kayhan (Kalhor, the Kemanche Master) do a solo show. I feel like he does the same thing, with time, and engaging people's ears...the patterns he creates, the patterns of the universe are all within it. And whatever he does, he finds the perfect combination of things, and this could be a set over a long period of time. 10 minutes, 20 minutes, 30 minutes. And he's taking you by your ear and just literally leading you along. It's sort of a similar experience to listening to the art of the fugue.

O: Yeah, yeah. It's like both unveil—Kayhan and Bach—like they understand all these laws of the universe, and they take you with them.

J: I wonder with Kayhan—and I wonder if it has any relevance to Bach—but with Kayhan, he's playing in spaces and looking for the resonance of the hall. Kayhan loves a lot of reverb, but I think it's because that's his way to engage the space, and that tells him when the harmonies are moving, and he can control the development...Similarly, those pieces of Bach were played in large churches, where the natural reverb could also have played a part in connecting those voices that might otherwise feel disjointed.

II. Born Under the Foot of Russian Giants

J:...I want to ask you about...how you...You've named a lot of sources of inspiration in your writing. When you were growing up, I know your mom was a pianist. What kind of music were you listening to at home?

O: Well she played the *Tempest Sonata* every day, even the day before she died. And other Beethoven sonatas and Bach, Schubert, Bartók and

Brahms. So that was the bread and butter. And then my father loved Beethoven and Tchaikovsky. And tango. You know, Troilo, who was the Duke Ellington of Buenos Aires. My father kept saying, when I was trying to do weird stuff, he would say, "Okay. But there are people who are universal. Like Tchaikovsky." And at that time I thought, "Ehh." But I think now that I get older, I think when you get older you realize that some people, at least in my view, that they resonate more with the human experience than others.

What do you think?

J: Well you know, I grew up in a household with—

O: Russian giants!

J: Yeah—

O: Under the foot of Russian giants!

J: Actually, under the foot of the piano of the Russian giants. Because I would play under the piano while my parents would practice.

O: But me too! That's my first memory! You mean like, not play the violin but—

J: Yeah, no, no, no, play with toys. I grew up in a household with musicians. Both my parents are musicians. My sister, who's 5 years older, is a violinist. And our household for the most part was all classical music. Like many classical musicians, it's really like the world view is complete. It feels like it's complete. Until your mind gets blown by something you've never considered. I'm trying to think of, what were some of the first non-classical things that I got obsessed with, like an album of Oscar Peterson. Or Stan Getz. And then hearing Romanian gypsy violinists.

O: What did your parents think about the Romanian gypsy violinists?

J: Oh, they love that tradition. I'm not sure how much weight is given to them. But it doesn't matter, right? Because if you listen to it, and you love it, you can just go into a rabbit hole of listening to that. And then it really affects how you think about everything else.

O: Right. It's the difference between a mind that thinks in categories, like your parents' or mine, and a mind that is more fluid and thinks: this is also an important and organic part of human experience.

J: Then there were other deep dives into classical recordings but before the 1930s...Recordings that put the composer not as an untouchable mysterious person that you would never ever reach, but it's like, Oh, this is a tradition that—here it is. You can touch it. Listening to Frederic Lamond's recording of *The Tempest*: it's mind-blowing! And most people today would say it's old-fashioned, it's inappropriate, etc. Lamond was a student of Liszt, who was a student of Czerny, who was a student of Beethoven, so it's a direct link to Beethoven! Much more direct than anyone today claiming to be a Beethoven expert.

I was wondering...I imagine that when you're deciding to be a composer, and you're in school, learning about a particular tradition, it can lead in a particular direction. But then your worldview, your ears, are so open to so many different inspirations. And you found a way to let them into your voice, in a beautiful and transformative way. And I'm just wondering, did you have to allow yourself to do that? Was it a conscious choice? Or did it start seeping into what you were hearing?

O: It's a confluence of things...I forgot to mention that the other big part of my musical childhood was the synagogue. And then of course the other thing that was a factor was distance...Growing up in Argentina, everything came from a very faraway place. When your parents tell you "Listen to this"... it comes not only from the past; it comes from across the ocean. It's a mythological thing...But there was one guy, Piazzolla, I would go to his concerts in concert halls or cafes and say to myself, "This guy's alive," and I understood everything that he was doing, every phrase. I would recognize, Oh, this is how people walk, this is how people talk. Or this is how people flirt. Or are heartbroken. I could understand in every note what he was doing, where it came from. Even when he wrote *Tango-Fugues*. Nothing was abstract. And to me that connection between life itself and music was very important. But coming here,

I was "in the closet" with Piazzolla. And then, when I was a student in Tanglewood, William Bolcom was visiting and he said, Oh, you're from Argentina, the land of Piazzolla! He didn't say Ginastera. And I thought, Oh. I can say "Piazzolla." And that helped a lot.

But also, a couple of years earlier, in the same week that my first child, Talia, was born, my mother died. And I said, you know, I don't give a damn about certain kinds of music. And I'm not going to do them any more. Because it's not who I am.

So those two things. The juxtaposition of Bolcom's permission to be free and the person whom I loved the most dying and the one who I would love the most being born at the same time. It made me think: Do what matters to you while you are alive. It was like the Hassidic story of Rev Zusyia…when he was in his deathbed surrounded by his students, they noticed he was anxious and asked him "why are you so anxious, Rev Zusyia? You were such a just, righteous man, and a great teacher to us, you'll surely go to heaven" and he responded "I know I'll go to heaven. But I fear that when I get there I won't be asked 'why weren't you Moses the Prophet?'" But, "Why weren't you Rev Zusyia".

III. Motion. Emotion.

J: It's so interesting that you were talking about how Piazzolla could capture how somebody walks, because when we were working on *Falling Out of Time*, you were talking about how does this man who is completely stricken by grief, how does one walk?

O: Isn't that what every composer does? Like the romantics do the horse gallop, or the wanderer's walk of Schubert, or the bluesmen doing the train…I think music is, fundamentally, motion. Once you find the type of motion that you're trying to embody, be that of a drunk man or a grief-stricken man or a paraglider, then that's a good feeling. It's like what you were saying about Bach.

J: That's interesting…to try and connect it to such specific things. How does somebody talk, how does somebody walk? And be able to first imagine it, then notate it, and then translate it to musicians who are going to play it.

O: Yeah. It's beautiful when you find the right rhythm and pitches and all the rest. It's a good feeling. But the one that went the furthest in this direction is Janacek, right? I mean he could really notate speech, the music of speech so well. But then, the thing about Bach is—he can do that but then he can also find the rhythms of the atoms, and the planets, and, you know, everything in nature, not just a drunk guy in Buenos Aires.

J: And with almost zero instruction for the performer.

IV. Schools of Interpretation

O: Right. So what do you think about these wildly different ways of interpreting Bach?

J: That's a hard question. I mean...I feel like—with violin, I'm not even sure I've gotten to the place where I can compare the way people play it. I might be too close to it. With the cello suites, with Casals finding them and then bringing them basically back to life, to the repertoire, and putting such a strong stamp of what they are about to him? I think that affected most people who play them.

O: And the "that"—what is the "that?"

J: I think about his version, the worldview. It's grandiose. It's full of pathos. And beauty, and seriousness. Also the time that he was living in and everything that was going on—it assumes a gravitas. Which obviously that music can take, because people have been doing it since he started playing them, and doing it beautifully. But—somebody like Anner Bylsma or this gamba player that I've been loving, Paolo Pandolfo, they can look at the same exact score and just imagine something completely different.

O: What words come to your mind when you think of Bylsma?

J: Well, the total opposite of grandiosity. So humor and lightness, you know, and joy—joy in finding little tiny jewels. Versus the grand totality.

It's kind of like making your opinion of things...Like when you look at a piece of music, you can hear it a certain way, and then you can find a bunch of reasons why that is true? You can find justifications for things. And in Bach you can see that grand totality, if you want to.

O: Yeah. That's how we started the conversation.

J: Right. But then you can also, if you're interested in it—you know, with Anner—he pays so much attention to very specific notations—we were talking about no instruction, right? Very little instruction. And yet, in Bach's bowings, there's actually a lot of instruction, *if* you decide that those bowings are important.

O: Right...

J: Which a lot of people ignore.

O: Are you following all the bowings?

J: In the violin sonatas and *Partitas*, I tried to follow the manuscript as much as I could. The cello suites feel different. What I see in the Anna Magdalena version is the implication for infinite possibilities, the way an incredible improviser can find endless variation within the simplest form. I'm thinking of one of my favorite musicians, the Irish fiddler Martin Hayes. Seeing Martin weave together a medley of Irish tunes is very similar to seeing and experiencing amazing magic—I'm always left dumbfounded, how did he do that??? His art is never flashy, never tries to impress—it flows directly from the source material. There is a delight to it that is very similar to Bach's joy we were talking about earlier. And there is also something very humble about the process. It's not setting out to change the world, or write the greatest piece ever written, or anything else like that. It's a scientist's pursuit in finding out what else might be in there, what layers might still be hiding. It's engaging one's imagination, but also being able to then actually do what you've imagined. That's a real gift.

Back to your question, improvisation is not something I'm good at, but my goal is to get to a place where I can feel like what's happening is created on the spot.

O: So you would like to get to a place where you don't know which bowing you're going to do that night?

J: Yes.

O: That's amazing.

V. Oneness. Freedom.

J: No, but it's not...The people like Kayhan, or Martin, or Bela Fleck, you know, people who are in the world of improvisation, they're so connected to—their hands playing the instruments, they're so connected to their inner workings. Or Chick Corea, where it's so like—

O: It's one thing.

J: It's one thing. And we interpreters of other people's music, for the most part, there's already a barrier. You know? And I'm trying to get to a place where the barrier is lifted...—

O: I see what you mean, but you could...right, right. I think in the case of Chick Corea, even if he didn't write music, he could be playing music of others and make it his own. You know what I mean? Even if he was quote-unquote just a pianist, it would be so personal, in that sense of his fingers being part of his brain. Right? So what I'm saying is, you yourself are there. With Bach and with others.

J: Yes! And people get to that place in different ways. To that place where they feel like it's completely the brain and the heart and the hands.

O: Does it mean that you would, on the spot, reconsider the construction of a phrase?

J: Yeah. It happens a lot. It could be in a hotel room or it could be in front of an audience. In front of an audience it might happen more, but only if you're really feeling the energy flowing back and forth.

VI. Freedom. Oneness.

O: Do you ever have an experience where you play one of the two sets entire and you actually, throughout, without any distraction, became all those fugues?

J: I haven't yet played the full cello suite set (it's happening next month). But with the violin set, the times when it feels special are when I've gotten in the middle, somewhere in the middle; sometimes it can take a full hour to just get to that place, or sometimes it's relatively quick... But it's a place where it can almost feel like, kind of observing from up in the air. There is a scene in *Kung Fu Panda 2*, where in a crucial moment, Po finally understands what his master has been talking about all along, time and space stop, he can hold a raindrop in his paw—he finds Inner Peace. That's the place I try to get to.

Some of my favorite musicians in the world, I feel like what they do comes from just enjoying, loving and respecting the thing that they do, the craft, the instrument, the history and tradition; and then just literally, just weaving and starting from nothing and seeing where it can go. There's nothing grandiose about any of that effort. And that part is truly astonishing. Like with Kayhan, when he plays in a mode he only a few notes. But good ones. And he puts them one after another, always in the right order. You know what I mean? Or like Martin—it's just one guy with a violin playing traditional Irish music. It's folk music, music that an entire people are connected to. And he just finds, continuously finds, new ways of looking at something that is so simple in its form, and yet so full—it has the world of Bach in eight bars of music.

O: I think this in a way takes us back to the opening of the conversation. Right? Because if all is really part of that long thread, you can reinterpret and re-weave however you want. Because it's the same thread.

J: Right.

O: Man, we just scratched a little.

J: We didn't even.

O: We didn't even.

CHAPTER 16

A BRIEF HISTORY OF THE PIANO-PERCUSSION QUARTET

RUSSELL GREENBERG

The piano-percussion quartet is a relatively recent configuration in contemporary music, dating back to the early 20th century. Despite its logistical hurdles, there is now a growing body of work that has been created, stemming from the intersection of the quartet's unique qualities paired with more recent trends in new music entrepreneurship and drive. It has proven to be flexible, timbrally-rich, dynamic, and able to evolve with emerging technologies. Newer groups in the United States and worldwide, including Berlin Piano Percussion, Icarus ensemble, and my own quartet Yarn/Wire have continued to develop personalized approaches to repertoire creation that will determine the next directions that this music takes.

In the 20th century, a few new ensemble formations that didn't exist before became commonplace. Two that are now widely recognized and long-lasting are the percussion ensemble (usually four to six players), which grew out of the work of Varèse and then Cage, Cowell, Harrison, and *Pierrot Lunaire*'s (Arnold Schoenberg, 1912) eponymous Pierrot ensemble, which is sometimes augmented with a percussionist. These two ensembles got their start in the early part of the 20th century, and were firmly established by the 1960s. Another now recognized ensemble formation that didn't flourish until the later part of the 20th century and into the 21st (though the first "official" work was in 1937) is the piano and percussion quartet. Once thought of as a unique or rare ensemble, there is now a diverse and expanding repertoire for this formation. This quartet in particular exemplifies and follows a trajectory of development that reflects diverging trends in American and European musical scenes today.

The piano-percussion quartet is quirky and cumbersome. There are always four players, but the exact instrumentation is never the same between two pieces because "percussion" can mean almost anything. For instance, pieces such as Steve Reich's *Quartet* (2013) are scored for two pianos and two vibraphones, while on the other end of the spectrum, George Crumb's *Music for a Summer Evening* (1974) has no fewer than thirty-three percussion instruments (more, if you count multiples of the same class as individual instruments) along with two amplified grand pianos. Other works, such as Catherine Lamb's *curvo totalitas* (2016) eschew pianos altogether and replace them with synthesizers. Such variability is part of the intriguing nature of this ensemble—the timbral possibilities are nearly endless. However, the potential for enormous setups and logistical performance hurdles (including space, sightlines and instruments needed) have historically been a stumbling block to presentations of this repertoire as well as the sustainability of dedicated quartets.

Rehearsal and performance of piano-percussion quartet repertoire requires significant resources. These resources include finding rehearsal spaces with two pianos and having access to massive amounts of percussion, presenters who are able to cover the logistics of concerts, and commissioners who are willing to fund an entirely new repertoire. Because of this, a few forces—specific ensembles that were active during a certain time, and music festivals/foundations that were dedicated to new work, have driven the repertoire for the instrumentation.

The following chronological overview of the piano-percussion quartet repertoire provides history and context for this music as well as some general trends. It is impossible to cover all of the works that exist, so instead, the discussion focuses on select works that have been performed multiple times, or else illustrate distinct features of the repertoire's development and sustainability.

The piano-percussion literature is one of the newest repertoires in modern music. With the exception of the Bartók *Sonata* (as discussed below), the repertoire has been in development for less than 50 years. A search for pieces of this instrumentation in IRCAM's "Brahms" music database[1] yields only sixty-six pieces, compared with one thousand fifty-one contemporary string quartets.[2] A similar search within the New York Public Library's catalogue turns up thirty-five piano-percussion quartet works (this time more Americans are represented), and five thousand, four hundred thirty-six string quartets

1. IRCAM maintains an in-depth database of contemporary music documentation called "B.R.A.H.M.S" or "Base de documentation sur la musique contemporain" at http://brahms.ircam.fr

2. It is also worth noting that at the time of this article, only one is by an American Composer (Michael Gordon), and only two by women (Misato Mochizuki and Diana Soh).

(including common practice scores). The repertoire is far from standard at this point—in fact, it is increasingly far-reaching, genre-fluid and difficult to define. This variability, flux, and flexibility make it one of the most alluring repertoires, all the more so because of its evolving potential.

Early Work—1973/74 (and Before)

The history of the piano-percussion quartet starts with Bartók's *Sonata for 2 pianos and percussion*. This piece was written in 1937 and is widely considered to be the first major work for this instrumentation.[3] While this is true with regards to the instrumentation itself, musically speaking it belongs to a different era than subsequent post-war modernist works involving percussion. The pianists and percussionists are treated as having different music abilities (in the score, Bartók admonishes the pianists to "keep an eye on the percussionists [to make sure they are doing things right]")—soloistic piano parts are essentially "accompanied" by orchestral-style percussion writing. In a sense, this piece can be thought of as a "proof of concept" that the instrumentation could work to support a composition as opposed to the start of the modern repertoire that came to define the genre. While a masterpiece for its time, it would take over 35 years for another set of works to cement the ensemble formation.

3. Igor Markevitch wrote *The Flight of Icarus* in 1932, but it is scored for two pianos and three percussion.

In the early 1970s, two pieces demonstrated the versatility and possibilities of the piano-percussion quartet for the modern era.[4] Luciano Berio wrote *Linea* in 1973 and George Crumb wrote *Makrokosmos III: Music for a Summer Evening* in 1974. Berio takes a minimal approach to his percussion arsenal, writing for vibraphone and marimba in addition to two pianos. In *Music for a Summer Evening*, on the other hand, Crumb fully explores the timbral possibilities of large percussion setups, extended piano techniques (strumming, plucking, preparations and more), and vocal effects (performed by the percussionists) resulting in a 35-minute exploration of sound and ritual. Though arguably opposites in terms of the instrumental forces employed, both *Linea* and *Makrokosmos III* remain some of the most challenging and virtuosic pieces of chamber music today. It bears mentioning that both pieces were well funded: *Linea* was intended to be performed with dance and was commissioned by the Felix Blaska et sa Dance company in France,

4. A third piece, François-Bernard Mâche's *Temes Nevinbür* was also written in 1973, but it remains rarely performed. This work includes a fixed electronic tape part.

while *Makrokosmos III* was commissioned by the Fromm Foundation to be performed at Swarthmore University.

These two pieces laid the foundation for the future of piano-percussion quartet repertoire and demonstrated the musical possibilities afforded by the ensemble's instrumentation. However, with a few exceptions, the next developments of repertoire weren't to occur for another 15 years.[5]

5. There were a few notable pieces that were written such as Roger Reynolds' *less than 2* (1978) [for the same ensemble as *Makrokosmos*] and Rolf Wallin's *Mandala* (1985), but these were isolated as compared with the cluster of works to come in the 1990s.

IRCAM, Europe and the 1990s

In the 1990s, activities by the European group, Ensemble Intercontemporain (the resident contemporary music ensemble at the famed French institute renowned for its merging of computer science and contemporary music, IRCAM) resulted in a significant cluster of new works. These were performed both by EIC[6], as well as other European ensembles. IRCAM established the Cursus Program for Young Composers in 1990, specifically for training in contemporary music and electronics. For this reason, many of the piano-percussion quartet pieces were written to include live electronics. The works from this time include Franco Donatoni's *Cloches III* (1991, for EIC[7]), Michael Jarrell's *Rhizomes (Assonance VIIb)* (1993, for IRCAM/EIC), Magnus Lindberg's *Related Rocks* (1997, for IRCAM/Strasbourg festival), and Philippe Leroux's *M* (1997 for IRCAM and the Donaueschingen Festival). Other notable pieces, including George Friedrich Haas' *...Schatten...durch unausdenkliche Wälder* (1992) and Wolfgang Rihm's *Schrift im Schrift* (1993, for the Schumacher piano duo) came to fruition during this time as well. The significant resources offered by IRCAM, EIC and other European festivals and funding structures (including state support) meant that these works were rarely restricted in terms of instrumentation, duration, and use of electronics. There was also ample rehearsal space and time to put the pieces together. In many ways the works of the 1990s are a fusion of the technical, modernist writing foreshadowed by Berio's *Linea*, and the timbral richness of Crumb's *Makrokosmos III*. Before the next significant developments in repertoire, another dry spell followed this flurry of piano-percussion quartet activity in the early to

6. I will be referring to Ensemble Intercontemporain using it's well-known acronym, "EIC" from this point on.

7. I am including the commissioning partners in conjunction with the date the work was written, e.g. (1991 for EIC), etc.

mid-'90s.

2000s and After: European and American Developments and Ensembles

With a small but growing body of repertoire now in existence for the piano-percussion quartet, the 2000s saw a new development—the formation of dedicated ensembles performing this repertoire, as opposed to subsets of larger ensembles like EIC. Similar to dedicated string quartets,[8] these groups formed and existed to exclusively play already written works and develop new commissions for the specific instrumental configuration of the ensemble. These quartets include Ensemble 2x2 (Germany 2007–08) Quatuor Makrokosmos (Switzerland), Berlin Piano Percussion (Germany ~2007), Yarn/Wire (New York, 2005), Ensemble Icarus (Baltimore, MD 2016), and Quarter (Hong Kong, 2016). From around 2005 onward, a continuing explosion of piano-percussion repertoire was (and continues to be) spearheaded by these ensembles.[9]

8. E.g. Arditti Quartet, Flux Quartet, Kronos Quartet, Takács Quartet, Beaux Arts Trio, etc.

9. It is worth noting that George Crumb's *Makrokosmos* and Roger Reynold's *less than*, both from the 1970s, were written for a group consisting of James Freeman, Gilbert Kalish: pianos, Raymond DesRoches, Richard Fitz: percussions. However, this ensemble did not become a lasting and permanent ensemble.

Because of the nature of dedicated quartets, the repertoire in the 2000s developed in different ways than earlier works. Ensembles directly requested and commissioned specific composers who then tended to tailor their works to specific performers, abilities, and quartet resources. In contrast, the previous method that work was generated included sprawling funding and possibilities afforded by the IRCAM and EIC-led process, including the eventual publishing of the works. To be sure, festivals and foundations still played a large part in the commissioning of new work, especially for European ensembles, but this was not the only way that new work came to be. Instead, there was more of a focus on interaction between a dedicated quartet and composers. This change in process and composer/performer relationship in many ways reflects the diverging trends in the contemporary music coming from the United States versus Europe. These trends seem to be encouraged by the differing funding structures and institutional support between the two places.

Some examples of works stemming from the European process include Stefano Gervasoni's *Sviete Tihi....* (2005–6) for the Makrokosmos Quartet and the Contrechamps festival (Arditti Foundation commission), Oliver Schneller's *Resonant Space* (2007) and Jérôme Combier's *Sables de vieux os* (2006/7) for ensemble 2x2 at the Witten Festival, and Martín Matalon's *La Makina* (2007) commissioned by McGill University. These works followed a similar sort of structural development as the earlier 1990s works, the difference being they were written for set ensembles dedicated to piano-percussion quartet repertoire.

On the other hand, the culture of making and presenting new music in the United States was undergoing lots of change in the early 21st century: musicians were arguably attempting to move away from a more academic/university-based practice to one in which performers sought to engage a public more actively through branding, self-promotion, and collaboration. The origins of this change in general began in the 1980s with groups like Bang on a Can[10] and Kronos Quartet, followed by younger ensembles that were inspired by this sort of activity, who began appearing in the 2000s. Groups that did not have significant resources and funding at their disposal instead followed a more DIY approach to creating repertoire. They began by working (often for free) with composers in a local scene and of a similar generation in order to build highly personal, logistically manageable, and tour-able repertoire. Piano-percussion quartet music readily fit this approach since creation of a new repertoire was necessary because of the nature of the instrumentation. Because a template for this ensemble formation was lacking, performance practice could be built from the ground up.

10. For very thorough discussions about many trends in American music, please see Will Robin's writing on Bang on a Can and more. https://williamrobin.com

For an ensemble such as Yarn/Wire, this was the trajectory that repertoire development took. It was a liberating activity and meant initially commissioning works for one piano (four hands) and the instruments that the percussionists could fit in one van. Works such as Alex Mince's *Pendulum VI-Trigger*, Eric Wubbels' *alphabeta*, and Kate Soper's *wolf* (all from 2010), were part of this initial push. Thus, rather than having an existing structure or festival where this music could take place, repertoire was initially built out of a need to tour and generate music to play, often with limited resources, including a venue. Ensemble members usually paid for pieces out of their own pockets, and the group rented venues such as Roulette and Greenwich House in Manhattan to self-produce events. Other works such as Thomas Meadowcroft's *Walkman Antiquarian* (2013) and Sarah Hennies *Primers* (2019), came to fruition years after the first set of works, but still benefited from a similar workflow. This mindset, born out of the need for repertoire but also the lack of funding for contemporary music in the United States, allowed for and enabled the flexibility to try many ways of making music—often outside of written scores. Yarn/Wire, freed from a "common practice" of new music creation was able to bring in experimentalism, improvisation, and minimalism into its active repertoire in pieces like Travis Laplante's *Inner Garden* (2016), Annea Lockwood's *Into the Vanishing Point* (2019), Marina Rosenfeld's *My Body* (2019) and Michael Gordon's *Material* (2016). For many of these pieces, performance practice was taught by rote; notation and performance directions were documented after the premieres. What is interesting is that this type of DIY, improvisational and hands-on approach to music making can still be seen in the quartet's later works that did receive funding support (such as Zosha Di Castri's *Tachitipo* (2016 at Miller Theatre) and Misato Mochizuki's *Le monde des rondes et des carrés* (2015 at Lincoln Center Festival) as well.

These collaborative processes and the stylistic breadth of the resulting pieces contrast to the European top-down approach to music making. They even hint at a rupture from a purely classical music practice which, after World War II, new music continued to be closely aligned with. In the United States, this split can also be felt as a reaction against a purely University and research-based musical practice, towards one that pays attention to operating in a marketplace (albeit an extremely small, niche and specialized one) and for a concertgoing public. The freedom to create work inside and outside of an historical repertoire (unlike a string quartet) as well as the cultural structures that impose a certain way of working, allows work to be created in a multitude of ways that spans multiple genres. The lines between experimental music, improvisation, and notated scores continue to blur. And the composer-performer relationship ceases to be hierarchical in this model. As a result, musicians who fall outside of the typical "new music" definition of composer are now freed to create works for the piano-percussion repertoire. These include noise musician Pete Swanson (*eliminated artist*—2010), techno artist Mark Fell (*core, self, oscillation*—2015), and indie musician Sufjan Stevens (*Round Up*—2015), all of whom worked closely with Yarn/Wire. Also important is the increased attention in United States ensembles to representing works by women, gender non-conforming, people of color, and other underrepresented groups to better reflect the communities in which music is made while experiencing new creative potential. This is a conversation that is conspicuously absent as a stated objective in other new music scenes around the world.

A 21st Century Ensemble Continues to Evolve

Openness to form, process, and genre may be one of the strongest and greatest developments in new music, and it is embodied in much of the recent literature for piano-percussion quartet as developed in the United States. As a fully 21st century ensemble, the piano-percussion quartet can explore music in ways that traditional ensembles have not been able to. (At its core it is, of course a prog-rock instrumentation.). The recent intersection of all of this activity—development of dedicated quartets, European festivals and commissioning history, "grit" and openness of the American working process, has led to a robust and richness of work that has started to be considered a viable repertoire. Rather than in fits and starts, since 2005, hundreds of works have now been written for this instrumentation.[11] Each ensemble has begun to develop its own "voice" or "sound", largely by choosing which composers to work with. While performance practice and sound may start local, the interchange of ideas is international with many groups starting to share repertoire.

11. It is worth noting that George Crumb's *Makrokosmos* and Roger Reynold's *less than*, both from the 1970s, were written for a group consisting of James Freeman, Gilbert Kalish: pianos, Raymond DesRoches, Richard Fitz: percussions. However, this ensemble did not become a lasting and permanent ensemble.

Small chamber groups of all kinds have begun to change the direction of classical music. This is largely because of their inherent flexibility and smaller overhead costs, but also a drive to explore new ways of making music. As one of the most recent of these formations, the piano-percussion quartet has joined Pierrot ensembles and percussion ensembles as a viable formation that will continue to play a leading role in the development of new repertoire and models of musical creation.

CHAPTER
17

THE VIBRAPHONE IN THE MUSIC OF JOHN ZORN

An Observation on the Evolution

SAE HASHIMOTO

I was in my final year of undergrad at Juilliard when I met John Zorn. Juilliard's contemporary ensemble, AXIOM, programmed two works by Zorn in the spring of 2016 for a concert at Alice Tully Hall, and I got assigned to play the vibraphone in his chamber work *Missa Sine Voces.* When I met him at the dress rehearsal, he carried a uniquely intense aura unlike any of the composers I had met before. About a year later I was given an opportunity to premiere two of his newest works for solo vibraphone and improvised rhythm section: *Naked Lunch* and *The Exterminating Angel.* I was absolutely ecstatic but also terrified. I was in the middle of my Master's degree at Juilliard at that point, and still being immersed neck-deep in the conservatory environment, I had no idea what *playing with an improvised rhythm section* meant. And I was too terrified to ask. I asked how many rehearsals I would have with the rhythm section, and John emailed me that we would just put it together at the sound check before the private premiere. This made me incredibly nervous, so I practiced intensely until I knew both pieces almost by memory. On the day of the premiere, I met my rhythm section for the first time—Tyshawn Sorey and Shanir Blumenkranz. By this point I was starting to realize the weight of this reality. We didn't even have time to go through everything during the sound check. But the moment we started playing, the fear and nerves went away and it was just pure joy. I had never felt so liberated and in control at the same time. I felt like this music brought another expression out of myself that I didn't know I had. Not only did I have time to admire Tyshawn and Shanir's mastery and sensitivity on their instruments, their presence was so reassuring that it felt like even if I lost control, they would be right there to pick me up. I had never had a performance experience like that before. I felt a strong force pulling me deeper into this new world that I caught a glimpse of that day.

It's crazy to think that that was only a little over 2 years ago. Since then, I have had the chance to premiere over nine works by John and have performed his music in venues all over New York and beyond, not to mention the incredible musicians that I've gotten to meet through his music. This dear collaboration with John has had a huge impact on my vibraphone playing. I would like to use this opportunity to write about these transformations from a musical and technical standpoint, not only as a means of self-clarification and betterment, but also in hopes of illuminating this composer's imaginative, constantly evolving writing that keeps pushing the sonic capabilities of the vibraphone to the next level.

Sound Production

One of the biggest challenges I faced early on was volume production. During my conservatory years I had studied contemporary mallet masterworks by composers like Manoury, Berio, Druckman, Andriessen, Boulez, Hurel, and Reich. These premieres with Zorn were the first time I played the vibraphone as a solo voice with bass and drums. Zorn's writing in these pieces are full of intricate phrases and complex lines, sometimes with huge leaps across the instrument, so the challenge was how to clearly enunciate these lines with a big enough sound that can match the energy and soar over the rhythm section. Although the vibraphone was amplified at many of the performances I've done of these pieces since then, some of the more intimate performances were not, and in these instances I needed to figure out how to make myself heard, pace my stamina and still play with a good sound.

The Stevens Grip

One way I approached this was through the four-mallet grip. For four mallet playing, many percussionists use either the traditional Cross grip, or the Burton grip invented by famous jazz vibraphonist Gary Burton. I use a grip called Stevens grip, designed by marimbist Lee Howard Stevens in the 1970s. For the following three reasons, I've found this grip useful for vibraphone playing, and especially Zorn's repertoire in terms of sound production.

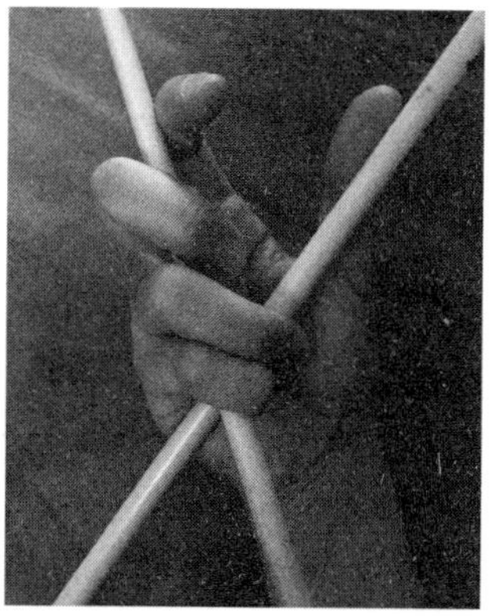

Cross Grip.

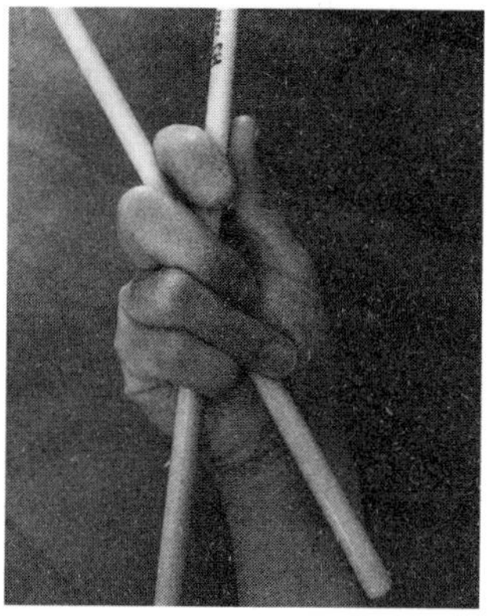

Burton Grip.

Stevens Grip.

Firstly, one unique aspect of the Stevens grip is its weight distribution. While other grips result in the player holding mallets at about ¾ of the way down, with the Stevens grip, both mallets are held at the very bottom of the shaft. This allows almost the entirety of the mallet shaft to be activated into the stroke and the maximum weight of the head to strike against the bar. (Think choking up on a putter once you're on the green vs. where you would hold a driver to get the maximum distance.) Additionally, this grip allows for a wider angle of wrist rotation, increasing the amplitude (height of the stroke) of both inner and outer mallets.

Another strength is the wide interval range. Because both mallets are held at the bottom of the shaft, I am able to comfortably reach a twelfth (C5-F6) in my right hand and a tenth (F3-A4) in my left hand. This allows for ease of playing chords with wide intervals as well as being able to use double stickings for licks with huge leaps instead of playing hand-to-hand, which would create extra traveling across the instrument, thus more room for error. I will further elaborate on the topic of stickings later.

Lastly, the Stevens grip allows for more independence between the mallets. With the Cross and Burton grips, the mallet shafts are in contact with each other inside the hand. Because of this, when the player strikes a note with one mallet, the other mallet naturally moves a bit in reverse motion. However, with the Stevens grip, because the two mallets are held with different fingers (inner mallet with thumb, index and middle, and outer mallet with ring and pinky), there is a bigger chance of striving for complete independence of mallet movement. This mallet independence ultimately develops the player's dexterity. The execution of subtle pulses, accents, inflection or lilt can be done with finger controlled fine movement instead of the whole wrist rotation. The Stevens grip gives me the skills I need to strive for more conviction in my playing, whether I am going for smooth, jagged, feathery or powerful.

Mallet Choice

Another angle I approach sound production is through my mallet choice. For Zorn's music, I tend to choose vibraphone mallets that are generally on the hard, and heavy side, even for contemporary classical taste. It is common in orchestral and chamber playing for the percussionist to have a tray full of different mallets, and incorporate a lot of mallet switches. In most of Zorn's writing for the vibraphone, there is usually little to no time for mallet switches, so I needed to find one all-purpose type of mallets that would help me achieve my ideal sound.

John Zorn writes intricate, chromatic, extremely virtuosic lines, sometimes at mind-numbingly fast tempi. Because it takes a lot of stamina to play his music, it often comes down to making choices that allow me to be as efficient as possible. I let the articulation of hard mallets help me enunciate every note in these gestures. Over the years I've grown fond of the green "Terry Gibbs" mallets. They are articulate enough but not too pingy or brittle. They are also on the heavier side, which is something I value quite a bit. The weight of the mallet is one of the key elements that impact the color of the sound. If the mallet is hard and lightweight, it produces a relatively bright tone. Because I strive for an articulate but full-bodied, warm tone, the heavy and articulate mallets allow me to activate the full sonic spectrum out of the metal bars, from dark and beefy to bright and crisp. Additionally, not only does the heavy weight obviously create more body of sound, it is also a great way to gain finger strength and chops just by using them on a daily basis.

Stickings

Stickings are like fingerings on the piano: it's determining with which mallet to play each note. Especially with four mallets, creative stickings can 1) increase the efficiency, and 2) enable more ways to add inflection to a line. For the purpose of further discussion, I will refer to each mallet with numbers 1–4, as seen below:

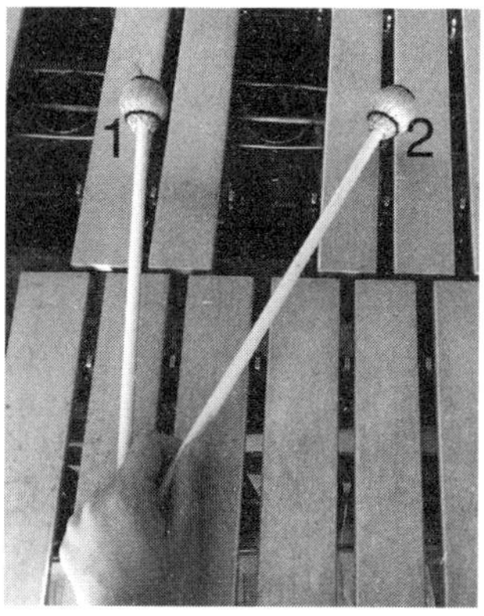

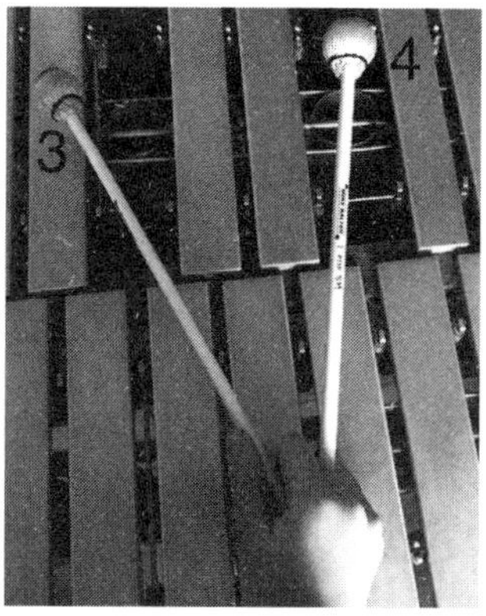

Over the past few years, I've become more of a proponent of

double lateral motion. It is simply when one plays a note with a mallet, followed by another note with the other mallet in the same hand. Here is an example of a double lateral motion:

I tend to use this sticking quite often in Zorn's music, for ergonomic and musical reasons. This is a line from *Naked Lunch* for solo vibraphone and rhythm section, one of the pieces I premiered in 2017, and the stickings I decided on:

The tempo here is quite fast, at quarter note = 100. This is also a climactic line at the end of the first movement, and I wanted to execute it as clearly as possible with a big crescendo into the chord. In the first ¾ bar, I incorporated some double lateral motion to minimize the hands crossing over, which would create room for error. Playing alternating or hand-to-hand sticking for the next two bars was, for me, out of the question, because of the tempo, the line's chromatic nature, and all the extraneous motion it would cause. I eventually settled on the above sticking, so I can lead each of the chromatically ascending melody with the preceding note in the same hand. In other words, the right hand double lateral motion (3-4) allows me to play almost a mini crescendo into each triplet figure, incrementally contributing to the large crescendo into the chord that I try to convey. I also liked the feel of this particular 4-2-3 sticking, rather than playing 3-1-2. I felt like 3-1-2 would "phrase off" each triplet, but I wanted to lead into each new triplet with the double lateral motion.

In order to use double lateral motion to add inflection in such a way, I needed to strengthen my technique so that I can play comfortably at any interval, wrist angle, speed, dynamic or accent patterns. I think that using the Steven's grip is advantageous in this regard, because of its aforementioned merits: power deriving from the low grip, amplitude, interval range, and mallet independence. In order to build strength and ease of double lateral motion, I want to share a warm-up exercise that I've been using for many years; I was introduced to it by Jacob Nissly, the principal percussionist of San Francisco Symphony, when he gave a masterclass at Juilliard years ago. I've added my own twist to it to adapt it for double lateral strengthening.

As it can be seen, these stickings allow the player to practice a wide variety of intervals and various wrist and elbow angles, sometimes very awkward ones. It could be practiced at any tempo, and sometimes I add accents to practice emphasizing a particular mallet. This warm-up is also endless: the player can keep going and end up practicing these harmonic progressions in all twelve keys! I use this exercise as a way to improve accuracy as well, and only moving on to the next chord if I hit all the right notes. This warm-up exercise has stuck with me because it's fun and more harmonically gratifying to play than some other exercises. I look forward to coming up with more variations in the future and hope that this warm-up could be useful on other instruments as well.

Extended Technique

One of the many joys of working on Zorn's music is the new sounds and possibilities that became part of my language on the vibraphone as a result. I love the experimental and inventive nature of his writing. In every piece, Zorn finds a new way to feature the instrument, and create unique sonic possibilities. The mouth vibrato is one of the earliest examples. Once I strike the note, I lean over and get my face as close to the bar as possible. I put my mouth above where the resonator is and use it as a resonating chamber, creating a vibrato-like "wah-wah" effect. I think it is such a cool and visually striking effect that shows the player physically manipulating the post-stroke sustain.

Zorn's writing was the first time I saw the use of motor in such an active and precise way. He often specifies the running speed of the motor, from slow, to medium, to fast and very fast. Sometimes the speed changes happen so frequently that the piece requires a vibraphone assistant who controls the motor speed, like in *Candlemas Eve* (2016) or *Altarpiece* (2017). It was kind of revelatory to me that all these different motor speeds can have such emotional effects. When paired with certain music, the motor speeds can really heighten or alter the expression of the music. Very slow motor can have a pulsating, wave-like effect, and very fast vibrato can make it sound muddy and dizzying, and give it almost a detuning feel.

Pitch bending on the vibraphone is another favorite of mine. It can be achieved when a note is struck (or bowed), by pressing a plastic mallet against the node of the bar and then rubbing down towards the center while exerting pressure. This works better on some bars, usually not in the higher register. When done successfully it creates a quartertone downward pitch bend. I like to use a soft plastic xylophone mallet with a very bendy rattan shaft, and put a little piece of moleskin or fabric tape at the very tip of the mallet for silent initial contact with the bar.

Creating harmonics that sound two octaves higher on the vibes is a relatively new addition in Zorn's vibraphone writing. It is a work in progress for me and I am searching for more consistency in my harmonic playing. In order to make the harmonic heard, I try to find a way to maximize the volume of the harmonic and minimize the volume of the fundamental pitch. I seem to find more success when I gently put my fingertip exactly on the middle point on the bar. This basically splits the bar in half to create the harmonic sounding two octaves higher. If the note is to be struck, then the timing is tricky—I strike the bar (at the very edge, since the center is occupied) then leave my fingertip on for a split second before releasing it. If it is to be bowed, I find that on some bars it just doesn't work immediately as well as others. In those cases, I sometimes start bowing it regularly then gently put the fingertip at the middle point while the bar is resonating, then the harmonic usually rises out of it and rings beautifully. A lot of these extended techniques don't work quite well on the higher register of the instrument. Usually the cutoff is about G5, with some fluctuations across different instruments.

These unique sounds often stand alone to create special moments in Zorn's music, but they are also occasionally combined. In *$R\mu\nu$-$\frac{1}{2}g\mu\nu R$= $8\pi T\mu\nu$: thought experiments for string quartet and vibraphone* (2019), there is one note that is struck, then bent down over a mouth vibrato—all of this floating over a cloud of airy harmonic gliss in the strings. In *Casting the Runes* (2019), one of the newest additions to the piano, vibes and improvising rhythm section repertoire, I strike a chord with mallets and out of the resonance a bowed harmonic emerges. It's a fascinating and mysterious sound. These new techniques and sounds make me fall in love with my instrument all over again.

The vibraphone has really become a huge part of my voice in the last couple years. And the joy I feel playing this music continues to grow. Every time I get to perform Zorn's music, whether it's with the JACK Quartet, with pianist Steve Gosling, or in a group of *Cobra*, I am filled with an incredible rush of energy and have an outrageously fun time like no other performance. 4 years ago, I would not have been able to believe for even a second if someone had told me in a Juilliard practice room that I would be playing this music with the people that I get to play with now. On top of being experts in their own fields, everyone is so open, inquisitive and accepting. It fills me with inspiration and gratitude. I'm completely mesmerized and astonished on a daily basis by this incredible avant garde community that I got to discover through John Zorn.

CHAPTER
18

DEEP RIVER...BUT HOW DEEP?

A Pianist Greets His Piano

DAVID HOLZMAN

The spiritual *Deep River* has become an intimate friend, almost a morning ablution when I first sit at piano. It happened for many reasons, profound and mundane.

Firstly, it is a rich memory from 60 years ago. Like many of us approaching 70, especially in these distressing times, we look to the perhaps imagined warmth and simplicity of childhood to give us strength and comfort. My memory was of Paul Robeson singing it on an old LP. I was young and had two healthy and receptive ears so his unforgettable voice never left me. I recall the little Krakauer upright on the other side of the living room from the phonograph where I would play this and countless other songs. My parents were devoted communists in the '40s and early '50s and my father had protected Robeson at the Peekskill riot of 1949.

Various losses gradually came my way. First, I lost the hearing in my left ear when a child. Pitch was still good, but resonance and spontaneity were diminished and without fully recognizing it, I became more introverted. 30 years later, I lost much of the hearing in my other ear and sounds became to a large degree in my imagination. My inner ear and digital sensitivity were enough for me to give convincing performances of modern masterpieces but hearing with pleasure and ease largely vanished. After this loss, I seldom listened to records and with the demise of my phonograph, LPs were forgotten.

The inevitable loss of family and friends began. My father, whom I never knew well, died 10 years ago, leaving me alone in a big house with my own memories. My struggles with epilepsy and hearing (both the ailments and the cures) were a permanent feature of my days, but things proceeded fairly smoothly much of the time—both musically and personally. My interests were few, and music consisted almost entirely of intense preparation for concerts and recordings, with the varying degrees of satisfaction all musicians face.

The return of *Deep River* started about 15 years ago but took off five years ago when hearing was slowly being restored to both ears-one with a cochlear implant and the other with a hearing aid with a music program. While still an ongoing struggle and balancing act, the experience of hearing close to fully for at least a few hours a day was a sensual revelation and part of my rebirth. I learned the joy of giving and receiving beauty—words, sounds, people—love. A more mundane but wonderfully touching addition to the above was when Joel Gordon, who has produced many of my CDs fixed my phonograph. Joel had heard me play *Deep River* as a prologue to recordings of Wolpe, Shapey, Sessions and others, and now I looked for, and found, my old LP—worn but playable.

With all these challenges of mind, body and spirit, plus the stress surrounding us, walking to the piano in the morning became almost a prayer of thanksgiving which began with my remembered, and I now realize, personal version of the song. It was a daily reminder of my returning hearing; it was an invocation of Robeson's nobility and strength; and it was a prayer of love for my father, which I had seldom expressed during his life. This revelation now came, happily, from my ears as much as from my hands, as had been the case for so long.

Getting from the breakfast table and the morning news was indeed an almost religious ritual. My first task was taking the devices out of my ears and putting them on the piano to change their programs. Hearing WNYC and hearing my Steinway grand was a different world. For a few years, I had to be careful that the blunt reality of my deafness, as evidenced by the sight of these impersonal objects, not overwhelm me. I learned to ignore much as I resisted nervousness when walking on stage to perform. I put a sardonic smirk over my mouth, narrowed my eyes, rather like Humphrey Bogart, and them simply moved.

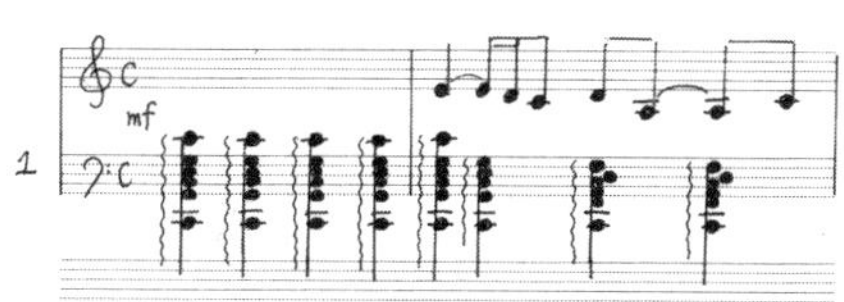

Figure 1.

I would then sit and, with a mere breath, would play the four opening chords (Fig. 1) They somehow must be in C, even though he sings it in

A♭. It is the same purity of white keys which John McDonald gave me in *Berceuse to Play With Devices.* He ends the piece with a poignant metaphor of the mud of chromatic black keys resolving to the solace of treble G's which he knew would last forever with two devices in my ears.

After the first of the chords, I already feel the magically rich sound of my piano and I let the chord wash over me. Playing all four chords, slightly broken and landing on top C only increases the thrill and the endless root position chords which follow makes for an even richer purity. The chords must be played mezzo-forte, which is more an expression of love than a precise dynamic. I use lower arm and some wrist. Fingers seem an afterthought of the gesture, though they are more present than I realize.

But now, I am Robeson, as the melody enters. How do I let it soar over chords, just a 3rd above, without a hint of percussiveness, ie. forte? I now realize that, over time, I have unknowingly created a richer mf with a bit more pressure from my arm. I allow it to swell over chords by lightening the touch of chords minutely with a bit of finger which is more shallow. Both my back and my mind tilt slightly to treble and any melody note requires a minute degree more weight than a chordal touch. It is a rich sound of three variants of mezzo forte which I both feel and hear. Perhaps nothing taught me this independence better than Schoenberg's *op. 23.*

Then the phrase repeats (Fig. 2) I do largely what I heard Robeson and piano do. The quarter note chords become sixteenth note accompaniment with hints of counterpoint and chromaticism. Somehow, this is always a liberating moment and my emotions expand.

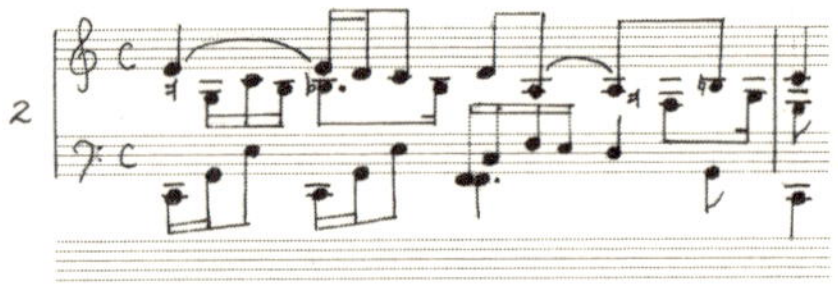

Figure 2.

The tempo is often a touch faster, and somehow my mf takes a further step up, while still not forte (my devices give a stern sense of forte). The chromaticism of V7 of IV is fully comfortable and I often bring out the counterpoint of G C B natural B♭ (Fig. 2) in the alto as stronger than melody itself. The *deja-vu* joy of dividing the melody between hands (one feels like one has a ten-fingered hand) occurs as the added soprano makes left hand part of right hand.

My only moral/aesthetic problem is the minor IV where A natural turns to A♭. It seems a bit vulgar in the purity of my morning ablution. Often, I simply ignore it but, lately I will let the A-A♭-G take place—just with a gentle finger touch of mp or less to appease my guilt.

When the middle section starting on A minor comes, I can seldom resist my ears and heart! (Fig. 3) I will rise to forte, maybe fortissimo and often play in octaves and be damned if it is a bit banged out. The return to the recap can go any number of ways but all involve fixating on the rich chromaticism of the transitory chords (Fig. 4)—always holding back and preparing a gentle return. I am often free enough to add counterpoint to the line as the final cadence approaches. Now the minor IV A♭ is fully convincing and I happily allow a rich, at times overbearing alto line with dotted rhythm A A♭ G.

Figure 3.

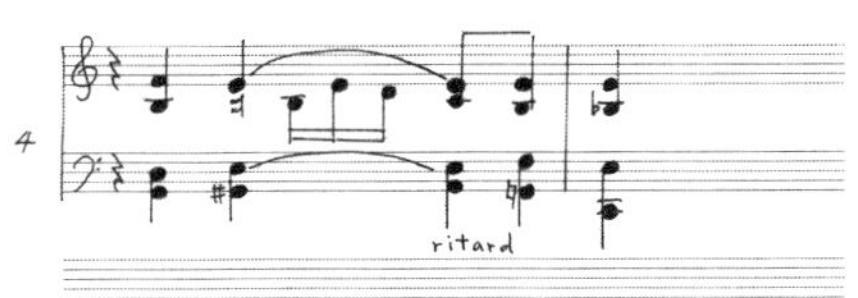

Figure 4.

Lately, I have been so swept up with the ear/finger wedding that I almost "take my clothes off" and play it all again with no break, now with melody two octaves higher and an accompaniment filled with Liszt-like arpeggios. One of the greatest thrills of hearing is that sounds sustain and, over the last few months, upper registers shine—a memory of what my piano sounded like 50 years ago.

It is over, but I don't want it to end. I can repeat the final cadence again and again, much as I do not want to leave the person I love. But I eventually stop. Without realizing it, I often put my hands together almost in a yoga posture and close my eyes. Every morning is slightly different and I wonder: does my mood cause the difference in speed, touch and freedom? Or does the slightly different sound I experience with first chord create my mood and interpretation?

Recently, events both public and private depressed me horribly. I woke up and did not think I could even go near piano, let alone touch it. However, almost as a research experiment, I did so. I started slower and softer—that fit my mood. Second verse was already picking up depth. A minor is even more intense and freer than usual. Recap came as sober and I cannot add a coda giving a schmaltzy sensual ending. Playing was fine, but it did not relieve me of pain and I was still upset.

Just as in much of life, Who or What is directing Whom? Am I the outside maestro confidently creating a work of art? Am I a needy human crawling inside a warm blanket of diatonicism to hide? Or am I finding a new world? My most memorable performances were like aerobic exercises—at a certain point, I lost almost all awareness of pulse, keys, audience. I was joyously in another universe. But it is a complex soup of all three plus countless other viruses.

I soon open my eyes and wonder: What now after that 5-minute ablution? Lately it has been learning a Verdi aria for a dear friend. I give myself a little respite and take out my fragile 50-year-old score of Beethoven *Sonatas*. I am mastering *op. 110*. When a youngster, my new teacher told me to learn one of the *op. 31 Sonatas*. I didn't know what an opus number was so started learning *op. 110*—the *31st Sonata*. Naturally I couldn't handle it but now, with slow hands-separate work, it is ready. Mrs. Scheiber would have been happy. The remarkable diatonicism of the opening pages is purer than the morning spiritual and the chromaticisms almost unnoticeable in their subtlety. I am slowly reaching a pathway back to devotion.

Next is a real break for my ears as I take devices out and enjoy the sound of silence. I can look at smart phone for messages; I can write a bit; I will eat lunch and watch a bit of news. I still am not ready for complex new music which was my life. But my health, happiness and musicality are still within and when I receive two new hearing devices in June I dream of an explosion of fingers, ears, mind and heart. A full day's work to give back to those who have given to me...the rediscovery of discovery.

My thanks to Yen Wen Chen for the illustrations.

CHAPTER
19

"VENIT ILLUMINATIO"— A PROCESS NOTEBOOK

AARON JAY KERNIS

> It seems as though some innermost core of my being, some childish holy of holies, secreted a supersubtle reminiscence, which, under some stimulus that now and again became active during sleep, exhaled itself in this singular dream—shadowy and slight, but invariably accompanied by a sense of felicity so measureless and so penetrating that I would always wake in a mystical flutter of ecstasy, the bare remembrance of which was enough to bless and make happy many a succeeding hour.
>
> —George du Maurier – Peter Ibbetson, 1891

Introduction—Not Dreaming

I can't recall my dreams—as much as I've tried; notebook by the bed, writing anything I can recall upon waking, meditation, vitamin B6—nothing comes back to me. I can more easily recall dreams from my childhood than any in recent decades. I have a sense that maybe my compositions are my waking dreams—possibly taking the place of my night-dreams. Who can know? The pieces have the vividness of dreams—where the inexplicable discontinuities, fracturing's of logic, and the most fantastical imaginings live so brightly.

In my early adulthood I developed a process of using logical, intricately worked-out formal structures that I applied before and during the composing process. In recent years this gave way to a far more patient, intuitive excavation of ideas and sounds, growing out of listening into silence, through which I develop my way of flowing into the course of a piece. I find a way to begin, it teaches me, and I keep adding and shaping while I find my way. This process is neither vague nor unconscious, but feels to be one lead by some mysterious super-conscious force that I view with a mixture of bemusement, horror and wonder. But I don't simply follow it, I'm not just a passive onlooker, I actively engage and have an ongoing dialogue with the unknown and unexpected, often letting the compositional process lead me rather than the other way around. Then suddenly I find myself taking the lead.... and have been leading all along....

The du Maurier quote above speaks to some of the most precious feelings that can come through the creative process—those special moments where one finds the unique internal correlation—the "supersubtle reminiscence" which makes the difficultly of making music, through all its twists and roller-coasters of emotions and internal pain—most worthwhile.

Composing

I can break down aspects of the composing process into the objectively observable and the subjective, which I can only describe in vague terms.

Elements that can be objectively discussed are things like how a melody is made and shaped, how harmony is constructed, how phrases are shaped, their overall contour, peaks—hearing the orchestration, details such as scoring of chords, layers of counterpoint... even after decades of experience these need to become as familiar, as necessary, and as natural as breathing. And I must know fully the DNA of the work that I'm mucking about in, (but without over-intellectualizing, since the last thing I want to do is analyze my own work!)

Subjective elements are those that only I could discuss: how chords make me feel, what instrumental color choices elicit in me, what synesthetic experiences a given piece holds for me, if any, what underlying concepts influenced the work and how; if the structure, melodies or any elements were developed out of personal experiences or internal feelings of any sort, or why the form is laid out the way it is. These can be discussed but not proven, and are the issues that interest me the most, but are the most difficult to talk about and convey meaningfully to others. They are intrinsically personal and not subject to any external artistic laws. It has to be taken on faith that these are essential parts of the composing process. I will attempt here to bring up many of these aspects, but truly, music resists being spoken about in words (except in the concrete, analytical elements mentioned above, which I resist going into...).

Process

Starting a piece can happen in any number of ways—hearing musical ideas and retaining them, singing them, writing them down on paper, jotting down ideas in images, signifying words, mathematical (proportional) concepts, taking walks and imagining sounds, textures, shapes, singing in the shower, having synesthetic epiphanies in peak experiences: over a plate of pasta, squash blossoms or other culinary dishes, or during sex… Over decades I've used all of these possible ways of working at one time or another.

After that initial gathering of ideas, some sort of structuring is usually put into action—often as simply as drawing a partial map of a piece, or some kind of schematic picture that helps to put musical concepts into perspective.

Then the hard, concentrated work begins…

Moving from the general to the specific takes the most time, hard work and is often agonizing. Walking, humming, becoming distant and self-obsessed—drawn inward, shutting out outside sounds and avoiding eye contact is typically the external mode. How do composers manage that to keep that disconnect from the real world while being thrust into what's most necessary in everyday life—parenting, domestic life, teaching, performing and all else….?

Most important in the process is remaining open to all possibilities, unexpected directions and tangents, while completely internalizing the simple and complex DNA of the piece and its meanings, materials, fragments, nuances and drama. Living the work completely is so important: a minute of music can take weeks, and holding on to the excitement and emotional need for it to be right, even as real time elongates and collapses into internal time, is arduous but critical.

Along with that, balancing the momentary and large-scale, the phrase that's of concern right now with the internal logic of larger phrases and sonic/timbral connectivity in instrumentation at all levels. Also keeping hold of the thread which will hold the listener tightly in the music's thrall.

{Now I include excerpts from the summer notebook I kept during the writing of *Venit Illuminatio—Toward the Illumination of Colored Light*, in 2019, for orchestra.}

Process Journal

…. First line… violin, high, with mist…. Multi-timbral mist with bowed percussion….

First schema—what is color? How can color move from instrumental group to group?

How do I translate the range of feelings I have onto music paper and into chords, lines, and color?

May 21

Right now I feel like I'm lacking inner vision and inner sight. I feel direction and certainty, but the sense of imagining color and sensations in orchestral color is pretty much deadened.

Even the subtlety of feeling the close movement and the physicality of harmonic shifts inside of the chords with voice leading is not experienced as distinctly as before—not sure why. Am I moving away from this chordal approach as I think toward vocal pieces becoming primary again? Am I not sleeping enough? I'm hardly dreaming at all.

May 24

At an orchestra concert, thinking about what internal feelings, colors, images happen when I'm writing, conceiving, walking. That's what interests me here—the internal mechanisms and subtle shifts of feelings that occur. Can I retrieve those feelings?—I've often felt blank and without sensation. It's been more like a miner excavating a tunnel in the pitch-black who's only able to see a tiny portion of the very narrow sides in front of him, and only straight ahead with the confusion of blinding light.

I know where the harmony and weight is going—I've sensed that for a few months, but only in the last few weeks has it helped the notes be created and allowed me to move forward—so I keep looking back and refining. Unusually most of the piece is in short score (a kind of shorthand score with many fewer musical lines than a full orchestral score)—with a bit of orchestral shorthand notated as I go, and most of it is sketched and developed in my head. Formally it is all very clear. The harmonic material is full of certainty—even if the melodic shapes are more amorphous than in other recent pieces. It's more important to stress the harmonies and formal weights that are built up. I've been so surprised to be looking/listening so much to Bruckner for the first time, really. How his spaciousness, open textures and breadth are giving me permission to streamline my orchestration and density in many ways. I feel like this is a very good development, especially as I head (hopefully) to opera. I want to have more patience with openness and space rather than feeling the need to fill in the spaces and silences all the time.

I'm not looking to explore generalized emotions but to see if I can hone in and maybe even name very specific sensations that appear as I work.

May 25

Getting to the end of this passage I begin to see rainbow colors—toward C major!!!

May 26

Toward Illumination
Ad Illuminare
Toward multi-colored reality

May 28

Even with the thickness of my chords (usually 5–8 notes at least), I'm beginning to feel their multi-dimensional character. I wasn't sure if I'd be ending in C or elsewhere—now it feels right. C is (of course) the root color of all, and I sense E major as green (as M Torke does) but rather than any one color being prominent there's lots of shifting color sprinkles and a kind of crackling sensation around the last (final) two sections of the piece. Before that, the chords change so frequently that there is little sense of rootedness, but a general sense of chord types and melodic shapes which repeat but are also rootless—not directionless on the surface but which are always shifting harmonies. There is a sensual if not sexual aspect to the internal sensation of voice-leading, or maybe it's more like tasting the strands of an amazing salad or complex entree. The chromaticism in the lines and chords can contain so much rubbing and friction. I can feel that in my stomach. Now that I'm ¾ths done with the sketch I'll keep on massaging what I have until all the choices feel right, then go on to the orchestration, which will be in much bigger strokes than usual.

June 2

Color and feeling is starting to emerge in the voice leading, making itself felt within moments that connect to larger sections, pivot to new pinnacles, and lead to the most significant arrival points. The internalization of nuance comes back out again as a fine gradation of expression, and what I do can have flickers of color and live inside the primary ideas.

Toward a Definition of Color Sensation

June 6

The issue of sensitivity to weight and instrumental color is paramount now. Most of the writing is done—scoring and winnowing are major concerns now. And two sections, layered string harmonics with bowed crotales and vibraphone, needs a lot of careful detail to find feathered, highly textured effect. There's nothing simple in this piece about moving from dark to light—even though that was the first idea behind the piece. The harmonic density is high a great deal of the time but there are clarifying moves toward greater tonality later on, its goals are toward bigger masses of orchestral sound with less counterpoint.

[Most of this "diary" was written after emerging from a dark period, where I'd sketched another piece that I wound up abandoning—I'd felt oppressed by it, but was trying to prove something through its intensity—it had some good ideas (and certainly the intention to base a piece on Hilma af Klint paintings was a good one) but it was too hard to play, would've been too hard to rehearse and too painfully frustrating to write.. then, after transitioning to this new, color-related idea, writing was no better for nearly a month. I was concerned I wouldn't finish in time, but suddenly all that accelerated and I was able to move forward without all the intellectual baggage weighing me down. What I had to do became clear, and I could just <u>write</u>—at last.]

It is shocking to write in simple rhythmic values—¾ especially—mostly quarters, halves, 8th notes—they feel too simple, but allow lots of room for directness of expression and direction from the conductor, I had to feel comfortable with their simplicity. Now I need to orchestrate heavily, look for any dead spots and go through it super-finely.

June 8

Getting to the very end, with the C/F♯ major oscillation, and the orchestration is nearly done. I instinctively knew the kind of resolution I was looking for at the end, but still was pleasantly surprised when I arrived there in the writing. After all that chromatic, wandering music it feels so good to get to this place. Last 8–10 bars, I see white light in the diatonic 8-4-5 note chords—the sense of home in C/F♯—the presence of all keys—the pull of the sharp 4th to 5 or the flat 2 back to C. And the sensory rush of reaching the point where the entire orchestra is phrasing together—a kind of ecstatic arrival—like the end of Color Wheel (an orchestra piece of mine from 1999)—holding back the final harmonic arrival to the very end. Maybe it's not only white light—it has metal of the perc/chimes/crotales/glock, and the coloration of silver and gold. Not sure if the #4 to 5 is red-to-red hot or another version of white. These colors are in my head more than in front of my eyes.

Interesting that I don't want to be around crowds of people right now—want to be alone....

Can I feel colors? They're in my brain with bands and flecks/sensations of multi-dimensionality.

June 11

Looking for ecstasy/earthly transcendence/weight and color. Finding sounds and harmonies that take one out of the earthly dimension and concerns, into mind and spirit, and always into sensation toward the fingertips. Very happy with the Latin title which is so wonderfully compact and complements the slightly ornate English.

There are levels, peaks, long transitions, that lead the orchestra through the last 5 minutes. I have to look carefully and make sure I'm not giving away all the intensity too early—the areas are like locks? Plateaus? Terraces? They lighten in intensity but build in ecstasy.

June 14

The shape is building as the orchestration is focusing. I can feel the chordal and orchestral weights—the balances—the colors as it moves from area to area—the sections transform.

June 17

Building a tutti—single color lines—rainbow chords, 4th with bluesy hues.

June 25

Much time has passed—so much teaching this month, now over—three seminars on my own—at least sixteen lessons—enough! And I am really in the home stretch... Two more sections left to complete—mostly orchestrating timbre, then fine listening for balances and layers and percussion—adjusting their dynamics and timbre details.

I'm ready to go on to a different paradigm—I can keep the clustery harmonies, but they probably won't work or be needed in vocal music.

Nearly done..... just about time to secure reservations for that celebratory meal.... Where will it be this time???

{Following the completion of the full score of the piece in late July, the parts for each instrument had to be created, and the final proofreading process was long and arduous, with a lot of careful detail and rethinking of small details. The work was fully complete in early August.}

Venit Illuminatio (Toward the Illumination of Colored Light).

Program Note

Written for the St. Louis Symphony Orchestra, Stéphane Denève, music director.

Though this piece no longer holds its original title, *Red Alchemy*, many of the ideas that got it started are the same for this new work, *Venit Illuminatio*. Alchemy is a seemingly magical process of transformation, creation, or combination of the two. I am always thinking about the transformation and exchange of emotions and musical ideas and the animation/creation of a wide range of orchestral textures colors deployed through a large group of brilliant musicians.

But what does this mean? Music for me is something magical. It goes beyond words, to places where the weight of chords and sounds, expressions of groups of notes and instrumental timbres take the place of language and punctuation. The syntax in this work has relationships to older music and to content which I have never expressed before. It is of a particularly personal nature to me relating to (among many things) sensory and sensual feelings that I have experienced inside my body while composing. Sometimes, if I'm very lucky, I will come upon a compositional moment where a chord or an instrumental idea will burst out inside my head as color, or even in heightened Technicolor! Hence its place in the subtitle of this piece, *Toward the Illumination of Colored Light*.

I don't want to weigh down the listeners experience with signposts and analytical reductions. This music flows in its own time, with its own shapes and hopefully, internal logic. It's not one thing, speed or idea, as it traverses many things that shift constantly over its 14-minute length. There are aspects in it (as in the last movement of Brahms' *4th Symphony*) of Passacaglia—melodic shapes and particular chords that are repeated over and over into different guises and characters, always in new contexts and with new meanings. One could take an x-ray of the entire work and see three large sections; beginning with a floating line that keeps returning, but mostly a highly changeable, always-in-flux first section; the second simpler and more steady in character, the 3rd more unified and dramatic, leading toward some ultimate resolution in the last moments. Much of the music is lyrical, mostly singing and slowish, with contrast coming from darting and passion-driven activity.

Some descriptive words from the score—searching, soaring, floating, with passion, intimate, spacious, heavy, aggressive, suspended, ecstatic.

This movement may be the missing *Adagio* for my *4th Symphony*, written in 2018, or it may be a stand-alone movement—or both.

If there's any overarching idea I hold onto while composing, it is to live actively through the compositional process, trying to leave the dark thoughts and conflicted emotions (which were so present in past years) behind and find a transformative experience of ecstasy and light. Not just white light of inspiration, but the colored light of change and imagination.

[Some musical influences on the work—Mahler's *Symphony No. 10 Adagio*; Scriabin's *Poem of Ecstasy*; Sibelius's *6th* and *7th Symphonies*, Messiaen's orchestral work.]

A few explanations of the Latin title:

> *Venit Illuminatio*—literally, "the brightness (of any kind, spiritual or otherwise) is coming."
>
> The word *venit* (from venire, to come) is Present Tense, implying we are not there yet, but heading toward a goal, stating most importantly that something indeed is coming, i.e. not to give up hope.
>
> The word *illuminatio*, a Late Latin noun meaning spiritual enlightenment, or brightness derives from the Classical Latin verb *illuminare*, to throw into light. *Illuminatio*, by its delayed position adds high expectation and answers the question, "what is coming?"...the light, the brightness, a cause for hope.

(Many thanks to Prof. Rosanne Gulino for her work to find just the right Latin words.)

CHAPTER 20

THOUGHTS ON COMPOSITIONAL STRATEGIES

INGRID LAUBROCK

Wayne Shorter, one of my biggest living musical heroes, once said that playing with his current quartet was "like being on a playground, a *serious* playground". He was putting into a few words what I have always felt when improvising with like-minded creative musicians. I go right back to being a 6 years old, running around with my best friend, making up crazy worlds and building all sorts of things. (This often involved knives, fire, electricity and molten lead—apparently there wasn't a lot of helicopter parenting back then). This sense of adventure is still important to me, especially when it comes to music.

I was an extremely reluctant composer at first. For years, I wouldn't even dream of putting a pen to paper to write a tune. I never saw myself as a band leader and was happy to tag along in other musicians' bands. I had almost too much respect for the art of composition and composers. That, coupled with perfectionism and a strong fear of commitment and failure was paralyzing me. I felt that if I committed notes to paper, I would show everyone my true taste and would be vulnerable to criticism. There is a finality to a composition that I couldn't face. The fleetingness of a saxophone solo at a performance that was over once it had been played was much more to the liking of the shy, introverted and under-confident person I was back then. At that point I also hadn't figured out yet that composition, like everything else, takes practice—and a lot of it! I thought it would just have to pour out of myself and be perfect. But enough of armchair psychology. The fact is that I had to jump over my own shadow, like I have done many times before and probably and hopefully will do many more times. I realized over the years that fear of criticism gets completely in the way of finding artistic truth.

It doesn't mean that fear ever gets eradicated, but while writing and playing it should *all* be about the writing and playing and not about how the result might be perceived, especially as that is something we ultimately have no real control over anyway. Focussing on the *process* as well as the love for learning, researching and experimenting has been an important tool for me to focus inwards and find myself more.

I now love composing and it has become as important to me as playing the saxophone. Composing is *own time*, time to go inwards, time to be on your inner playground as opposed to a playground with other musicians.

Growing up in nature, I have always paid close attention to its sounds. Like many musicians and composers, I am attracted to the "irregular regularity", the way sonic events repeat but are never quite the same and form unpredictable collages. Superficially these can sound repetitive but they never truly are. Sound in nature is not static but a big kaleidoscopic organism. Take rain on a roof for example. There is much variety in the sound of raindrops depending on their size and speed and the variety among them creates that amazing phasing sound. The almost impermeable shimmering wall of noise of thousands of frogs singing in Costa Rica is right up there with the best music for me. Once I moved to the city, I realized it's is no different there. Cars, horns, drills, footsteps creating a combination of rhythm and overtones everywhere.

I find the same sense of this irregularity in improvised music. In an improvised context we don't know what the other musicians are going to contribute. That, coupled with the fact that we often don't play in a tempo or are disguising the pulse we are feeling, can invoke a similar sense of phasing and collage.

As a lot of my composed music includes freely improvised sections. The fun part for me is finding strategies to frame these improvisations with composition in ways that are meaningful to me while leaving the musicians room for self-expression.

I like to blur the edges between both but have also found that sharp tears in the fabric and sudden shifts can be what I want. This can be useful to counteract the "nature" approach and to yank the listener out of being too comfortable. My music often has a collage aspect: I frequently have two or more unrelated events happening at the same time that do not react to each other but co-exist in their own spheres. Space, micro-tensions (rhythmically or tonally), dynamic contrast, range and gradient changes over time are also important colors on my palette as a composer.

Here are three examples of how I used some of these aspects as well as others in my compositions.

All examples are notated in concert unless specified.

1. The Same, but not the Same and Collage

Vogelfrei (from *Contemporary Chaos Practices,* 2018)

I like reusing material several times in a composition but disguised or altered to the point where it becomes harder to recognize. I am hoping a part of the listener's brain ties it all together, even if subconsciously.

At rehearsal letter C of my orchestral composition *Vogelfrei*, the Piano plays a melodic statement.

(Fig. 1). It is played dreamlike and in a fragile way.

Figure 1.

This motive is elaborated on and extended a little later at rehearsal letter D (Fig. 2). It still has the earlier fragility at first, but quickly grows fiercer before ending literally with a bang. The melody gradually seems to speed up through gradual use of faster and faster subdivisions. I wanted to impart a sense of irregularity by using a mix of subdivisions and odd tuplets in combination with even ones.

Figure 2.

At the end of the piece, the original melodic motive becomes the material for an extended line, played by double basses, violoncellos, bass clarinet and electric guitar (Fig. 3). I am keeping some of the intervallic structures intact and augment and diminish intervals in other places. I change tuplets and rhythm in general and add material as well. This is done to extend the line (Fig. 4) without ever completely repeating anything verbatim. I tend to avoid easily recognizable vamps in my music to create a sense of forward motion.

Figure 3.

Figure 4.

At this point in the music there is nothing dreamlike about this melody anymore. It serves as an underpinning to a completely rhythmically opposed piano cluster/snare drum part that does the opposite of the piano line at D—it gradually slows down in time, using longer and longer note durations. On top of this, woodwinds and brass color this section with fast flurries and harmonized melodies. All of the material at this point is connected to material that was previously used but altered and superimposed in a collage.

2. *Contrast and Texture*

Chip in Brain (from *Serpentines*, 2016)

Chip In Brain uses a very simple "high-low" contrast. Tuba, drums and electronics create a drone reminiscent of doom metal drones. The piccolo trumpet part is freely improvised (by Peter Evans on the recording). Koto, piano and Glockenspiel have seven miniature pieces to choose from, that interrupt the improvisation. All the entries and exits are cued by a musician other than the soloist.

The soloist has the choice to react to or ignore these interruptions and not all of them have to be played.

These miniatures are inter-weaving looped pieces of varying lengths with one set of pitches shared between the voices per loop. Except for Number 4 and 7, only (major and minor) 7ths, 9ths and their inversions, seconds, are used. I wanted to undermine the cute and childlike sound combination of koto, piano and Glockenspiel with tense and dissonant intervals as well as clashing rhythms to make them sound more unnerving and unsettling—a bit like the echo of a nightmare.

The loops sound almost random but are actually rhythmically tightly composed. They gradually become rhythmically more complex and I use mixed subdivisions in the three parts to create a phasing and shimmering texture. Piece #7 is meant to be the release. It has a pretty melody and makes use of 3rds and 6ths and is supposed to give a sense of closure.

Here are loops #1, 4, 5, 6 and 7.

Figure 5.

Figure 6.

Figure 7.

Figure 8.

Figure 9.

3. *Phasing, "Revealing Over Time" and Open Instrumentation*

Pothole Analytics pt. II (from *Serpentines*, 2016)

Pothole Analytics is an open instrumentation piece that has been performed by groups ranging from three to ten musicians, but can potentially be played by any number of players bigger than three.

It involves no improvisation. The idea behind it is the gradual revealing of a skeleton of trills (Fig. 11) from a dense but controlled wall of sound (Fig. 10), similar to a sculptor carving out detail from a rough block of granite.

Exact pitches aren't as important as the general shape and intent and individual parts can be read at pitch or in their transpositions. While it is not required to be metronomic, the parts need to be played with rhythmic propulsion and a strong sense of inner pulse to achieve the desired phasing effect and to keep a sense of overall intent. In this piece, even when parts are doubled there is never any real unison due to the independent tempos.

When composing this *Pothole Analytics* I often stepped back to look at the score visually. I wanted to make sure I could *see* the sparsing of events, visualize where rhythmic tension was missing and that the tremolos were evenly distributed. Especially the tremolos in the relative silence of section C are most striking when they are coming from different directions in the room.

All the melodic material is derived from a 12-tone row. I use intervallic expansion, contraction, retrograde and inversions to have general cohesion within the material. The sections are open length and repeated many times. On cue, musicians jump to the next section wherever they are within their individual parts at that point.

Figure 10.

Figure 11.

In *Pothole Analytics Pt I* we play the pitches of *Part II* in any octave and in extremely slow individual tempos, usually ranging from 30–50 bpm. The rhythmic writing is suspended and we just let the notes float within huge swathes of space. Each note is played with a completely different attitude, dynamic, articulation and color so that it sounds like more instruments are present and every event becomes its own universe. Although many of these compositional tools are used in 20th Century Classical Music, I usually don't follow any rules and go into some sort of freehand mode at some point in the process. The above mentioned techniques just help me to generate and extend material which I use to avoid stasis. Repetition says "composition" very clearly and when I want to smudge the edges between improvisation and composition I like to avoid it. Ultimately, I like following my inner ear. I also somewhat "dance" the rhythms to make sure they are personal and felt. Imagination remains the ultimate guide in my music and the "serious playground" the place to be.

CHAPTER 21

A MEANS OF PRODUCTION

Showing Up for the Recording Session and Delivering the Magic Take

BRANDON LOPEZ

All thanks to John Zorn and the community of individuals who continue to push me to question everything.

I am a musician and not a writer.

I often find myself confronted with a mundane, distressing internal dialogue while in the throws of improvising. It's often fed by a seemingly dire need to produce an experience for those involved; those involved being the players, the listeners, and myself. It's often the fact that indulging these thoughts and feelings leads to the detriment of the music, while ignoring them does much the same. It seems important in my process to let myself make decisions and interjections, while remaining actively skeptical and discerning of the material produced.

There has to be the acceptance of human error while creating and the issue of making such a thing integral to a piece.

For me, it's important to remember that the mind will make sense of whatever it chooses to let in. I've often fell into an obsession with so called "rational" musical forms (standards imposed by classical and jazz pedagogy), when it's evident to me that there aren't any inherent laws that govern beauty or what make a musical form viable.

* * *

It seems evident to me that if you consider yourself an artistic radical, should be built into the fabric of your work, as your process and the way in which you live your life will decide the outcome of what you produce.

Yet, in today's day and age, it seems difficult for many artists to resist the allure of commodifying radical politics in their work. Branding your work as social justice themed, creating wordless suites supposedly aroused by violent acts against a marginalized people, the dedication of a set of improvised music to the "children at the border"; If your audience is of a privileged class in the so called "developed" countries, Aren't these kinds of platitudes little more than a comfort for the very people who should be disturbed to action?

As artists who benefit greatly from a country with unbridled military and financial hegemony, and who have access to a wealth of information about how every facet of the capitalist market is based on the violent subjugation and suffering of the poor. How can one protest the violence of an inherently classist and racist political ideology, by creating work that actively participates in the very nature that drives it?

* * *

I struggled with the limits of my own intelligence. Growing up as a working-class-striving-to-be-middle-class, attending a private conservatory with a highly educated, largely wealthy student body, often lead me to question my own abilities and education.

I came across Samuel Beckett's *Gnome* sometime after I exited.

"Spend the years of learning squandering
Courage for the years of wandering
Through a world politely turning
From the loutishness of learning"

It brings me to ease that human intelligence is vastly limited. That limit is also horrifying.

Postscript: Seems to me that wealth/power codifies information through the higher education system and gives the keys to its wealthy offspring. The "elite" schools seem to farm the capable and docile/complicit members of the lower classes in order to continue to codify information. What a joke.

* * *

On Perception

An anecdote from a friend on chance meeting Misha Mengelberg:

It was at the Stone. It was cold night. I'd never met him. I was walking to the front row to sit next to my wife. The place was packed and he was behind me. I said, "oh you found a coffee." He said something like, "it's not bad." I sat down and he continued talking to me. He said, "when I was at conservatory, the cafeteria had coffee that was so bad that the only way I could drink it was to imagine that it was not coffee at all, but a coffee-like drink."

* * *

I was at a premiere of some works in Chicago.

There was an unfortunate start to some casual conversation with an older composer.

He said, "Is it not wonderful how music can aid in one's perception of time?"

I said, "Look at a clock."

* * *

Lachenmann on Nono's Exclusion:

This mutual process of estrangement had less to do with Nono's declared communist beliefs—which were still regarded as a minor offense forgivable in a "naive artist" who would then be expected to conjure up in concert halls and theaters pleasant idylls from the romantic, folkloric, picture-book world of anti-fascist resistance. It was only when Nono insisted on identifying potential sources of fascism in capitalist post-war society—not least in the dominant political culture of West Germany—that these activities started to cause offense.

CHAPTER
22

A MENTOR

BRIAN MARSELLA

The smell of his single room shack was the first thing that struck me. A mix of wood, books, and dog, the smell was quintessentially colonial. Located along the Delaware River in Bucks County, Pennsylvania, this particular shack stood outside of time. Inside, the walls were lined with books, sheet music, and opera libretti. Against one wall was a sofa (that looked only moderately clean) on which the dog, Cesar, occupied. A small area in one corner housed a sink, mini-fridge and a single gas burner. There were two chairs in the room—one by the front door (in which my mother sat on) and another stately looking chair a few feet from the Steinway B. The piano, a late 1800s rosewood Steinway caught my eye; it was the most beautiful instrument I had ever seen and I was eager to hear if it sounded as good as it looked. But in my first moments of being in this new environment which was to become the cocoon for my artistic spirit, one thought pervaded my consciousness. Where did he go to the bathroom? For a bathroom was noticeably not present. The thoughts of 9-year-old me.

My first meeting with David occurred a year before in a different location. It was at a barn not far from the shack. My teacher at that time was a student of David's. She was my first piano teacher whom I started studying with when I was five. By the time I was studying with her, I could already play simple tunes by ear and was both improvising and composing short melodies. My music journey began quite early on; in fact, my first memories are of sitting at the Kimball organ in my family's dark-paneled family room. I would try to imitate what I had just heard my father play. (He was an amateur multi-instrumentalist that played clarinet, flute, all the saxes, organ and vibraphone.) It was the vibraphone that really caught my attention—there was something both athletic (the sight of four mallets flying through the air!) and almost wizardly-like about seeing him play the vibes. But being too short to play the vibes I must have coaxed my parents into sitting me on the organ bench. (Which was also too tall for me to reach on my own. I was only two after all.) I had been studying with Georgia Fragale for 3 years when she brought me to David's barn where he hosted a monthly masterclass for his students. In that time, I learned to read music (I had fooled Georgia for close to six months into thinking I could read music because she would play the pieces I was to learn first and I picked them up immediately by ear), built up a small repertoire of pieces, and studied much music theory. I had fallen in love with Scott Joplin's rags when I was about 6 and remember the milestone when my hands grew large enough to reach an octave so I could tackle those pieces which fascinated me. I'd also like to think that the stretching exercises Georgia gave me helped!

Georgia brought me to that masterclass because after 3 years of teaching me she said, "There's nothing more I can teach you. I'm going to take you to meet my teacher... he only teaches professional musicians but he agreed to meet you." At that barn was the same Steinway I would see a year later at David's shack. A semi-circle of about ten chairs were there for the performers/students. I was not surprised that I was by far the youngest there; of course I had not known any 8-year-old "professionals." I probably was unaware at the time that this would be an informal audition as I was to play alongside the "professionals." When it was my turn, I played an arrangement of *Hooked On Classics*—a medley of several well-known classical compositions set to a disco beat—my left hand supplying those iconic disco bass lines. (I laugh now remembering I used to play this.) I don't remember what the other students played unfortunately, but I do remember David's comments to me. Something about me having the best rhythm out of all the performers. Even though it was a compliment directed to me, I felt as if it was more an admonishment to the others. But more than any of David's words that day, it was the *tone* of his voice which stuck with me. I had never heard such power, such conviction, such articulation. The kind of voice that shakes you to your core with the deepest levels of truth and understanding. It was both awe-inspiring and frightening. But hell, he complimented *me*!

At some point after David first heard me play, he agreed to teach me. But before we were to begin, he gave Georgia a list of things I needed to accomplish first. Included were scales and arpeggios in all keys, a 2-part invention of J.S. Bach, and a Haydn piano sonata. I was to see him after these had been learned. It was a little less than a year later when my mother and I made that 30-minute drive to the shack on the Delaware river.

As I stood there with my "waste management" queries, David invited me to take a seat at the piano. After a brief exchange of pleasantries, I was asked to play. I was ready to perform a few things, including the Haydn *Sonata in C Major Hob. XVI:35*, and the *Maple Leaf Rag*. I chose to play the Haydn. After I was finished David asked, "So Brian, what do you want to be when you grow up?" "A pianist," I answered quickly and resolutely. "Do you know how hard that will be? How many sacrifices you will have to make and the work involved?" Without hesitation I said, "Yes. Can we start now?" My conviction won him over! "Yes," David said calmly with a warm smile. And with that he turned to my mother, who was reading in "her" chair by the front door, and stated, "We are going to go for a walk along the river."

As we made our way down to the river, I noticed what I identified as an outhouse. That put an end to the bathroom conundrum. (I was later to learn that David bought this property because he loved the river front land, not the dwelling itself. He was to build a house himself, along with his good friend and master builder (another David) in the following years. In fact, it was a very short time after my initial lesson when he had built a "proper" bathroom.) When we reached the Delaware, David asked me, "What do you see when you look at the river?" I was always eager to impress, to be inventive. But in this moment, and perhaps because of the banality (or so I thought at the time) of the question, I answered, "I see water flowing," and motioned to express the downstream movement. "Yes indeed." David then explained that the flow of the water is called current and that downstream refers to the direction toward the mouth and upstream as the direction toward the source. From there he started to discuss that current is created by gravity and to explain the role of gravity on current in relation to velocity. Furthermore, he talked about the current below the surface sometimes even moving in the opposite direction and that whirlpools can exist in which the water is moving in all directions. As we were walking north along the Delaware he continued the discussion of the river. After the lesson on current, he started to talk about the ecosystem of the river and all of the life that the Delaware contained. I was amazed not only with how much David knew about the river but by the fact that he was even this interested in it! Continuing on, he talked about light as waves and vibrations and how that affected the life in the river. There were so many topics that he touched on that related either directly or tangentially to rivers. I don't remember specifically but it's probable that there was also mention of rivers in literature and the metaphors contained therein. David also discussed the role of the Hudson River and the melting of ice that sometimes would cause flooding of the Delaware. (One disastrous flood occurred many years later that destroyed his rosewood Steinway.)

We walked along the river for 45 minutes and I remember at one point my head started spinning and I was developing quite a headache concentrating on trying to keep up with all that David was saying. As we made our way back to his shack I was thinking, "What is going on here? I came here to learn the piano. All I have learned about is this damned river!" When we were back inside and I was seated at the piano again, David gave me a piece of music to sightread. I thought, "Finally!" and sightread through the piece. After I was finished, David said to me, "You see everything on the page. All of the ink—the notes, the rests, the dynamics, the phrase marks, the accents... That is like looking at the top of the river. That part of your journey is over. Now we will look at everything that is behind that page."

The "everything" behind that page has been and continues to be my journey. A journey that has transformed my life and how I relate to all things. My music is a reflection of that relationship. I remember those words that David spoke to me so clearly. I remember how I felt in that moment—exhilarated, thunderstruck, full of optimism and joy. I had fully understood what he was saying. Man, did he get his point across to that 9-year-old! As the saying goes, "When the student is ready, the teacher shall appear." And I knew I had found my teacher. It was not until many years later that I would realize how rare a true mentor is and that many people never really find one. My feeling on the car-ride home that day was one I was to experience repeatedly after my lessons; I was high. My mind was racing with thoughts, with possibilities. Everything seemed possible. I couldn't stop making connections; it was beyond my control. And sleep that night was difficult.

I studied with David for 10 years. In that time, he never raised his rate; it remained a consistent 25 dollars (which was a lot of money for my parents at the time). And never did he charge "by the hour." A lesson was as long as the *lesson* took. Until there was some transformation in me—an epiphany, a concrete movement in my being, a tearing down of self, the lesson would continue—sometimes as long as 3 hours. David was never short of analogies or metaphors to make a point. And he wouldn't stop until he knew I understood. I remember one particular lesson where we were working on Mendelssohn's *Rondo Capriccioso*. There was a passage that I couldn't quite communicate the feeling of. After suggesting numerous visual images and many trials on David's part to bring the phrase out of me he stopped and exclaimed, "I know why you're not getting this! You've never made French pastry. You have to feel what's its like in your hand to roll pastry dough for croissants." And then we went to the kitchen (by this time, he had built his two-story house where the one room shack had stood) and made dough and he showed me how to roll it. "Now you know how it feels." And we went back to the piano and damn if that phrase didn't just roll out of me!

There were numerous lessons like that one. When I was learning the Bach *French Suites*, he taught me how to dance the baroque dances: a sarabande, an allemande, a courante. He described the ornateness of the snuff boxes of Beethoven and Mendelssohn and of the elegant gesture of unfolding a handkerchief over one's hand. He described European architecture with the detail and understanding of a master mason. He taught me the politics, the culture, and the cuisine of the periods of the composers I was studying. Many lessons I would never touch a piano; in others we would just sightread 4-hand piano works by Mozart and Debussy for an hour. I learned tai chi and the plays of Tennessee Williams which he was so fond of. David had me recite poetry and instilled a love of reading in me. The first book he told me to read was *The Little Prince*. Others he had me read included *The King and the Corpse*, *The Inner Game of Tennis*, *The Dancing Wu Li Masters* and numerous by Karl Jung whom he discussed often. I was introduced to the ideas of Gurdieff. He harped on me about understanding the Latin roots of words and what words really meant. I remember one lesson on "terrific" and the root coming from the Latin for terror. David would often pose koans to me. I rarely had a clue what he was asking! And after his cryptic questions he would never utter a sound until I had said something. And usually I was so confused I would just sit in silence. My mom would later tell me that sometimes there would be 10 minutes or more of silence, but David would never speak until I said *something*, *anything* first. One of my favorites, which he asked me often and that I now ask all of my students is, "How do you know that you know what it is that you say that you know." Or to put it another way, "How do you know what you don't know?"—one of the most important questions a student must ask himself.

There were times I cried in lessons. The level of truth he got me to see inside of myself was sometimes too much for me and I would burst into tears. But I knew it was always in my best interest, out of pure love. David told me recently (as we have remained dear friends) that before our first lesson he prayed. He said "Please don't make any mistakes with Brian. He deserves it that much."

There was an internal stillness to David I had not encountered before. It was almost like he wasn't there. He could quiet his thoughts and emotions to such a degree that he became a mirror that reflected me back to myself. And it was in those moments where sometimes the truth of what I saw about myself overwhelmed me. But David was also a master at managing my ego. When he knew my ego needed a boost, he would set me up with an underhand pitch that he knew I would knock out of the park. One such example was when I was thirteen and he put me in the role of music director, harpsichordist, and "conductor" (of a string quartet) of a production of Mozart's operetta, *Bastien and Bastienna*. (Which Mozart wrote at the same age.) David knew I would acquit myself admirably in that role which I did, and led to my first good press. I felt great giving radio interviews, being in the newspaper and on local television. And at that time it was just what I needed. David was equally attuned to when my ego needed to be deflated. When I was fifteen, David had me audition for the Curtis Institute in Philadelphia. It was the first audition I was to do and I thought I was the shit. Even with the great education I was receiving I had relied on the skills I already possessed and although I always heard what David was saying, my actions in terms of practicing (which David always referred to as "dirty work") didn't follow. I was very lazy when it came to doing the "dirty work." I loved improvising, composing and playing the music I adored, but my playing was sloppy. *Really sloppy*. I was underprepared for the audition (and of course David knew this.) I butchered the audition and in particular, Chopin's *Winter Wind* etude (in which I had a major memory lapse and had to start one phrase over three times). I was mortified, particularly after hearing some of the pianists before me and one after me. I wasn't even in the same universe as them, but somehow I felt I was still a better *musician*. The lesson after my audition David asked me how it went. After I told him he unleashed a fury towards me that I had never personally encountered. (I had seen him go off on other students—some of which would be reduced to rubble, leaving his studio in tears never to return—but never did he go off on me before.) Everything he said was entirely true of course and cut me to the core. He basically said that I would waste my talent if I didn't do the work and that in fact I *should* have played circles around the other pianists. He told me that the only difference between them and me is that they did the "dirty work." And it was then, at age 15, that I adopted a self-discipline to do the "dirty work" which I still carry today. In fact, I learned to love doing the dirty work—that the work itself is the end, the joy.

Throughout our studies, David often referred to himself as a psychologist. His observation skills were quite sharp; he could tell by my body posture if my parents had an argument before our lesson. He would say, "I don't teach music. I teach students how to teach themselves." David was a gifted problem solver; he was incredibly adept at getting to root causes (in large part due to his persistence and unwavering patience.) And not just in dealing with musicians. Other teachers would send their students—actors, dancers, playwrights—to David when they had a problem they couldn't solve. It might have been hereditary too. David's father (an engineer) had realized his true gift was in designing other peoples ideas or solving their problems so he started a business in Philadelphia as a professional "problem solver!" Without a question, David got to the root of many "weeds in my garden."

David was (according to him) the first Juilliard student to get a full-scholarship to the piano, organ, and opera departments. He would never tell you that, though. He prefers to live out of the limelight. To live and die with an empty footprint. He loves cigarettes and scotch. In my lessons, he would smoke compulsively—one cigarette after the next. In a long lesson, he would go through two packs! I used to think it was because he was so frustrated with me. And perhaps that is partly true. He still smokes, even after recovering from esophageal cancer. A young student can't always see the flaws in their teachers. I know I couldn't. But now, I see the Juilliard full-scholarship student turned hermetic teacher the way he sees himself. As an empty footprint. So he shall remain known only as "David".

CHAPTER 23

MUSIC AND...FOOTBALL?

CHRISTIAN McBRIDE

When talking about music, I often find myself mixing metaphors. I like to say that being a bass player is similar to being an offensive lineman in football. As a bass player, my primary job is to support. Play the rhythm and anchor the harmony. Spotlight is not something we get often, nor should seek, just like an offensive lineman. No bass player has ever gotten a gig because they're flashy. If they do get a gig because of that, I can't imagine that gig will last long. Flash gets old quickly. In football, the offensive lineman's job is to anchor the offense, protect the quarterback, make holes for the running backs, to make sure the flow of the play isn't disrupted. In music, bass solos happen way more often than offensive linemen carrying the ball or catching a pass, but you get the comparison. We're workhorses first.

Growing up in a family of music, it was almost predestined that I would have some type of career in music—broadcasting, performing, administrating, teaching, etc. My father is a bass player, my mother raised me on classic soul and R&B—Motown, Stax, etc., my uncle was in radio as a promotions and advertising manager, my great uncle is also a bass player and my grandfather was a lover of classical music. I was surrounded constantly by James Brown, Mongo Santamaria, Beethoven, Aretha Franklin, John Coltrane and Mahalia Jackson. Lucky for me, nobody in my family ever heard of the word "genre." It allowed me to fully embrace all of these different types of music as one big tree, with these different styles as branches. By the time I heard the word genre, I'd already been studying and practicing both the acoustic and electric bass. Learning Bach's *Brandenburg Concerto No. 2*, *A Love Supreme* and *Sex Machine* was all one in the same to me.

Around the same time I started to become serious about learning the bass, I fell in love almost as hard with sports. 1980 was an amazing time to be a Philadelphian. The Eagles, Phillies, 76ers and Flyers all made the finals that year. Like most kids, I played a lot of street sports—dodgeball, stickball, kickball, basketball and football. I was always physically bigger than most of my friends, so I was always picked to play basketball. Except I can't play basketball for shit! Never could. My sport was football. When we would play football, I felt like Jim Brown. Nobody could tackle me, and I was pretty quick for my size. Had good hands, too. I think I would have been a good tight end! When I first started really paying attention to the science of football, it was mesmerizing to me. What was an "I" Formation? A "Nickel" defense? A "Dime" defense? A long snapper? A pulling guard? A spy? How did all these things come together to make the game of football? Likewise, what did it mean to play "behind" or "in front of" the beat? What was a tritone substitution? What's a drop 2? What's a canon? What's a "sus" chord? What's a fugue? What's a tremolo?

In any endeavor, study is paramount. Sure, talent is important, but everyone is talented at something. Not everyone, however, studies and works hard at developing that talent. Strangely, I've found that often, underdeveloped talent goes a lot further in music than it does in football. Most underdeveloped football players I'm guessing have about a 3 or 4-year average career length, if they even make it into the pros. In music, if you learn to simply touch someone emotionally, it doesn't really matter if you're well trained or prepared. You just need to find what that place is in a person's soul that needs to be touched. Now by no means am I suggesting that young musicians should stop studying and just randomly figure out what notes or phrases will get you the most applause, I'm saying the opposite.

I fell in love with James Brown's music as a kid. After I got past the surface of it being "funky," I pulled my metaphorical goggles down and got inside of the music like a doctor about to do surgery. Why did James Brown's music sounds like it does? What makes it sound like that? Who are his musicians? That transferred to other music I liked. I analyzed Ron Carter with Tony Williams vs. Ron Carter with Jack DeJohnette. What made Charlie Parker admire Stravinsky so much? Why do McCoy Tyner's chords sound so big? Why did some country music I had heard sound like Ornette Coleman's music? Let me explore both.

I was studying their playbooks. I was preparing for the "game."

Once it became clear that I was going to be a professional musician, I strived for a gig. Who did I want to play with? Whose music touched me the most? It turned out to be the music of Art Blakey and the Jazz Messengers. In high school, many of our ensembles played *Moanin'*, *Blues*

March, and more modern tunes like Bobby Watson's *In Case You Missed It*, and James Williams's *The Soulful Mr. Timmons*. But pragmatism came into play. If I actually get an opportunity to ever sit in with Art Blakey one day, what songs will they play? Surely, they play more songs than those four, if at all. I became obsessed with learning the Art Blakey playbook. Preparation became the most important thing for me. Yes, I had to learn how to walk, I had to develop my sound and feel, I had to learn not just Art Blakey's repertoire, but standard repertoire. What if I don't get to play with Art Blakey, who will I play with? James Brown? Ok, I knew his playbook really, really well. I'd studied all the bootleg shows my uncle recorded for me, so I was ready to go. Unfortunately, he got sent to jail my senior year of high school. So much for that. What about McCoy Tyner? Freddie Hubbard? Bobby Hutcherson? Steve Coleman? Ornette Coleman? The reason why I struggled so badly my senior year of high school is because I immersed myself in nothing but music. I wanted to learn everybody's "playbook."

Bear with me on this probably-boring football story.

In 2008, the Washington Redskins signed free agent defensive tackle Albert Haynesworth. Haynesworth had been one of the most dominant defensive players in the NFL. When he got to the Redskins, he was a disaster. He complained about his role in the defense, saying he didn't like playing the 3-4 defense. (That means 3 defensive linemen and 4 linebackers as opposed to the 4-3 defense of 4 lineman and 3 linebackers which is more common in football) When the legendary old-school defensive end David "Deacon" Jones was asked about Haynesworth's complaints, he said, "It ain't about what he LIKES. He needs to be a professional. He knew it was going to be the 3-4 when he got there. If that was me, whether I liked the 3-4 or not, I would play my ass off, because that's what I was brought in to do." As I got to New York and started to hear musicians complaining about the bands they were in, I just couldn't imagine why they'd take the gig in the first place. If it's that much of a drag, then just friggin' quit the gig! If you need the gig, then shut up and play. Seemed simple to me.

I look at bands like teams. I take great pride in learning a band's playbook. Whatever I need to do to make a particular band work, I love the challenge of figuring that out. I want every bandleader I work with to know that I have their back. You need me to play in, I'm in. If you need me to play out, I'm out. If you need me in-between, I'm in-between. If I don't know what the hell I'm doing, I'll ask and figure it out. It's all about selflessness and empathy, which seems to be in short order in every endeavor these days. Everyone's too eager to be an individual instead of being a team player. You already ARE an individual. No need to drive that point home and jeopardize your gig.

There is one thing that trumps all study in all areas of life, I believe, and that's imagination. Think about all of our greatest innovators. Why are they innovators? They had imagination. But they had imagination AND empathy. I'm not sure imagination is a good thing in a vacuum. You have to meld your imagination with someone else's, which is why I love the man who asked me to write this, John Zorn. One of my greatest moments as a professional musician is when I played a gig with John, Steve Coleman and Tyshawn Sorey. As we played a completely open and free set, I remember John busting out a quick bebop line. I wanted to laugh so loud. Not because it was funny, but because it was John's way of saying, "See? I know all that shit, too." John is one of the most complete and imaginative musicians I've ever met. I love working with him and his body of work shows that he's a total and complete musician.

My advice to all of you, be a professional and LEARN THE DAMN PLAYBOOK, use your imagination to the fullest and most importantly, show empathy. It'll get you a long way. Believe me.

By the way, I DID get to play with James Brown after he got out of jail.

CHAPTER
24

WHERE I'M AT

BILL NACE

I've always been drawn to art that feels both immediate, with an almost accidental quality to it, yet is also very considered and crafted and feels like its own universe with its own rules, gravitational pull and idiosyncratic impulses. A sense of sculptural precision mixed with the feeling that THAT particular shape should not be able to stand, yet somehow it does. A combination of assertion and getting out of your own way, and ultimately out of the music's way. How do you gauge what is true or real to the moment, or to the other players or to the situation, yet still maintain a feeling of immediacy and "roughness." I guess there are a lot of approaches. I try to clear my mind and be present to the moment, and simultaneously listen to and ignore my feelings. Which isn't a unique approach, but is the one that has always made the most sense to me, and allowed for a clear site through to those spaces that feel very uniquely me and also alien and not me at all. A space where I can hopefully surprise myself and still feel like I'm developing an ongoing thread. This has led to some of my favorite musical experiences and to some that, in retrospect, were awful. Why does the bad show feel SO bad if it came from an honest place? Is it a feeling of failure? Doubt? Comparison to another show and the feeling that you know you could do better? Is it fear that the audience didn't like it—and if so… for the audience is a bad show just as "entertaining" as a good show. The process is still the same it's just that the results on that particular night are different.

In an interview with Bill Murray, he talks about an early experience with acting that saw him leave the theater in a despondent and suicidal mental/emotional space. He made his way towards a park with a lake thinking if he died he could just kind of… float. On the way he came across the MCA in Chicago and wandered in. Upon entering the gallery he saw Jules Breton's *The Song of the Lark*, which is a painting of a woman working in a field with the sun coming up behind her and he thought "I too am a person and get another chance everyday the sun comes up." This really resonated, because although I have certainly had shows that left me feeling ecstatic, I've had others that left me feeling so low that I professed to quit music altogether. But the more I play and the more it becomes just another aspect of my life the more that it is merely part of a narrative and part of an approach to how I live my life. Something always becoming and always containing a "sameness." If I pay attention to one (the high) then I have to pay attention to the other (the low). Music, like life, doesn't have to make any sense outside of the shape that I try to give it. So as I zoom out from some of these individual experiences it doesn't become so much about a failure or a win, but an approach to my life, and how I interact with other people/players. This has been a very liberating feeling and can also be a bit too freeing if there is no context. It's good to be your own compass in a way, but without any pushback or dialogue or sense of birthing something it could lead to a kind of basic "I don't care what anyone thinks"… an "I decide what is good" mentality. Which in a way… fair enough!

I certainly have aspects of this at the core of my thinking and approach. But we all thankfully have our limitations that make us fallibly and uniquely us… in life and in music. The goal for me is a kind of heterogeneous mix of collaborators/approaches that pushes and pulls and allows me to feel simultaneously elastic, yet grounded enough to root downward and really explore a space and sound as long as I think it is interesting—not in the space of one gig, but over the course of years (or however long a collaboration may last.) Improvised music takes so many forms, but due to its group nature, I think this is something it offers that I had always wanted growing up and that has been such a big part of my musical life. The goal is not to say what the music is in my mind. Improvisation seems to me to be, at its worst, so concerned with its own history sometimes, that it can run the danger of losing the very promise of its best—which is pointing to something that has yet to be heard or at the very least something that feels honest and true to that particular combination of people. Is it jazz? How is it jazz? How is it not jazz? Is it non-idiomatic? Is it noise? Are these even interesting questions anymore?? It seems that there are so many touchstones for kind of slipping out of the grip of genre… Captain Beefheart, Ornette Coleman, Outkast, Nina Simone, Bob Dylan, Twig Harper, Daniel Higgs… yet we still keep clinging to it or looking for answers there.

I think, for better or worse, tradition has become more complicated and perhaps more regional than how it was thought of before. We are always trying to catch up to ourselves and the world we've made, but in this I think we can allow for not necessarily an aesthetic, but an approach that allows ourselves the freedom to slip between the personal and historical in a way that feels real to ourselves, our collaborators and our community without paying too much attention to the new or the old, but to the personal, the idiosyncratic and whatever other ineffable aspects of music making we want to draw upon, regardless of how much sense they do or do not make.

CHAPTER
25

SHAPES

A Memoir

MILES OKAZAKI

I'd like to share some pictures that I've been collecting. They are variations of a certain preoccupation that started early in childhood, when I spent most of my time creating imaginary worlds on paper. I made thousands of intricately detailed drawings of epic battles, alien landscapes, undersea adventures, and especially mazes and maps. In May of 1980, Mount St. Helens erupted and covered the town where I lived in ash, so volcanoes became a big subject. Here's a maze shaped like a volcano, drawn sometime that year:

Figure 1.

There are some themes in this image that I'm still working on, the main ones being motion along pathways within limited space and fascination with forms from nature. I picked up the guitar around this time and I remember liking the surface of the fretboard, a grid that moves chromatic one way and pentatonic the other. Like the drawing paper, it was two dimensional and I could make designs on it, like these:

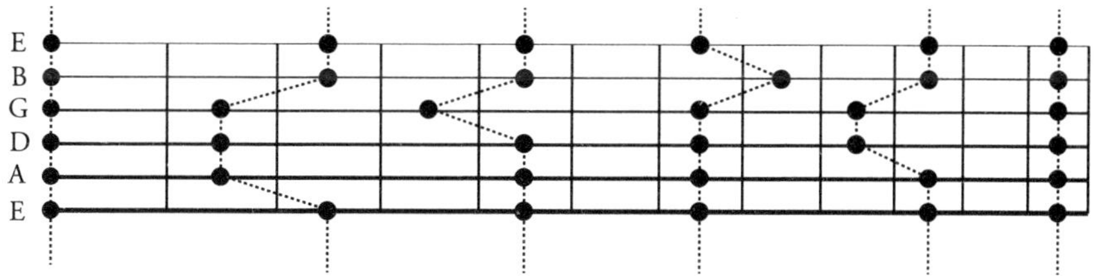

Figure 2.

As I explored the instrument, I came to believe that music was a kind of magic and that certain combinations of sounds could open the door to hidden worlds. Actually, I still feel the same way, probably more so. I learned how to play easy classical pieces and popular songs, but I wanted to know what the sounds were made of. I stumbled upon a few of the ghostly bell tones from the world of natural harmonics, and much later made a picture of their locations:

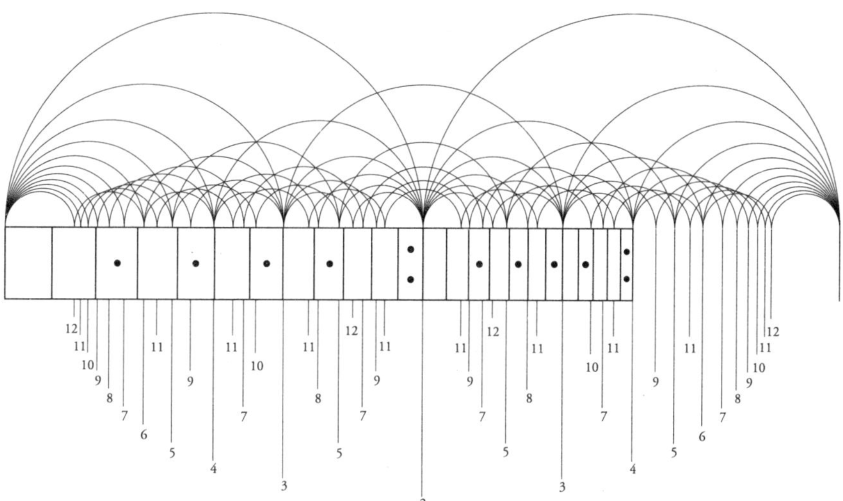

Figure 3.

The harmonics lived in a different dimension from the fretboard, with its arbitrary division into twelve parts. I didn't understand the exact geometric/logarithmic relationship at the time, but I had a feeling that there were two realms coexisting, the fretted notes going about their day on Earth while the harmonics floated above in the firmament.

I learned the symbols of the musical staff but the format didn't reveal meaning to me in terms of how things work under the hood. Around the age of 12, when I began studying improvisation, a teacher showed me the circle of 5ths. This was big deal, which got me from crawling to walking in terms of theory. The elegance of the diagram was a revelation. I began working out ideas on circles, endlessly fascinated by the way that information on the line curves into itself and connects to become a shape. The figures would uncover symmetries, like major and minor:

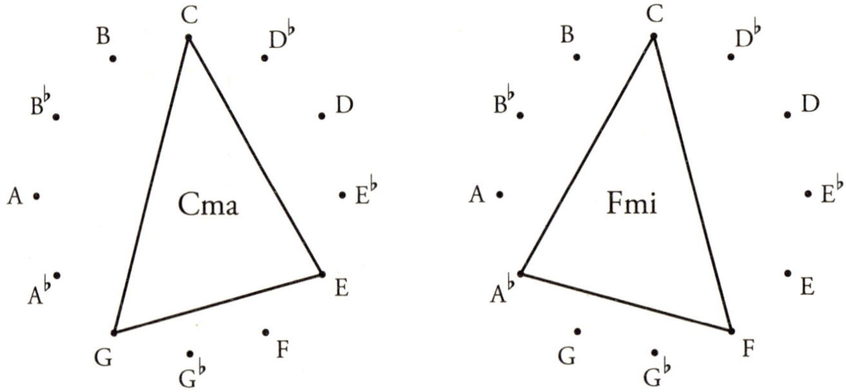

Figure 4.

And how the modes become a mutating shape as it passes through keys:

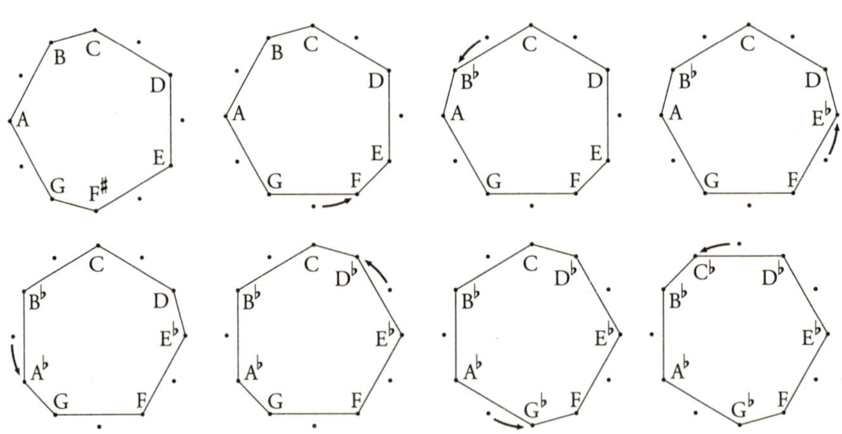

Figure 5.

Over time, visualizing musical concepts expanded into its own pursuit. I purchased a lot of theory books and finished reading a few of them, usually mining for ideas more than systematically digesting. I enjoyed the process of finding puzzles, translating them into pictures, and finding a musical application. For example, buried in Nicolas Slonimsky's *Thesaurus of Scales and Melodic Patterns* (p. 178) is the passing observation that a major, minor, diminished, and augmented triad can be combined to make twelve tones. I made a mandala of this to verify that this can only be done with one configuration, and put the triads into an order that sounded like a cadence:

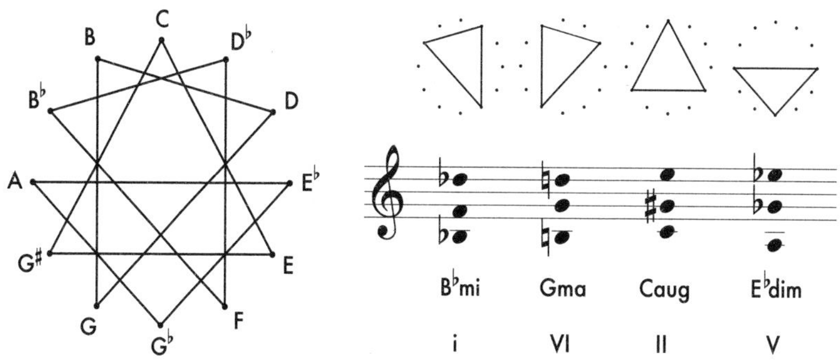

Figure 6.

This progression entered my musical language at an early stage, and has been an important sound for me. A kind of magic symbol.

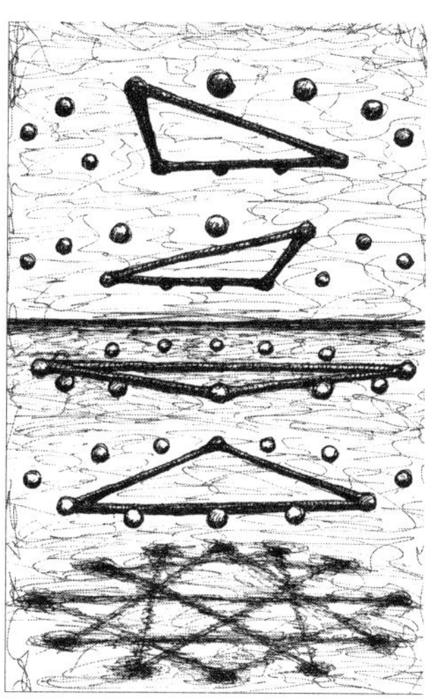

Figure 7.

I got ahold of Elliott Carter's *Harmony Book,* and became preoccupied with the idea of making some sort of personal reference dictionary. After all, every imaginary world needs an imaginary language. I had been working on four triads, but wanted to get to the rest of them. But how many are there? It depends on the criteria. Carter lists twelve (p. 44), but connecting dots inside of circles makes 19:

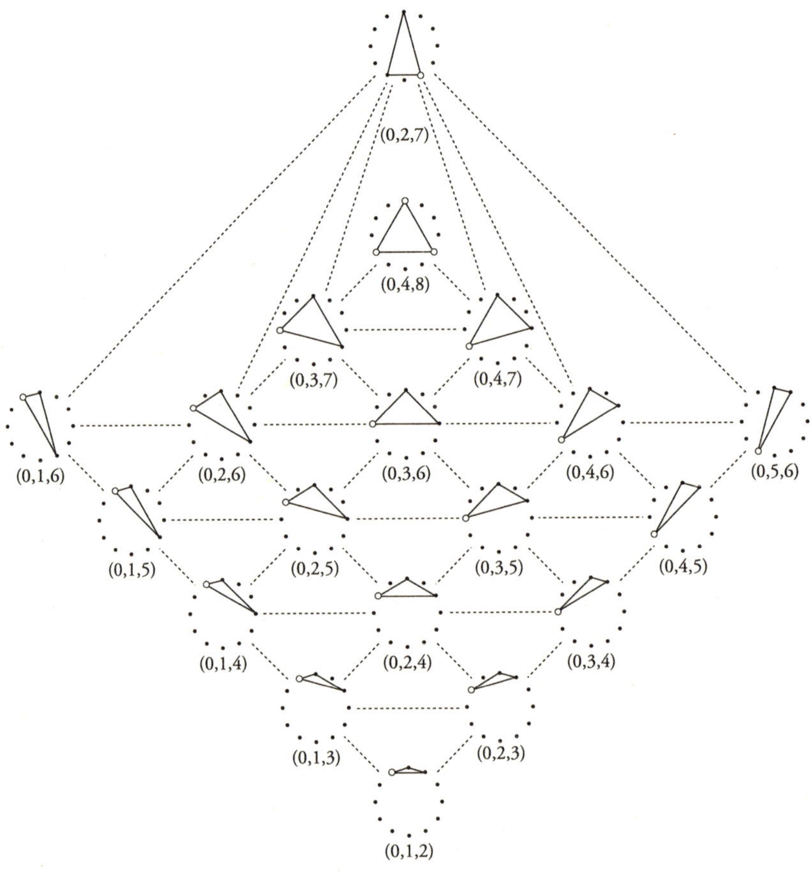

Figure 8.

This is a spine made of five symmetrical triads with reflected wings of seven offspring triads on each side. You can get twelve triads by cutting off one wing, which would represent inversional equivalence (e.g. where major = minor, intervallically). I let my ear make the choice and went with the two-wing version. The first question that came to my mind was, how might progressions work here? If you arrange the nineteen shapes connected by the closest possible voice leading (two common tones, one semitone movement in 3rd voice), you get some isomorphism of the map above.

Although there's no way to move along the dotted lines without repeating a triad (look up the "Königsberg problem"), I've found many useful pathways. Here's one tour around the map, which generates the harmony for a song of mine called *The Calendar*:

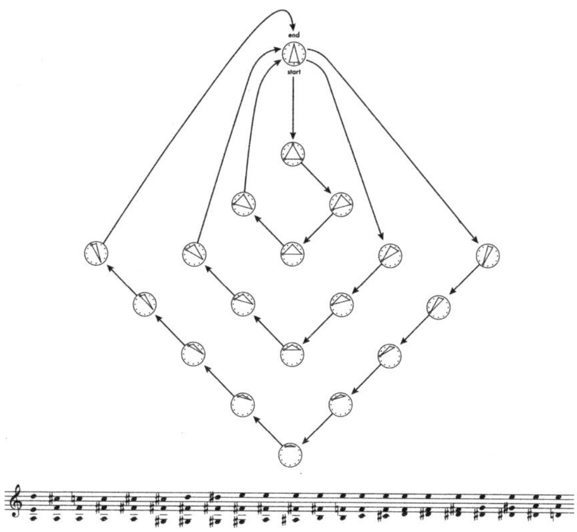

Figure 9.

Spending some time making these mandalas allowed me to meditate on each shape in terms of its sound and symbolism. For example, the triad at the apex (0, 2, 7) is used to shift between inner, middle, and outer rings. The singular position of this triad seems to indicate that there's something special about it, and in fact it's the only one of the nineteen that can't be pinned down to a single smallest inversion. There are two versions of it that exist inside a perfect 5th (e.g. C, D, G and G, C, D are inversions of the same notes bound by the same intervallic range). It makes sense to use it as a pivot because it can exist in five keys, more than any other shape on the map. It is the most open and mutable of the nineteen. Interestingly, it's also the sound that begins John Coltrane's *A Love Supreme*.

I studied (and continue to study) improvisation in a typical way, learning solos from albums to internalize and imitate the language, phrasing, and vibe. But I was never very interested replicating a style—I wanted to figure out process and concept, which can be applied to any context. I used shapes to analyze all kinds of music, looking for buried treasures. I felt that the music made by John Coltrane in the last years of his life was full of hidden symbols. I would try to decode some of the melodic movements with shape theory:

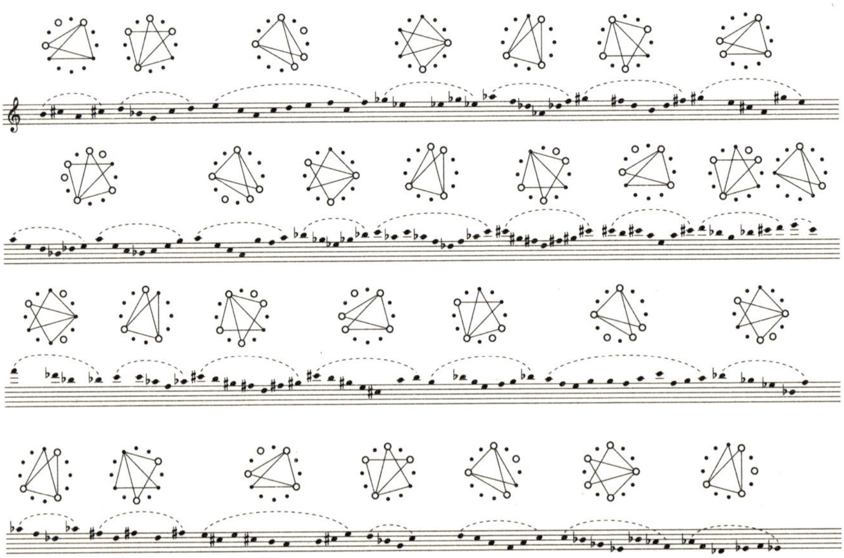

Figure 10. PASSAGE FROM JOHN COLTRANE'S IMPROVISATION ON "BRAZILIA" Recorded May 17, 1965, Van Gelder Studio, Englewood Cliffs, NJ Released on the album *The John Quartet Quartet Plays* Notated an octave above concert pitch. (11:42–12:08).

I began to understand of a way of improvising with cells, linking them together into melodic chains. While fiddling with this triad concept I met with saxophonist John O'Gallagher, who was preparing an enormous book on the subject. He had found a totally different and fascinating way of approaching the same material. It was a reminder that this is well traveled territory—the numbers have been crunched if you want to see them, but the value is in the personal process, wrestling with the raw data until it gives up some secrets.

I wanted to move from triads to some picture of all possible pitch sets. How many there are is not that difficult a question, but getting from theory to practice was more my issue. After doing my best to comprehend the tables and nomenclature of Forte and Rahn, I came upon Edward Tufte's *The Visual Display of Quantitative Information,* which articulated something I had been thinking about. Meaning can be revealed in a complex set of data if it is visualized with clarity and elegance. I followed a similar methodology to the 19 triad study and made pictures of the 351 possible pitch sets, then started grouping and moving them around into pictures. Here's a mandala I arrived at for the forty-three possible four note shapes:

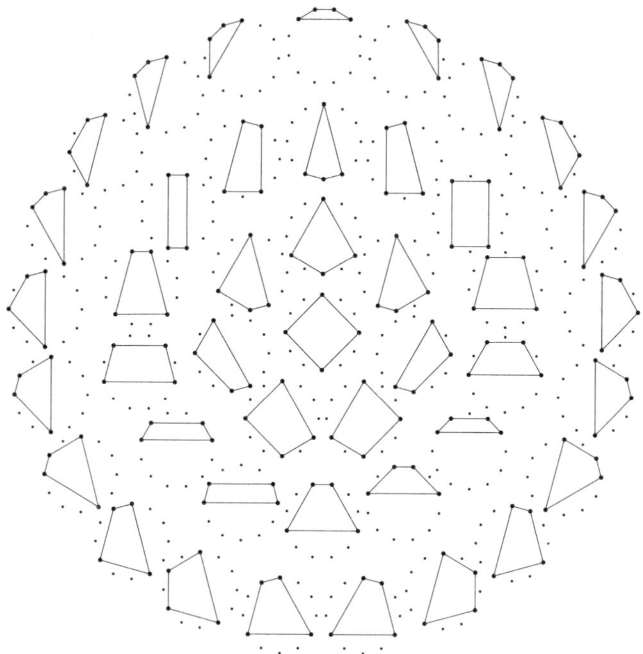

Figure 11.

It's almost symmetrical, but not quite (more on this later). While playing around with these shapes, I would sing melodies from each one to try to get to know them. Each one has a personality—expansive, prickly, elusive, heroic, honest, deceptive. In this picture, the central "noncommittal" diminished is flanked by the four "mercurial" all-interval tetrads and the more "assertive" dominant 7th and its reflection, the minor 6th chord.

Mazes and maps. When I started composing, it seemed like it could be useful and fun to make environments to generate musical ideas—I was reading Borges and wanted to make some gardens of forking paths. Finding ways to represent my favorite themes of infinity, paradox, and illusion. Every student of basic geometry knows about the Pythagorean 3, 4, 5 triangle, and the observation that these are the intervals of a major or minor triad has probably been made many times. Connect them in a lattice and you could build an infinite pyramid (or volcano):

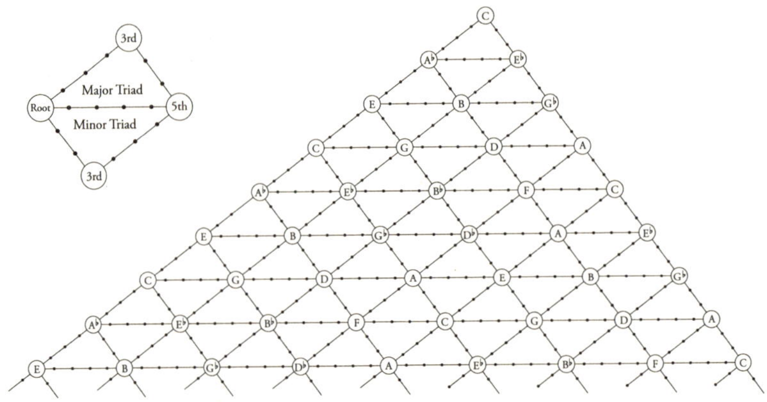

Figure 12.

But this literal spatial rendering of intervals doesn't work for the other triads (try it with diminished and you get a straight line), and certainly not for larger structures. And what about lists you would never want to make, like the 479,001,600 possible 12-tone rows? For this kind of thing, you could use something that represents the idea, without the brute force of comprehensive listing. Consider a 12x12 array of pitches where every row, column and 3x4 box contains a complete row. It seems to me like you could use this one table for a long time, reading the rows or boxes in any direction from any starting point. It doesn't contain all 479 million melodies, but there are plenty:

C	G♭	A	B♭	G	B	D♭	A♭	E♭	D	F	E
G	D♭	D	A♭	E♭	G♭	E	F	B	B♭	A	C
E	F	B	E♭	B♭	A	C	D	G	G♭	A♭	D♭
A♭	C	E♭	E	D♭	F	B	G	B♭	A	G♭	D
F	D	D♭	A	G♭	B♭	A♭	E♭	E	G	C	B
G♭	B	B♭	G	A	E	D	C	F	E♭	D♭	A♭
D	E♭	G	D♭	F	C	G♭	E	A	A♭	B	B♭
B	A♭	E	G♭	D	G	A	B♭	D♭	C	E♭	F
B♭	A	F	C	B	A♭	E♭	D♭	G♭	E	D	G
E♭	B♭	G♭	F	A♭	D	G	B	C	D♭	E	A
A	E	A♭	B	C	D♭	B♭	G♭	D	F	G	E♭
D♭	G	C	D	E	E♭	F	A	A♭	B	B♭	G♭

Figure 13.

This is nothing more than the popular Japanese game of Sudoku, with pitch names replacing the numbers 1–12. It's a simple diagram, but the endless combinations of pitches in every direction gave me a kind of vertiginous sensation, like the infinite honeycomb of Borges' *Library of Babel.*

Repurposing structures can lead to some interesting results. Here's another—suppose you wanted a map that seemed symmetrical, but not quite (as was mentioned earlier). Broken symmetry, with its combination of expected results and surprises, can be more interesting than perfect mirroring. The aperiodic tilings of Sir Roger Penrose have this quality, almost repeating but always a little different. We could put pitches on the kite and dart shapes to make a map with endless pathways. Here's a pentatonic garden to have a stroll in:

Figure 14.

* * *

When someone on the street asks whether I play rhythm or lead guitar, I choose the former, since it seems closer to the truth. One thing about shapes that fascinated me from the earliest days was that they could work for both pitch and rhythm. I imagined the contour of Thelonious Monk's *Evidence* as an object that was dropped, broken, and glued back together, the melody in the cracks. Any scale could be translated to a rhythm in 12/8, and any amount of time could be thought of as an area to be filled with shapes. As my musical training became more advanced I was still drawing pictures, but usually to investigate some idea about musical form. Here's a golden ratio tree that I made to serve as a reference for several compositions:

Figure 15.

In the late 1990s, percussionist Dan Weiss introduced me to the music of India, which led me down a rabbit hole of rhythmic shapes. After some years of study, I notated a book for my teacher Ganesh Kumar that bent and chopped the Western staff into the geometry of Carnatic compositions. The first song on my first album was a kind of culmination of this period, a long reduction in three speeds. The drum part explicitly imitates the structure of a "Korvai":

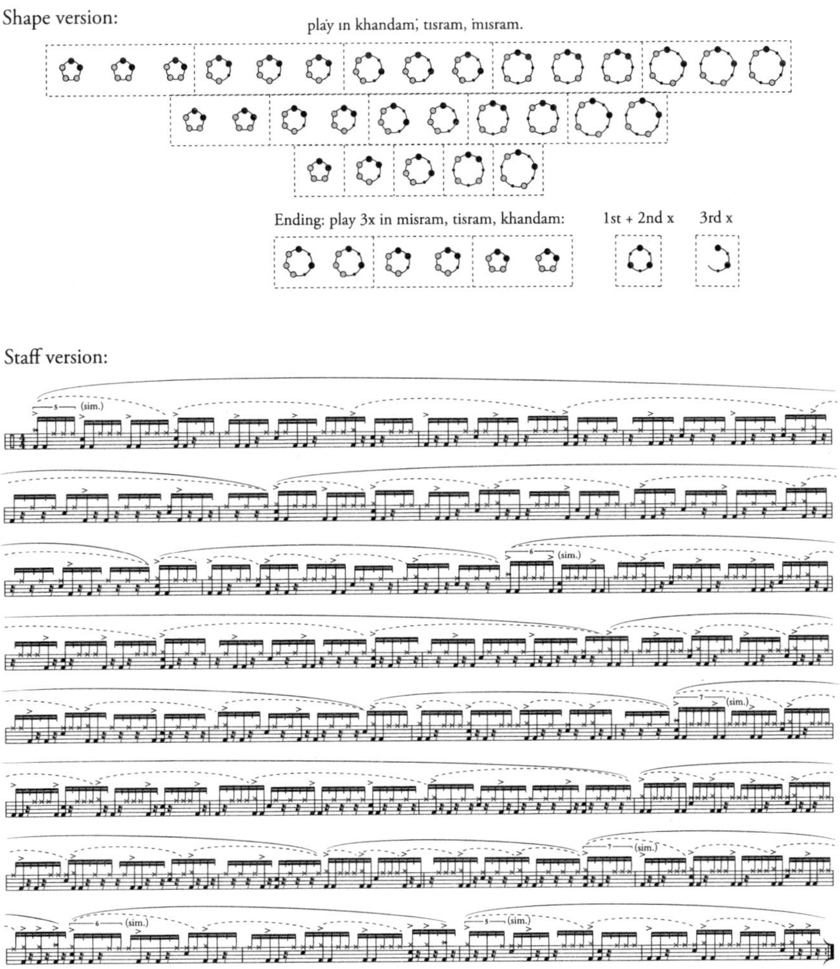

Figure 16. Drum part for *Spiral* (2005).

These contortions fill eight cycles of sixteen beats. I made a pile of compositions in this vein, and although it was satisfying to solve the calculations and aesthetic challenges of making the structures, they were prohibitively difficult to perform (at least for me) and weren't really amenable to my main interest, which was in making forms for improvisation. I was looking for something with smaller pieces, more fluid, modular, and contrapuntal.

For several years at the University of Michigan I've taught a college course called "Fundamentals of Rhythm," an aural musicianship class where we sing, clap, and stomp. Working with a diverse group of students has got me thinking about what it means to build a theory with minimal assumptions, which means imagining what it would be like to start from scratch. Suppose that the simplest rhythm is a single sound, with empty time extending infinitely into the past and future. If the sound has a certain length and begins to loop, it marks time like a metronome. If the length is within a certain range (not too long or short), we hear it as a pulse. Simultaneous pulses at different speeds make symmetrical composite shapes. Joseph Schillinger described these as "Interferences of Periodicities" (*The Schillinger System of Musical Composition, Book I, chapter 2*), and drew them as rectangular graphs. I tried a version using the numbers 2 through 8, using arcs and dots:

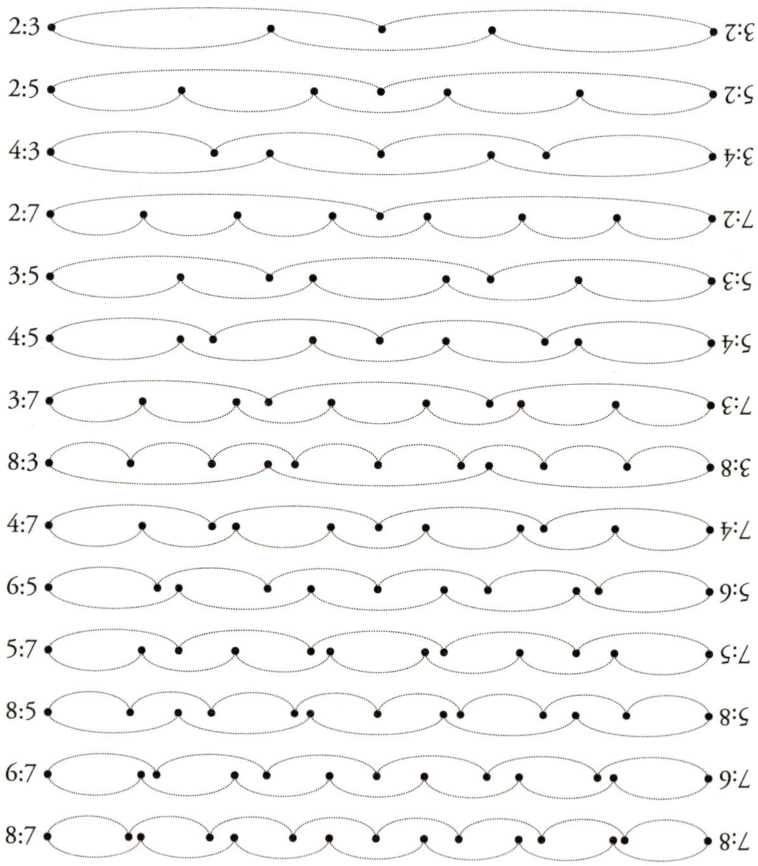

Figure 17.

This covers a useful range of single pulse against pulse textures. Now add an event to this lonely sound make a double pulse. In this looping rhythmic dyad, the two events can either be the same length (which will sound like the original pulse), or of different lengths, which will make a lopsided rhythm (like a heartbeat). I was first exposed to heartbeat concepts by Milford Graves and Steve Coleman, who were light years beyond my comprehension level (see *Arcana V*). But to get some basics together, I went to my circle drawings to puzzle out a workable version. In order to generate a useful (non-infinite) table of rhythms, the lengths of events need to be limited. Let's say they can be lengths of 1, 2, or 3. You could choose anything, but these will work well, since larger lengths are often felt as composites of these smaller numbers. If we look at rhythms with two events of different length, we can make three heartbeats:

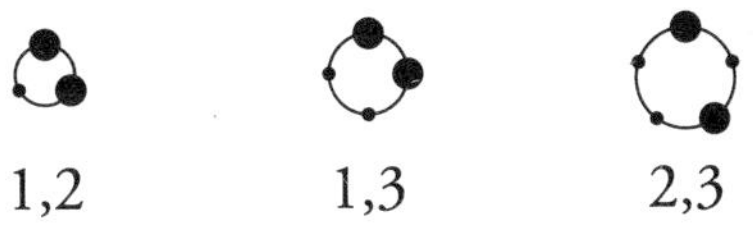

Figure 18.

Like the pitch circles, any rotation of the same shape is equivalent. There is a lot of material here already. Consider playing the second two shapes simultaneously in a triple feel—it's a simple idea that eats up a lot of staff notation:

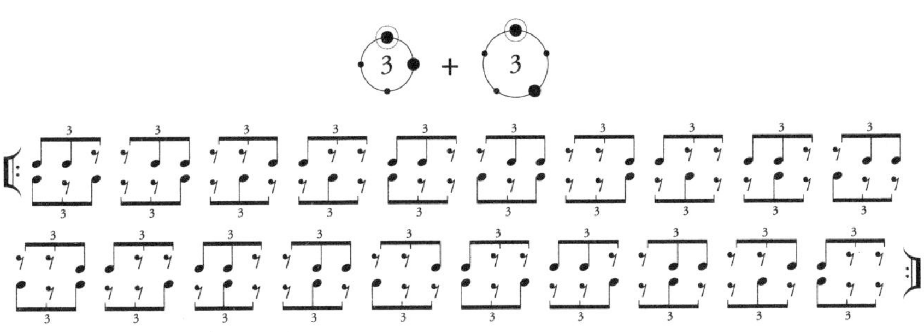

Figure 19.

What happens when you add more events? It's just a matter of finding all combinations and removing the redundant shapes. We could use this method to generate complete lists of rhythms of any number of events.

Using numbers of events from 2 to 5, we come up with seventy-seven unique rhythms. Arranging them in rows and columns of common events and lengths produces this shape:

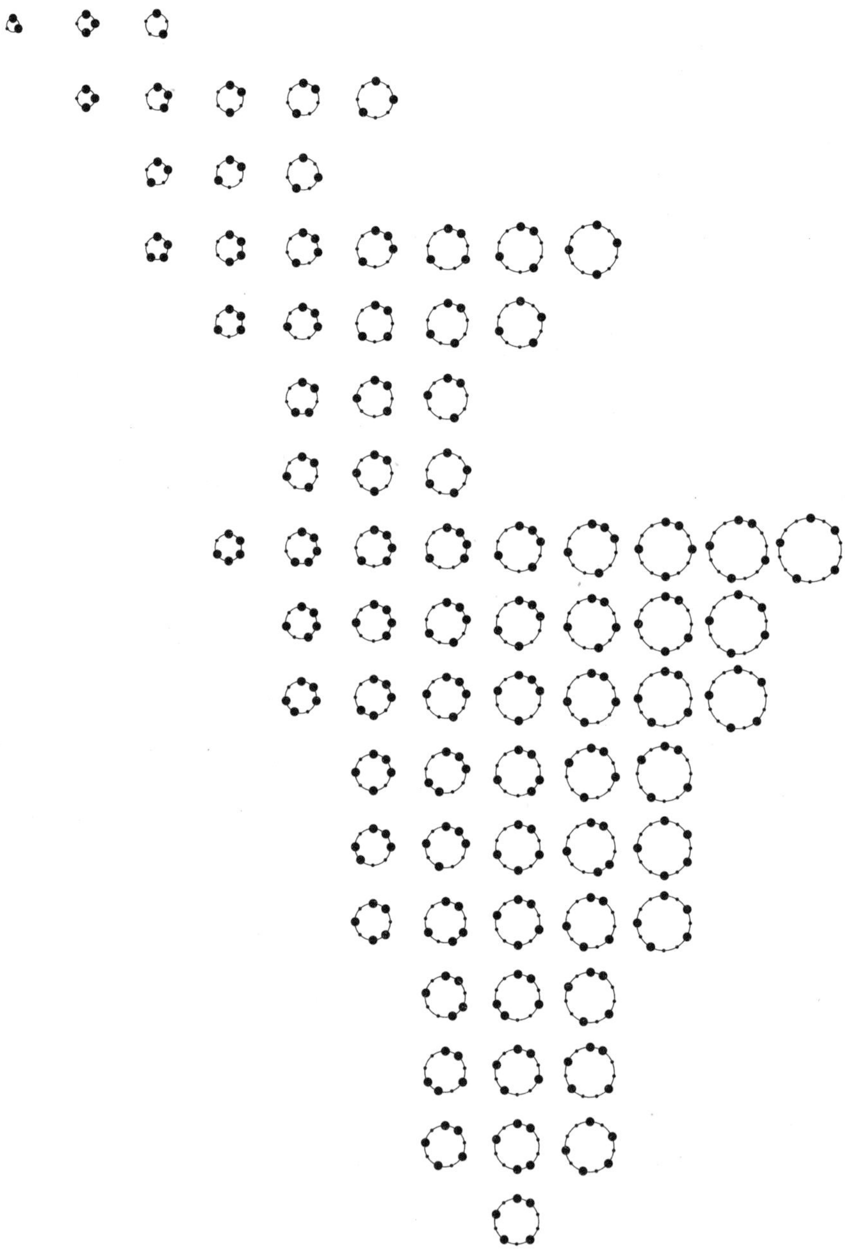

Figure 20.

In my visual library I made tables of these rhythm circles up to seven events, after which the numbers become unmanageable. For events 8–12, they jump up to 810, 2,184, 5,880, 16,104, 44,220 shapes. For my purposes, the simplest shapes provide inexhaustible options. Here's a percussion part that is just a map of the first eleven rhythms and how they can mutate from one to another via two types of transformation. The performer moves whenever they are ready.

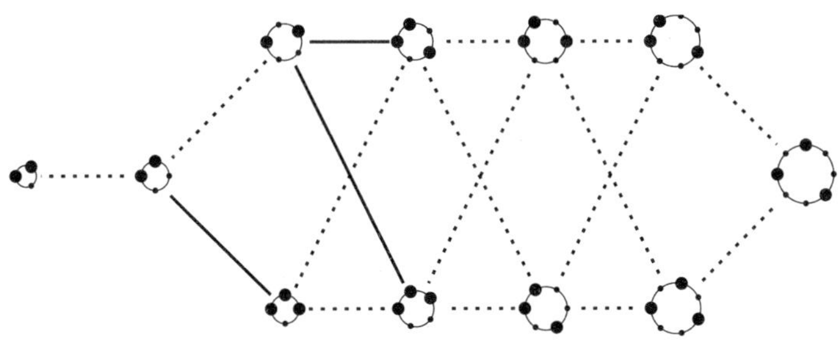

RULES:

add or subtract an event (rhythm length stays the same) (solid line)

change the length of an event (number of events stays the same) (dotted line)

Figure 21.

The scores for my projects have decreased in length with each recording, I suppose in search of more concise ways to express the same basic set of ideas. I feel proud of one of my shapes if it survives the various levels of doodling to become a composition, passes the test of live performance, and finally gets recorded. A very small percentage of them make it to the finish line.

This visual library, my compendium of mandalas, tables, maps and diagrams, is a work in progress. I'm constantly revising and tweaking it, tinkering with dots and lines. I realize that this may all sound more like a time consuming diversion than creative music making, but I enjoy it. It's a way to connect to the curiosity of childhood. Some people have chess, cards, or crossword puzzles—I play with shapes. And once in a while they snap together into an elegant design, and I get a tinge of that feeling from when I first saw the circle of 5ths.

* * *

As I write this, I'm wrapping up a two week European solo guitar tour playing the music of Thelonious Monk. This material might seem far removed from the topic at hand, but to me it's all of a piece, and Monk's music is actually the model that I have been following for the last 30 years. Monk's world is an environment that you can enter and inhabit, where you can get lost, be tested, and find solace. It's internally consistent and recognizable. You meet the same characters in different stories, and they greet you and notice that you've changed a bit since the last visit. This is a model of creativity concerned with imagining a world that you want to live in, building and populating it, learning the language spoken there, and inviting people in to explore and expand the territory. I'm not very far along in this process yet, but it's natural for me to work slowly, just trying to be ready to capture the ideas that occasionally form out of the cloud of passing thoughts, trying to trace the contour of their shapes before they disappear.

—Amsterdam, November 16, 2019

Figure 22.

CHAPTER 26

INFLUENCES

CHRIS POTTER

I would like to discuss the concept of influence in jazz music, and how jazz musicians use their influences to create a unique voice. This article is a way for me to try and get some of my own thoughts in order; as a musician, this subject is naturally very interesting to me.

The sources of inspiration artists use to create are feelings such as nostalgia, awe, sadness, anger, and love; memories of experiences they have had; impressions of people they have known, etc. These raw feelings themselves are not art, they must be channeled into forms in order to be communicated. These forms of musical expression can only be learned through the study of other musicians' styles and approaches.

In a form like jazz which is based so heavily on improvisation and is so stylistically diverse, what rules can there be for the aspiring musician? If there are no "wrong" notes in jazz, how can one know what the right ones are? How is meaning conveyed, what kinds of values (technical, emotional, spiritual, etc.) are worth conveying, and how does one find a way of conveying them? Expressing meaning implies using signs that belong to a common language. How can this be balanced with a desire for innovation?

Jazz exists in a unique space between being a folk music and a classical music. At this point in its development it has been taken in so many directions by so many different artists that it is impossible to make any true generalizations about it (I think this may be its biggest strength, and why I predict it will endure despite little commercial visibility). For the purposes of this article, I will restrict my focus to the original stream of jazz music that started in New Orleans in the early 20th century and has continued in a fairly direct line from Louis Armstrong and Duke Ellington to Charlie Parker and Miles Davis and beyond, reaching into the present time. I see my own style as trying to follow in this very diverse vein. Harmonically this music borrows a lot from the Western classical tradition, which has an established theoretical system of pedagogy, though of course its beauty must still be appreciated and understood by the ear. In contrast, the rhythm and phrasing that make jazz so distinctive have ultimately African roots, and must be learned through imitation rather than the written page. There is great importance placed in jazz on the way something is expressed, equal in importance to the notes themselves. How do we learn what "swings" and what doesn't? What kind of phrasing sounds "authentic"and why?

The magical human capacity for language is relevant here: the way we create and combine signs which point to concepts that can be transmitted from one brain to another, in a way that simultaneously transmits cultural attributes. Nobody needs to be told what sounds natural and correct in their native tongue, we know it when we hear it, through constant exposure. Music exists in a more mysterious and alchemical space than written or spoken language, since the signs are completely abstract and point towards feelings and states of mind rather than specific things or ideas, but the concept of a shared syntax that renders ideas coherent must be similar in both music and speech, and must also be internalized through exposure and imitation. The syntax of music is based on the physical properties of sound and our perceptions of it: the harmonic series, the feeling of time passing, the connection of musical rhythm to the rhythms in our bodies, etc.

Jazz also takes full musical advantage of the huge amount of social information humans pick up through tone of voice. These subtleties are expressed through control of myriad variations in phrasing, from shy whispers to friendly greetings to full-throated declarations. Besides musical fluency, a master jazz musician must have the social skills needed to conjure a certain state of mind in an audience using these tools.

If all the student of jazz does is imitate other players, how to come up with one's own way of playing? Jazz music places a special premium on authentic individual expression, and mere copying will not suffice. To help find a way through this problem, it is important that students not limit themselves to studying only one stylist. The more influences one has, paradoxically the more individual one's voice can become. A wide perspective of the choices made by different players over the same musical material helps the student realize what options have been tried and what their implications are. The student then gravitates to whatever sounds and strategies resonate the most with his or her own personality. These will naturally be different than any other individual's choices, and will reflect the student's own tastes and values, consciously or unconsciously. The development of fluency in the jazz language through imitation gives students the tools needed to begin constructing their own musical words, sentences, paragraphs and eventually perhaps their own musical worldview. The analogy with spoken language continues here: a child learning to speak doesn't only imitate what her parents say, she also experiments with her own linguistic creations in order to express herself.

As a musician develops and gains more experience, she or he sees new connections between the approaches of different musicians, and gains insight into how the music of the past can be reinterpreted and adapted to the expressive needs of the present. Webs of musical relationships are built in the musician's mind, between the styles of the past and among one's contemporaries as well.

To illustrate this, I would like to briefly consider a web of influence starting with the tenor saxophonist Lester Young. To a certain extent this is conjecture on my part, since my conclusions are drawn from recordings, and most of the people I'll discuss are no longer with us. I would also like to point out how this conjecture becomes an important framework I build for myself in order to clarify my own artistic point of view; a different musician might reach different musical conclusions by noticing different connections. Also, my understanding of these connections grows over time, which affects my musical approach.

Lester Young's playing was characterized by lightness of sound and by highly imaginative and often surprising turns of phrase. He expressed himself through a graceful and cool indirectness, yet his playing had arresting emotional intimacy. His strong yet relatively unadorned sound was revolutionary at the time, it was in marked contrast with both the heavier vibrato-laden sound and arpeggio-reliant approach of Coleman Hawkins, as well as with the more openly extroverted style of Louis Armstrong.

One strand of this influence was picked up by Charlie Parker. It is instructive to look at what aspects of Pres' playing Bird found useful for his own style. Bird eschewed the sweeter, heavier sound of other prominent alto saxophonists like Johnny Hodges in favor of a much drier and sharper tone, akin to Lester's, which gave his playing a plaintive, direct cry, and provided a contrast with his intricate and virtuosic turns of phrase. The feeling of inner awareness that you find with Lester Young is also present in Bird's playing, in his use of unpredictable and irregular phrases which convey a stream of consciousness. On a deeper level, while they each projected a strong sense of personality and style both in and out of their music, they seemed unconcerned with pleasing an audience in a "show business" way. They focused on their own expression, without trying to tailor it to the "square" tastes of the dominant culture. This attitude corresponded and contributed to a growing African American artistic and political consciousness flowering at the time. It seems to me Bird was probably influenced by Pres not just musically, but also in his vision of himself as an a jazz artist. Bird's approach was perhaps a little more virtuosic and "classical" than Pres, but still followed a similar line of thought. From the little bit of audio we have of these two men being interviewed, we hear the same dichotomy: Lester Young's speech is full of sly innuendo and innovative use of metaphor and wordplay, while Charlie Parker tends to speak very properly and carefully, but with a constant sense of wry "put-on" detectable to those who pay enough attention and are capable of reading between the lines. Clearly these considerations go way beyond the actual notes and phrases they used, but these extra-musical issues go to the heart of their importance as artists and must be addressed when assessing their influence.

Another strand to examine is the influence of Lester Young on Wayne Shorter. Shorter came along a couple of musical generations after Pres, and was influenced by all the intervening stylists, like Bird, Sonny Rollins, John Coltrane, etc. who themselves absorbed Lester Young's influence. However, I feel there is a strong direct connection between Wayne and Pres, in terms of personality, sound, elliptical ideas, and a certain otherworldly coolness. Listening to Wayne's playing in Miles Davis' band recorded at the Plugged Nickel illustrates this well, since it gives us an opportunity to hear Wayne stretching out over mostly standard chord changes, similar to the forms Lester used. Wayne, like Lester, creates highly unexpected and irregular phrases, and uses a similarly strong, even, broad tone, though the aesthetic of the music is more risk taking and exploratory than in Pres' time. In addition to their musical affinities, they were both famous for talking in riddles, koans, and a unique personal slang. I imagine as a young musician Wayne, like Bird, looked to Pres as a guide for how to behave as a unique spirit in a conformist world.

It's also interesting to consider the influence of Lester Young on John Coltrane. Coltrane consistently mentioned Young as his first major influence on the tenor. However, these two artists were temperamentally very different: Pres was a master of indirect allusion, while Coltrane was much more earnest. Nevertheless, Lester's musical ideas helped Coltrane develop his highly personal and influential language. Coltrane's direct assertiveness and his emphasis on spirituality fit well with the ethos of the sixties and the Civil Rights movement (when he did most his work as a bandleader), while Lester Young's subversive innuendo may have partly been a response to the oppressive racial environment he encountered in the thirties and forties. One could look at the progression from Pres to Bird to Coltrane in this social/political light as well as in purely musical terms. In any case, the influence of Lester Young through Coltrane would go on to influence the styles of many other saxophonists who would never be mistaken for Lester in a million years: people like Pharaoh Sanders, Albert Ayler, Jan Garbarek, and Michael Brecker, just to name a tiny but diverse handful. The jazz saxophone family tree has many branches, but all related.

A jazz musician in the 21st century has a great deal of musical history to digest, and greater access than ever before to recordings from the past. In addition, the aesthetic of jazz suggests an openness to new cultures and ideas. From the very beginning of my serious interest in music, I was listening to Buddy Guy, Stravinsky, Bartók, Debussy, Aretha Franklin, Hank Williams, the Beatles, Ravi Shankar, Joni Mitchell, and many others, in addition to the jazz greats. I know I share this musical omnivorousness with most of my musical peers. There is a danger in having a web of influences that is overly wide but not deep enough, especially in a world where perhaps too much information is too readily available, but I find that the obliqueness of influences from stylistically far afield can be an important key to finding new approaches. Consider Coltrane, who absorbed influences from India and Africa to help create his own musical universe. Also consider Steve Reich, who has more than once referred to how Coltrane's extended use of a single tonality on his recording Africa/Brass influenced Reich's ideas about minimalism. Nobody would mistake Coltrane's music for Reich's, still the musical kinship is there.

Fortunate is the artist who sees a way to use ideas from the past in a new way. We are all engaged with the culture of the past, down to the very tools we use for our constructions. Yet somehow every generation seems to find a way to put its own unique stamp on its creative endeavors. By putting our art into the public sphere, the work we do today may eventually become material for some future artist to come along and re-purpose it for his or her own artistic needs. In this way the tradition of creativity is in a constant state of renewal. By following in the footsteps of those who have influenced us, there are limitless new forms of beauty for us to find here and now, if we only have the imagination, courage, and persistence to bring them to life.

CHAPTER 27

TOMEKA REID INTERVIEWS DIEDRE MURRAY

TOMEKA REID

As I became interested in playing jazz and creative music, I sought out musical role models and checked out how other cello players were approaching the music. I learned about what I call the "bass" cellists, players like Oscar Pettiford, Sam Jones, Doug Watkins, Ray Brown and Harry Babasin. Then I discovered the "cellist" cellists like Abdul Wadud, Erik Friedlander and Fred Katz. My mentor Sais Kamalidiin took me to my very first live improvised concert with an improvising cellist, in 1999, at Blues Alley with a group called trio Synergy lead by cellist David Eyges. Delving deeper into the music, I wondered if there might be any African-American female cellists who participated in this music. That's when I learned about Akua Dixon and her Quartet Indigo, Eileen Folson in the Uptown and Black Swan String Quartets and through the recordings of Henry Threadgill, I learned about cellist Diedre Murray. I was really excited to learn that Diedre also wrote compositions and played with the legendary Chicago bassist Fred Hopkins, who I unfortunately never got to meet but learned, after purchasing my home on Wabash Avenue in Bronzeville, that his family's backyard was basically on the other side of the alley diagonal from my house. I really loved her playing on those records as well as her two duo records with Fred Hopkins, *Stringology* and *Firestorm*. In recent years, I have become interested in meeting as many of these cellists as possible, to speak with them and to learn about their individual journeys because they are all such wildly unique players. I really love that about the cello in improvised music, everyone takes their own unique approach! Having recorded over ten records, Murray has been an inspiration to me as a cellist, composer, bandleader and through my getting to know her, an inspiring human being, story teller and friend.

DM: I started studying privately at 11 years old, and by the time I graduated from college I received a degree in ethnomusicology from Hunter

College however I was a child musician, I mean, I did gigs almost from the day I first got my instrument.

I was born in Brooklyn Jewish Hospital, 1951. My father was a postal worker; my mother was a semi professional dancer, who danced with the Nicholas Brothers, so did my aunt. My aunt did it longer than my mother and as she got older, she formed a children's theater company called The Turnabouts, which performed for kids, that's how it all began. I started playing the cello in JHS 217 in the NYC public school system in the 1960s. When I was in junior high school you could play in the school orchestra, so they gave me a cello. I can remember almost from the first day that I brought my instrument home, my aunt happened to be visiting and she said "make some sounds for my movement"; then she gave me my first gig.

Both of my parents were from Virginia and they probably met up here in New York; I would say, in the late 1930s. They were part of the WW2 generation and I had two older brothers, one is deceased now. My mother was very forward thinking, talked a lot about DuBois and Dr. Kenneth Clarke. My aunt was a card-carrying member of the communist party, my grandfather a Garvey-ite. Moms had bourgeois ideations but not bourgeois money so she dreamed through me about having another type of life, an artist's life.

My grandfather played the clarinet in a band and there were many, many people in my family who played instruments. A great aunt played a mean stride piano up in Alaska for the miners during the gold rush, great uncles who played the violin and banjo in bands everybody played so I've always seen myself as kind of like the culmination of the lot. My grandmother was a church soloist who sang solos at church. She was an Eastern Star, which didn't mean that much to me at the time but seemed to be a big deal sorority back in the day. If you look it up you'll find out that that's where black women went who had social ideations and so I saw a picture of my uncle who had banjos, all of them played instruments, all of them and I think that music and art, but especially music, kind of runs through the family. Another aunt played a mean rag piano, stride piano and was in the Alaska gold rush. I mean these people... you know... really... it was crazy. Everybody played. I've seen pictures of my ancestors with banjos and violins and everything else. I didn't understand it when I was young then though, since most of them had passed away or lived in other places, you know. My little branch came to New York in the 1930s but the other ones still stayed in Virginia or Chicago.

Eastern Shore, Machipongo Virginia—that's my fathers' side and my mothers' side—is in Norfolk Virginia. So I always felt that culturally we had a southern household but my mother was very attracted to show business she would tell tales of hanging out with Lena Horne, Pearl Primus, Marlon Brando when they were just beginning, and those kind of people. They were the cool people of her day. And my aunt was a radical who held study groups for revolutionaries and believed in revolution of African nations from colonialism. Matter of fact, my folks forbade me from go over there for a while because, you know, they used to get raided by the FBI. I mean this is the 1950s, you know. So, she was very politically active, very forward thinking and I was exposed to jazz very, very early. I would probably say from the beginning, not only doo-wop which was the music that my older brothers liked. I can also remember ESP records that he listened to when I was a child. He loved Albert Ayler, Eric Dolphy and Coltrane; while my mother loved to jitterbug to Ellington's *Take The A Train*. There was also 1960s acid-rock, anything British, movie music, soul, theatre music, folk rock, experimental jazz as well as classical music especially Bach and organ music, that I had been introduced to in school. That was like the music of the household.

TR: Why did your parents move up here?

DM: Well, it's part of "the great migration". I think they moved up here for a better life, more money, less racism, the big city life. I know that my father said he hopped the train, just like in the movies, to get here. I don't know how my mother got here but I would imagine my grandfather and my grandmother brought her up here. Granddaddy owned a little Laundromat, and basically was in business for himself. I would say that they were like strivers but they hadn't gone over into the next level of money. You know, when I was born my grandparents had a brownstone in Brooklyn. Herbert probably bought that brownstone with the money from his cleaning business, or the laundry business. He was also an inventor and held some copyrights. Even though he was a businessman, he did some gigs as a clarinetist. I was always encouraged to be an artist and I always loved music. I mean, I knew I was going to be a musician since I was 5 years old. I mean, it wasn't even a question.

My father was from a farm in Machipongo, which is on the Eastern Shore of Virginia. It's in the middle of Perdue country, there's nothing but big farms around it... but my family that I have left there still have their plot of land. And... actually... you know, it's the main story of that area. In the past families were broken up and half the children went in one direction and the other went somewhere else. After a while they don't know each other, which is what happened to my family. He ended up (even though all the family were Virginians) being raised in the Carolinas on his grandfather's farm. His grandfather was very cruel and forced him to live in the hayloft or something, on a small farm, so of course he escaped to New York.

My father was born in 1906 or something. We're talking about a long time ago. My grandparents were born in the 19th century, I read this on their death certificates, sometime in the 1880s. My father had me when he was 50 and mom was 40 or thereabout. So, my reference points are somewhat older than my age. My father's father with his brothers were a gang that used to go to the local towns and raise the devil. My maiden name is Johnson, and they were called the "Johnson Brothers." He'd tell these stories about going to town with their rifles on them. Shooting up the place because of card games... I don't know, it sounds wild. My granddad William Grey Johnson (who I never knew), died from a bullet wound he got helping his brother commit a robbery. Another brother was sent to the penitentiary for killing a romantic rival. If you're a kid in New York, listening to the stories of the Johnson gang, you know! I can't even imagine, because by the time I came along, most of them were dead, one was only halfway alive and he was poisoned by his wife.

My early memories of Virginia are going down there on a Greyhound bus. They were clammers, and small farmers. My dad was actually born in a shack on a pier. Matter of fact my father's name was Wellington, and Wellington's were the high boots used to fish in.

What I know about my mother is that she was from Norfolk. As I told you, my grandfather had a Laundromat and cleaners. Some place along the line they came up here. My grandfather's father was a minister, I think. Also my great grandmother was a maid that worked in the Andrew Carnegie household, probably in Scotland. I have a photo of her in her maid uniform. They came up to New York, you know, probably for a better life, and more opportunity. That's what all those migrations were about, you know. My grandmother once told me, though, that they had always been in Virginia and worked in the salt mines. It was right out of the history books. I can't remember the people, but they were the original founders of Virginia. I had a friend of mine trace my heritage and they go back to the 1600s—the original colonists. Whatever the truth is, I've always considered myself to be an ancient American with African, European and Native American heritage. A friend looked into my ancestry and discovered ancestry from the West Indies; a boy that came from Jamaica as a toddler who was already an English slave. But my grandmother talked about Captain John Smith. She said that they worked in the salt mines. The only thing that's missing is Pocahontas!!

(laughter)

No really, it kind of reads like that, but that's how long they've been in that area. I know less about my mother's side, even though they're from Virginia. On my father's side, he knew one of our African relatives, an aunt, who was born in slavery, she was up in age, so if my dad was born in 1906 then she was perhaps 100—do the math. He called her a "Guinea woman" and never knew her name. He was a child when she died. I don't remember her name—but I think it started with an "m." That's what I remember.

TR: Okay, and what were your parents' professions? What did they do?

DM: They both worked in post offices because that was a good job, and security...

My father worked in the main post office as a mail handler. He used to lift the heavy bags. He used to take me there and I used to play in the main post office in the big sacks of mail when I was a child on 34th street, in main post office. And what did my mother do? She worked at Lord and Taylors—then at the main post office in Brooklyn. Ah... memories! She worked in a bubble gum factory, a Bazooka bubble gum factory. She also worked at a blinds factory. I remember she did that. But it was considered shameful that my mother had to work—that she couldn't afford to stay home with her kids.

You know, she was the one who was supposed to stay home and take care of us and I remember them fighting all the time about that. That she was not going to get a job. My mother had gone to college also, Hunter

College, the same as me. It's part of the New York City university system and she was only like ten to twenty credits from graduating.

TR: What did she study?

DM: I don't know, but my mother spoke French, fluent French and German. She had passing knowledge of Latin and Greek. So, I think she wanted to be a linguist, because I think her dream job, besides being a dancer, was to work at the UN. That's what she dreamed about. You know, that's what I think, but I don't know. In other words, they always wanted... the things that we do easily now, but back then, were very way out. That's what she wanted to do.

TR: So, did she dance for a living or did she earn money from dancing?

DM: Yeah, she was in the chorus of the Nicholas brothers show and she was supposed to go overseas with them. But her mother thought it was the work of a devil, you know, and that she was a harlot or whatever, and WW2 happened and her mother said "you can't go" and that was it—"you've got to get a job."

TR: So, she just stopped dancing completely?

DM: Yeah, yeah, she just stopped dancing. She went and got a job, you know. Like I said, back then, your parents tell you to do something, you'll likely do it. A woman, a young woman, sure—you are going to do it.

I always knew I wanted to be a musician. I became a cellist through the New York City Public school system. I always like to say that because of how they have taken orchestras out of schools—but then, they were there. They had really robust programs. I used to see this commercial for melody bells on TV. They were bells, and you could ring and it actually had a staff, and you learned the notes, and you could play—and I carried on, I could remember crying and crying and crying and you could not make me happy without these bells. So, even though, you know, as a kid, I was always trying to make something that sounded like a note—I was also surrounded by instruments. My aunt's husband was a guitarist, so there was constant music and you know, there was a piano in the house.

TR: Yeah, and you said you were born in Brooklyn? Were you raised in Brooklyn? When you said you went to school with Akua (Dixon) and her sister...

DM: That's high school. I went to elementary school at PS 54, I think, in Brooklyn and actually you can drive right by it when you get on the Long Island Railroad, there's a school in Bedford-Stuyvesant. If you look—that's the same school, it was built in the 1800s.

TR: So did you grow up in Bedford Stuy?

DM: Yeah, what happened was my family broke up, my parents split. I lived originally in the Marcy projects, and then when my parents split my mother went back to live with her father, which was in a Brownstone in Bedford Stuy. That school is still there. I don't think it's still the original school. The original was like a civil war hospital, I can't remember, it's either PS 54 or 45. I went to schools in that area.

TR: When did you start taking lessons? Was Kermit Moore your first teacher?

DM: The first thing that happened—that I can remember—is as soon as I got a cello, my aunt happened to come over and she said "you're coming with me" and she had me plucking out sound. I had no idea. I couldn't tune the instrument and I made my own tuning. I was just eleven. I guess my first teachers were at Van Wyck Junior High School in Queens. I couldn't read, but I was doing what my aunt told me to do. So that's first. Then I had a teacher... Evelyn Steinbach—you know how it is when kids have an aptitude for music. So in junior high school I could play a cello to some degree, and I was in little bands. So that's what I'm saying—I had my aunt and her dance company, and my aunt gave me my first gig playing in New Jersey. So I got on a bus, I must have been eleven or twelve, and she paid me to play behind the dancers. Then I had a little band, and my aunt had a daughter who sang, so we had a little group.

TR: What was the instrumentation—do you remember?

DM: Yeah, my cousin Alida played guitar, and there was another guitarist… a woman on the same floor of her apartment. We used to practice in the hallway because it had good echo. We were supposed to do the Ed Sullivan show—and we did gigs down in Greenwich Village. I was 11, 12, 13. I was doing little gigs, folk gigs, folk jazz, singing.

TR: Were they pieces that you guys wrote?

DM: Yeah. We played the Cafe Wha? We played at Café Rienzi. Agents came and saw us and liked us and Quincy Jones came—but we were like little girls. We got a little manager, and the manager started making little demos—I actually found one of those demos! When you listen to it (I can't play it now) but when you listen to it, it was like kind of Crosby, Stills and Nashy-ish, it was kind of on that tip. So we did that, and by the time I went to the high school, which is like 14, we were doing good and making a little bit of money. I went to The High School Of Music and Art, and the drummer started working as a baby sitter, this is a white kid—her name was Susan Evans. She had a pretty big career as a studio musician. I don't know whatever happened to Susan, but she became a babysitter for Judy Collins' children. So we used to go over to Judy Collins' house and we started making real music. We were like the talented kids hanging out with known adults who were really playing… like Santana. But we were still little kids, hanging out. Susan also studied with Warren Smith a wonderful percussionist and teacher who is still around—we used to rehearse in his studio. All the people who were playing with Aretha, Frank Zappa—all those bands—were coming there, and we were allowed to stay and listen and be go-fers, get them coffee, whatever.

TR: This was at Judy Collins house?

DM: I remember Judy Collins because we had a record producer, or manager that worked with her. In other words, this happened, that happened, Quincy Jones—all these people happened. This is my earliest memory about being on the scene… and I haven't talked about it in a long time. I don't remember the order of it happening, but somehow I remember meeting Joan Baez and all those people—and we started playing real gigs. I mean, we would open the festivals in the Park. They use to call it the "Rheingold" Festival.

At those big park gigs we would open for an act—it would be me, my cousin (I think her name was Norma) and then Norma left and then when I got into high school I went to school with Janice Ian. I don't know if you know Janice Ian, but she wrote this song called *Society's Child* which was a very big song. That's where I met Akua and all of them. We were young professional musicians at The High School and at Music and Art which at that time was full of the children of people like Leon Bibb and Eric Bibb—folk singers you don't know about today. There were young musicians who were playing with Eddie Palmieri's band as well. All those kinds of people had their kids at that school. I was at that school, too.

And I finally got so many gigs that I couldn't even go to school! So I went to a Professional Children's School for people who actually had careers.

So, I'm playing the cello and singing, right? We did that back in the '60s—little folk rock bands. You would see cellos in folk rock bands back then. But then when they started getting interested in boys or whatever, I don't know why, but I liked jazz and the guys in those bands were like, "Hey, why don't you come to this gig?" I remember Julius Watkins—who was a very great French hornist—even tried to get him married to my mother! I was 14 or 15. Anyway, he used to play with Charlie Mingus so I met all the different Mingus people and I would ask Charlie Mingus if he would teach me 'cause he played the cello and he was like, "Little girl, I play the bass, you play the cello!" It was, like, crazy! And I started meeting all those cats, so I knew them. All the people that I played with later on in life, I've known since, I was 11–12–13 years old. And by that time, I was also studying classically… I now was 17 or 18 years old, you know. Those girls that I had been playing with had kind of fallen away, but I asked myself "what am I playing?" I thought, "I think I'm playing jazz." I didn't know what it was—I would just play, improvise and play and do little Christmas gigs and stuff on the cello. I was still doing, you know, little orchestral things, or string quartet stuff as well—but I didn't like how I felt. I used to feel very... uncomfortable, I'd be the only black person there or if there were other black people there they were so snooched and weird. I couldn't even believe how they would behave. If you went and talked to them, they would turn away from you, because they were so intent on hanging with other people. I finally decided—I said, you know—"I don't think I'm gonna go into that career" because I thought that maybe I could do it all at the same time like Akua did. Akua used to do a lot of session work... she used to do a lot of studio work... she used to play with James Brown. She even let me sub for some of her James Brown gigs! She actually had those connections. So who did I meet? I was a young woman and meeting many guys, and 1960s music, which was great music, and people were very open-minded, musically and stuff. And then I had to decide what I was gonna do and by the time I was 17/18, I was pretty much on the road to jazz. One evening I went to check out The Gil Evans Orchestra who featured, at that time, a charismatic trumpet player. After the gig he asked me for my telephone number. He called and the rest is history. Hannibal Marvin Peterson and Larry Young (the organist) were my first experiences being on the scene in jazz. Hannibal used to call me the "teenager", and he said, "hey, come by" and so I did, I came to his house and he put me in his band. And that's the real beginning of me doing gigs on the scene. I also played with this visionary organist Larry Young who used to play with Miles and those people... And so, I met all these people and we used to go to this place called Slugs. Those are the early gigs. So basically by the time I was 18, 19, I was a jazz musician. But it really comes back to that earlier stuff, if you really think about how it happened. And I didn't really realize how weird it was. I started realizing how weird my career was when I was about 30—I said "wow, this is really strange, you know there's no jazz cello chair... you're just out here in outer space, aren't you"? And I said "well, it's working so far!"

CHAPTER 28

THE FLEXIBLE ROLE OF THE BASS

Observations on the Instrument's Use in Composed and Improvised Contexts

JORGE ROEDER

"You're playing too much," was the first piece of criticism I ever received from a fellow electric bass player. It was 1996 in Lima, Peru, and at 16 years old, I was playing my first show with my high school soft-rock band. The older family friend who shared his thoughts about my playing wasn't wrong.

Only months before, I had gotten my hands on two bootleg-of-a-bootleg instructional videos by two virtuosi of the instrument, Stuart Hamm and Jeff Berlin. Hamm, who was best known in the prog-rock world, imparted not just slapping but "tapping," a technique that involves using fingertips on both hands to step on the frets to produce a sound, and achieve polyphony, without needing to pluck the strings. In the video, Hamm tapped through an excerpt of Beethoven's *Moonlight* sonata on a four-string electric bass, which I found quite impressive.

Berlin had come from the world of jazz fusion, and though his musical language was much less understandable to me, it was no less appealing. I was mesmerized as his scales and arpeggios went outside the key at will and magically there were more options of notes to fill out the bars. I wanted to play like them, and I was eagerly forcing these concepts into vocally-driven soft rock. Calling this "too much" was generous.

Of course, as with any critical remark that rings true, I was deeply offended. But I did suspect that I really was using my instrument in a way that wasn't conceived for the context in which I was playing. The instrument had a role in that band, and I was forsaking that role for my own selfish pursuits.

At that time of my musical life, virtuosity ruled. Not only was I entranced by the virtuosity of others, but what passed for my own *virtuosity* was dramatically improving my life. Before the electric bass, I was a meek, awkward, insecure teenager, and not a stranger to bullying. But suddenly I had found something that garnered at least a bit of respect and admiration, enough for some of my classmates to back off. I stood out for the first time. It felt almost magical. Now I was in a band made up of popular kids, and my status was rising. Of course I was going to play as many notes as a I possibly could.

At this time I was also studying the cello, but my secret crush all along had been the double bass. I was most interested in an instrument that has the tuning of the electric bass, but the shape, fretlessness, and bowed qualities of the cello. In my high school orchestra, I quickly developed the urge to play the fundamental—the lowest note in the ensemble. This note seemed to carry all the higher frequencies with it everywhere it went. A symphony orchestra's cello section traditionally sits in front of the bass section, often playing the same part separated by an octave. And the tone of this low-vibrating instrument was something that drew me like a 20Hz siren's call. The double bass demands greater physical effort and gives you fewer notes in return, but I found those notes to be exactly what I needed. At age 18, more secure in my abilities, I finally made the switch. I had found my calling.

A couple of years later I began to play alongside my teacher in the bass section of the Orquesta Filarmónica de la Universidad de Lima, a budding ensemble that had absorbed most of the musicians that had lost their jobs upon the dissolution of the Lima Philharmonic Orchestra. It was an intern-esque position, with a fraction of the salary of a tenured player, but it was a dream come true to be able to play double bass with a professional orchestra. Here I connected deeply with the orchestrating styles of several composers, and the way they treated the bass. I got to play the classical "hits," and to form opinions about the works. Some bass parts were fun from beginning to end, some were unbearably boring, and most were somewhere in between. I thought the better composers wrote parts that are fun to play for all the instruments in the orchestra, not just for a few. During rehearsal breaks, I would find out what other instruments were up to in certain sections that I found compelling. I remember trying to understand why certain middle voices resonated so much with me. I was constantly drawn to harmonic motion that is more democratic, and doesn't live just to serve the melody. And I learned that the bass part didn't necessarily have to be fast or challenging to be compelling—I just had to find it interesting. To contrast (perhaps unfairly) just two popular works: *Blue Danube*, by Johann Strauss, while masterfully crafted and very memorable, gives not much substance to the bass part, while Beethoven's *9th Symphony* offers the bass a myriad challenges in the form of constant *soli* features, contrapuntal lines, fast, out-of-reach notes both high and low, and a level of dynamic contrast hard to parallel.

After stops in the lands of soft and very hard rock, and a classical orchestra, I finally came to jazz. In this form, and in contemporary jazz in particular, the bass had the most to do: traveling the full range of the instrument, the full gamut of tempos and keys, playing melodies and countermelodies, playing *obligato* lines, soloing and accompanying in complex meters and harmonies, all these being absolute requirements to a professional bassist, beyond the quintessential requirement of holding a bass line and grooving along with the drums, as it is with most other music styles.

In the context of instrumental music, one of the most compelling elements is contrast. The bridge of a song, the change in instrumental texture, the breaks, the dynamic changes—to name a few—are the elements that help tell the story of an instrumental song, in lieu of the lyrics. One of the less obvious but most valuable forms of contrast comes about when one goes to perform a set of music. These days, jazz concerts last from 45 to 90 minutes—usually in one or two sets, but sometimes in three or even (though rarely) four. The musicians decide how many songs to play, in what order, and which songs will contain which solos or areas of collective improvisation. Sometimes, depending on what kind of rapport a band has, some or all of these elements are not agreed upon beforehand. It is in these settings—when an ensemble needs to move as a unit seamlessly between composed and improvised material—that listening and focus become paramount. One of the most difficult but satisfying aspects for me when improvising as a group is choosing when to introduce change one end of a spectrum to another, be it slow to fast, sweet to gritty, manic to calm, all the while playing with intensity, focus, and an open mind.

In dealing with improvised music, more often than not, I get to create my own bass part in an ensemble. Sometimes there's a written part that needs to be followed exactly, but mostly there is a suggestion of the general flavor the bass part should have. And in some ensembles, I get to choose to modify the part from one concert to the other, according to the needs of the moment. The knowledge of the varied musical styles I acquired over the years has allowed me to understand that the bass can and should play several roles in order to keep innovating and creating. In my mind, the bass can play an innumerable number of roles in an ensemble, and how many notes a bassist plays can be informed by the context. Later in life, I have been guilty of playing "too little." This reluctance to introduce more variation in some settings may be my subconscious way to compensate for my teen-age failings. I am still working on that.

25 years down the bass road, I understand better the role of the bass in the bands in which I have the immense pleasure to play. I hope I serve that role better now, or at least that my selfish pursuits happen to fit the role instead of overshadow it as they once did. I treasure the joy of locking with a band, of melding together, of choosing when to change things up, of the interaction and camaraderie that occurs on stage. It feels ritualistic: a ceremony of getting closer with each other and with the audience, while creating a unique, unrepeatable moment. I am now happy to be "playing too much," when it's in the right place.

On Role and Gender

If I had a penny for every time I was asked by a stranger if I wished I played the flute instead of the bass, I would long be among the 1%. Yes, it is a large instrument and it's not always easy to move around. The bass teacher in my high school courted me into switching from the cello by telling me over and over that I had "bass player hands." I was flattered, and it worked. But of course any person that is tall enough to get their arms around the instrument (which itself varies in size) can develop the strength to play the double bass. A proper setup would allow virtually anyone to play. It is a shame that anyone should get discouraged from learning to play because of sub-standard setup (the action or tension is too high, or the strings are simply bad) when they don't know what a bass that is set up correctly feels like.

Unfortunately, set up is not the only obstacle for would-be bassists. At the beginning, the role of the bass in a jazz band is quite defined, even though most of the aspects that define it are left unsaid. That is because the role is intertwined with notions of tradition and certain aspects of "masculinity," including notions of the unwavering "father" figure, watching over the noodling children.

In latin music, this phenomenon is especially pronounced. I grew up listening to a variety of Afro-Cuban and Afro-Caribbean styles which reverberate all over the South American continent. When learning to play these styles in a band setting, I noticed an implicit requirement: to play this music, one must be "macho." The fear is that the music wouldn't work or sound good otherwise. But traditional "macho" attitudes in a musician are in my view often at odds with collaborative improvisation. Indeed, one of the greatest complements that I've received as a bass player is that I don't project a macho energy when I play.

This male energy is one of the roots of gender inequality in the world of jazz, and specifically for bassists. Every single one of the masters whom I listened to and transcribed when learning how to play was a man. The Wikipedia entry on famous jazz bass players refers to only fourteen women out of a list of nearly 440. And the adage that men are judged on their potential while women are judged on their accomplishments holds strong in jazz. When a male bass student doesn't play as well as he might, instructors or critics will say that it's a matter of time—a work in progress. But when a woman doesn't play as well as she might, her playing is often attributed to her gender: "she'll never play 'strong' like a man."

Today, more women have been recognized for their greatness and individuality on the instrument, including Bridget Kearney, Linda May Han Oh, and Esperanza Spalding, but this is only the beginning of a movement in the right direction. Until the same number of girls as boys are encouraged and invited to play bass—and especially jazz bass—great voices will remain unheard and phenomenal talent undiscovered.

CHAPTER
29

UNTITLED MUSINGS ON CONNECTION, CONSCIOUSNESS, INSPIRATION, AND PURPOSE

DAN ROSENBOOM

Throughout my life in music, I've been drawn to the nexus of the intellectual and the spiritual. That perfect balance where the mind and heart dance in tandem, where insight and purpose are revealed. This is where we artists create our collective reality, and shape the future through honest expression, and the pursuit of truth and joy. These things are difficult to quantify, especially with the written word. They are feelings, intuitions, and often their genesis is mysterious, their trajectories unknown. But they define the most captivating and limitless pursuit I've found in my life thus far. My intention here is not to provide a scholarly perspective, but to strive to reveal something inspirational, rooted in personal experience, and to explore these concepts that swirl constantly in my mind.

I grew up with parents who were heavily involved in avant garde music and art, so the scope of what I understood music to be was quite broad from the start. I was exposed to radically experimental music from before the time I could form memories. From this early experience I developed a mutual and deep appreciation for both highly intricate composition and pure uninhibited improvisation. These may not be polar opposites, but they do reach toward the edges of a spectrum, and certainly place different demands on the brain and the soul. The music that inspires me most strives for an intersection between these trajectories, a sort of "x marks the spot" where the intellectual and the spiritual coincide and move fluidly together.

In my youth, I was surrounded by highly accomplished and innovative musicians, and as I got more and more involved in music, I developed an intense set of expectations for myself. I was serious about music from a pretty young age, and being immersed in both classical piano and trumpet trainings, "getting good" was a primary focus. Intelligence, ingenuity, and innovation were paramount qualities in the way music was discussed at home, and the adjectives that were used to describe music were often weighty and intense. Once I started buying albums on my own, I found music that I thought was "fun," but in my mind there always had to be some kind of justification for its quality. This way of viewing music as a child was a double-edged sword that definitely distorted my relationship to music. It *did* instill a deep appreciation for practice, performance, experimentation, and boundary pushing, and it gave me a way to access strong emotions, and release them through my instruments. What it *didn't* do was instill an appreciation of music purely for joy or fun. I had fun with music, but the basis for having fun was *being good*, and *performing well.*

Throughout my education the stakes and expectations got more and more serious. By the time I finished college, I was really good at my craft, but riddled with anxiety and questions about self-value. It was all entangled with quality. In my mind, I was only a good person if I could perform with excellence and achieve great things. My perspective was seriously warped.

One of the most liberating moments in my personal development as a musician came during my first year of graduate school, though not *at* graduate school. I was searching for ways to be an innovator. Up until that point, I had primarily been a classical musician, but I knew I wanted something else out of music. I was exploring strains of experimental improvisation, prog rock, metal, jazz, and some folk music from far-off cultures. I was looking for *something else*. This led to an invitation to play with PLOTZ!, a band playing Balkan dance tunes mixed with elements of free jazz and metal. I went to my first rehearsal with an open mind, and after we ran the first tune and took a round of solos, I remember putting my trumpet down and having the profound realization that *playing music could be fun!* The sense of connection I felt between my bandmates was deep, and the experience of playing music together without any preconception or expectation amounted to sheer joy. That moment changed my life forever.

Connection

In the 15 years since that time, I've been fortunate to take part in a wide range of music making, from highly structured and composed music to completely improvised projects. Exploring the spectrum between structure and intuition, searching for a balance between rigor and freedom, I've found a beautiful reflection of my general experience as a human being. Wherever a project falls on this spectrum, sharing that connection, letting go of expectation, and enjoying the moment allows not only for a joyous experience of music, but spiritual and intellectual insight as well.

Intricate composition showcases a level of intellectual consideration and detail that can be awe-inspiring. Improvised music explores gesture and intuition on a profound scale.

Much of my work blurs the line between composition and free space, and explores how structure and intuition intermingle. Often, the structure of improvisation is not dictated, but the entry into free space needs to draw from the composition for motivic material. By playing with shapes and ideas from within the written structure of a piece, the improvisation develops in a way that is unique and specific to the composition, the context in which it develops. This can simply act as a launch pad into outer space, or it can be an intricate weaving of specific material that unfolds through group interplay. Sometimes, it can be exciting to completely change course in the middle of a piece, but usually a relationship to the written material makes for a more interesting development. This is where the process gets highly personal and intuitive, and ultimately boils down to a musician's conviction. If a player has a powerful belief behind their gesture, it really doesn't *have* to relate to anything. But in order to communicate with the other performers, if there are any, and the audience, the gesture must ultimately result in something that can be shared—it must connect to the shared energy of the performance.

There are myriad approaches to completely free improvisation, but by definition intuition drives the process. Some approaches are derived from systematic concepts, which can range from simple to complex. In order for these systems to work, all the active participants must be on the same page and speak the common language. However, free improvisation is often driven by emotional gesture, wherein players and audience engage in riding waves of emotion and sound, which can even reach a fever pitch akin to shamanic incantation or ritual dance.

Ultimately, it boils down to listening and reacting. In any kind of music, an open ear and quick reflexes lead to nimble, sophisticated, and engaged communication. It's totally possible, and sometimes even preferable, to slip in and out of systematic playing along intuitive lines. It's possible to practice a system to the point it becomes intuitive, so that in the moment of performance the system requires no thought to be expressed. A system can be honed to the point of instinct or reflex. However, sometimes systematic playing can choke the life out of a musical moment, just as sometimes completely intuitive playing can bear no relation to a particular situation. In either of those cases, the reason these approaches fail is that the performer is simply not paying attention. If one pays attention to the situation and the moment, truly listening, the choice is obvious and the balance is natural.

One thing I find particularly interesting in this spectrum is what I call "spontaneous composition." Of course, any improvisation could be characterized as spontaneous composition, but what I mean when I use that term is creating motivic or structural material in real time to shape an improvisatory performance. My long-time friend and colleague Gavin Templeton and I started doing this many years ago in our band DR. MiNT. It has since developed into a prominent tool in our improviser's toolbox, and has helped us develop a signature sound. We start a performance with a piece of blank staff paper, and as the improvisation develops, we jointly write out phrases that can then be used throughout the performance, and can be transposed, inverted, retrograded, or otherwise transformed through hand gestures. Significantly, these motifs are accessible to multiple band members throughout a performance as well. This not only allows for some potent moments of convergence in otherwise freely improvised music, but also can create a through-line in a performance that is almost akin to the use of leitmotifs to construct a larger structure for the spontaneous composition.

Ideally, the use of structure and intuition are fluidly combined, and the seasoned improviser knows when to use structural material and when to let that go. It's using intuition to collaborate with other musicians, the energy in the room, the audience, and one's own emotions to create something expressive in real time.

What makes an improvisational moment "work" is a sense of synergy between the improviser(s) and the audience. That can be highly subjective, and different musicians and audience members can easily disagree about moments that "work." But what I think most improvisers strive for is a flow state, where spontaneous moments of synchronicity between themselves, the other players (if there are any), and the "vibe" in the space. It's feeling the peaks and valleys of energy, the build of tension and release, and the timing of impact...much like comedy, or really any storytelling. Ultimately it's about the connection shared between the performer(s) and the audience.

Consciousness

An inordinate amount of my time is filled with music in my head. There are moments of quiet, but there seems to be an almost continuous stream of music flowing in the background, or foreground, of my thoughts. I don't need external input to be experiencing music. The majority of my waking life is spent experiencing music on some level. It feels like being tapped into a continuous stream of consciousness—possibly a collective consciousness that exists beyond the reaches of my own mind—and that the act of performing improvised music is like opening a tap on that stream. When you're tapped into that stream, music ceases to be a song or a piece that you're hearing, performing, or composing, and becomes an experiential "trip." You're taken somewhere unexpected and new, on an intellectual, emotional, and sometimes even spiritual level.

The inward contemplation that happens in both compositional and improvisational mindsets, as well as practice and preparation, is akin to meditation. It might seem to be a more active practice than meditation, but in my experience composing and improvising are often about "getting out of your own way." It's about accessing the subconscious or even the non-conscious part of oneself and unblocking a channel of creativity. Musicians often speak of letting ideas flow through them, as if they are conduits for some larger energy that directs their action. Some musicians speak of a collective consciousness or a sense of ESP when improvising. Historically, composers have often referred to divine inspiration as a factor in their work. I think all of these experiences speak to a removal of "self" from the process—a clearing of pathways to creative action. This clearing allows for inspiration and instinct to work in real time and can unleash some of the most direct and potent creativity we ever see.

In thinking about spectrums and balance, another aspect to consider is the dichotomy of "the serious" and "the fun." I feel strongly that if the practice of music skews too far to one side of this spectrum, it loses potency and relevance altogether. Serious music can speak directly to people's pain, deep contemplation, societal ills, intellectual pursuits, etc., and "fun" music can offer people a relief from the same things. Of course, there is a place for both, and really anything and everything in between. But to pursue music as a personal practice weighted to *only* one side of this spectrum is to be out of balance and to miss the full range of expressive possibility.

The extremes of this spectrum are not equal. To engage with music on a purely fun level is an inherent good, albeit a potentially limited experience. Any pursuit that brings levity and joy into our complex, and often difficult human experience is a worthy and necessary contribution. Of course, musicians should do serious work if they feel compelled to do so. Serious work often brings groundbreaking and transformative insights to fruition. But maintaining a connection to the pursuit of joy is vital to elevate our collective experience. The pursuit of joy can only enhance one's communicative, emotional and transformative potential.

Recently, I've had the opportunity to teach college students, pursuing degrees in musical performance at different institutions. The most jarring common thread for all these students is that in the pursuit of refining their craft, they have become disconnected from their sense of purpose, their sense of "why" they are doing this. They are so far down the "how" rabbit hole, that in some cases they are practically paralyzed by fear. Playing a simple melody seems inordinately difficult for many of them. This is *not* due to a lack of skill. It is due to an almost paranoid mental state, one I could recognize from my own past, that can warp a musical mind to its core. It's the feeling that self-worth is a function of how well one can play.

To me, this is musical dysfunction. When I first typed that sentence, I used the word "death" instead of "dysfunction," but corrected myself because this state is not permanent. It's a serious and dangerous condition to lose sight of the joy of playing music simply for joy's sake. One *can* reconnect, though, at any time. In my experience, that reconnection happens by remembering to strive toward an expansive shared consciousness.

Pursuing joy doesn't necessarily mean the music must by outwardly joyful. Actually, the truth is quite the contrary. How does one pursue joy while exploring and reacting to the ugly side of the human experience? In putting together and creating protest music with my band Burning Ghosts, I've had to think about this quite a lot. In our case, we funnel our emotions around the subjects we are reacting to with potent, sometimes angry, sometimes even despairing playing. Tapping into that nerve, connecting with that raw emotion, offers both the band and the audience a chance to feel connected, to sense their own pain is shared. And in that shared experience a momentary exorcism takes place. Even if the audience feels fired up or enraged, the opportunity to feel solidarity with the musicians and people around them provides a window to a way forward. Often, the experience is rousing and reaches an exciting almost jubilant point where the shared emotions become overwhelming and empowering all at once. And in that pursuit people are moving toward a better life, a better experience—they are in the pursuit of joy.

This has nothing to do with the content of the music one plays. It has only to do with the mental state one embraces *while* playing. And when the pursuit of joy fuels one's musical drive, the relevance, potency, expressive and transformative potential of a life in music is limitless.

Inspiration

Inspiration is an ineffable thing. Often the origins of inspiration are mysterious, nebulous at best, and in truth inspiration can come from anywhere. For me, the inspiration for a composition, or really any project, can be an interesting word heard in a conversation, or a joke, or a political moment or movement, or a potential technology...the range is enormous. When I try to distill it down, there's something elusive about what triggers the process. Here's an example:

I was recently listening to a podcast about A.I. while driving, and somewhere along the way I realized I was simultaneously riffing melodies in my head. I don't remember the first ones, and I don't think the composition that resulted looks all that much like the riffs that were flowing in the car. But something about the character of those riffs, and the way the ideas from the podcast mingled in my mind was potent enough to motivate me to write a piece when I got home. The origins are murky, but I enjoyed these musings enough to put pen to paper.

That's the biggest thing for me: I have to enjoy what I'm hearing in my mind enough to start writing. There's a background level of musical thought going in my brain fairly constantly. So there are a ton of ideas that I don't write down. The ones that make it out are the ones that are interesting enough to hold on to, or at least to build from, and the ones the align with the opportunity to write them down.

Unfortunately, I think some of my best ideas have never made it to the page, because when they happened there was no way to document them and they were too momentary to remember. Sometimes, I try to remember them when I get to a place to write them down, but they always mutate from the original idea. Usually, you can spin them into something interesting, but sometimes you just have to abandon them and move on. It really becomes more about the confluence of life circumstances that allow the compositions to materialize. So far, there's no way to take a snap shot of the melodies and grooves in my mind as they happen, so they've got to align with the opportunity to write them down or record them in order to make it out into the world.

Ultimately speaking, I think the inspiration for new compositions is fairly constant. How could it *not* be? In a world so rich with stimulus, and in a human culture that is so connected yet so confused, the need to express and share ideas is so important. We see our communities being fractured and polarized, and our political and social viewpoints are getting so intensified that we feel the impulse to shut down communication rather than have the difficult conversations. And while I have no illusions that a wacky tune will fix the world, I think any opportunity to create connections, no matter how small, enriches the world.

Purpose

The essential ingredient to making original music is honesty. But what does that mean when applied to creativity? More than anything it means honesty toward oneself, honoring one's true interests and ideas no matter where they lead artistically. In a culture that is constantly being measured in artificially quantifiable yet substantially vapid terms (money, fame, likes, shares, re-tweets, mentions, followers, etc.), it's more essential than ever that musicians follow their inner creative impulses, whatever the ends.

The lasting impact of an honest statement is inherently immeasurable. We never know whose life might be touched by something we create, and can never know how far-reaching that connection might be. It can stretch across unknowable distances in both space and time, and has the potential to alter the unfolding of human events. And in an age where human events are having a lasting impact on our planet, our solar system, and our universe, a single honest creative act actually has the potential to ripple through the cosmos and change the very fabric of reality.

This is the essence of creative magic. And often the results manifest far beyond the intentions or even the imagination of the creator. A turn of phrase can inspire empathy in a listener who may have forgotten their capacity for human connection. Or the energy of a performance could inspire a social organizer into action. An obscure and unusual composition could inspire a child of a future generation to pursue a life in music, and that choice could have an immeasurable and unknowable effect on the course of human history.

Honest expression inspires people, and inspired people can create a better reality.

Why do we do this?

To create a reality we can believe in.

CHAPTER
30

ART IMITATING LIFE

JOEL ROSS

Something that I've dedicated a large part of my life and career to studying and understanding, is communication. In the context of my career—as an instrumentalist, bandleader, improviser and composer—there's communication between musicians and the audience, as well as a musician to another musician. In the context of my life, there's communication with the earth, with animals, with other humans and etc. We are able to communicate with each other through language and voices, as we speak and host conversation and discourse. In this Black American Music popularly known as jazz, we're able to communicate and converse with each other through a common musical language—and just as everybody has their own unique speaking voice, the same applies to our voices as instrumentalists and improvisers. I believe there is a direct correlation between, not only the way we speak and the way we play, but also in our personalities, and the way we live and behave.

Focusing primarily on small group improvised music, there's a lot to discover about voice and communication. Consider one of my favorite examples of groups with fantastic interaction and communication, Miles Davis' *Second Great Quintet,* with Wayne Shorter, Herbie Hancock, Ron Carter, and Tony Williams. Miles uses a fairly common group set up in the jazz idiom—a quintet with trumpet and tenor saxophone as the front line, and piano, bass and drums as the rhythm section. One of my favorite recordings of the group is the complete, *Live at The Plugged Nickel* sets, and what they do with the music is incredible. Each one of them demonstrates a unique voice as an improviser—Miles, for example, has such a strong influence on the direction of the music, using just a few notes and/or inflections; and what they do while "comping" with and behind each other (especially in the rhythm section) tends to hold my attention most when listening. For those unfamiliar with jazz terminology or vernacular, comping refers to the term accompaniment or, to accompany—this is typically attributed to the rhythm section using their shared knowledge of melody, rhythm, and harmony to support and accompany a soloist—but I believe it gets much deeper than that.

For a chance at optimal group communication, a group must be completely focused—on the music at hand being created, and on their fellow musicians performing with them. Playing a tune is quite similar to holding a discussion; The melody is the subject and the start of the conversation, the topic that everyone is speaking about. The way that the melody is presented sets the tone of the tune. It's important that the band centers everything they play and "say" around the melody, the skeleton of the tune. Far too often a group will play the melody with everything afterwards, or even during, being completely divergent and unrelated to what the song is about. Even when we're improvising and moving away from the melody, we should keep that information in mind as we play and communicate; whatever path the group chooses to take should keep the melody in mind, explicitly or not—the melody *is* the tune, and we should build our improvisations from that.

After stating the melody, we tend to jump right into improvising or "solos"—normally it's approached as a soloist improvising with the rhythm section supporting, but I don't think of it like that. If this is really a conversation, then sure the soloist might "have the mic", but they're also receiving a constant stream of feedback from any number of different individuals. Often times, improvisers come out and play without any regard for what the rhythm section is saying right behind them, and that lack of inclusion misses out on some amazing discourse that could be taking place.

There are so many conversational opportunities that can happen between a soloist and an accompanying rhythm section. Thinking of a traditional situation of piano, bass and drums behind a soloist, each rhythm section member can hold an individual conversation with the soloist, as well as amongst each other. For example, while all four members are playing, the soloist can be playing off of and responding to rhythmic ideas from the drummer, while the bassist and pianist can simultaneously be matching up on some spur of the moment chord reharmonizing—the possibilities for rhythmic, melodic, and harmonic conversation and interaction are endless.

Things can be taken even further in the role of the soloist, where it's much deeper than just "taking a solo" in front of a rhythm section—we have the chance to lead and mediate a conversation with the band, while simultaneously crafting a story for the audience to witness and follow along with. Now here's where that focus I mentioned earlier comes into play; with so many tools like rhythm, melody, harmony, dynamics, etc. at our disposal, a soloist has the ability to dictate the direction that the rhythm section can go, similar to driving a car—everyone's going to the same place, yet when it's the soloists' turn to drive then they can decide how to get there. If the rhythm section acts as passengers, then the driver can choose to listen to and travel with the band to various agreed upon places, or ignore them and go their own way—only one of those options sounds like a favorable car ride, and likewise, the music can come across as such.

When a group is at their peak communicative prowess, they're focused on and listening to each other as well as focused enough to allow the music to evolve organically.

There is so much more that can be discovered and discussed surrounding this topic. When everyone in a group is thoroughly in tune with, actively listening to, and clearly communicating with one another, there isn't much need for verbal instruction. If properly executed, that group then has the capacity to weave beautiful tapestries and interesting narratives and storylines for audiences to follow—and in time, instead of dictating what a particular "story" may be about, the audience is able to create their own interpretations, which makes for a much more personal experience and creates a deeper connection between the band and its audience. My goal as a bandleader, composer, and improviser is to be honest and in the moment; meaning that I want my ideas to flow naturally and to be conveyed to the audience through clear correspondence amongst each band member—just as I'd prefer to engage in clear verbal conversation with other individuals. In the same way that we express emotion when we speak, with clear communication, we can demonstrate the same emotions musically. This is one of many instances where art imitates life.

CHAPTER
31

LOCKWOOD'S PIANO

CORY SMYTHE

Is there any sound more confined than the piano's? Push a key down and there it is. Piano. A trumpet is readily a length of intestine, a mist; the violin a windowpane, the air slowly vacating a room. But the piano is a piano. "*Piano Piano*," says Pauline Oliveros in her piece of the same repetitive name. "Each tone a key for life." For life, under lock and key.

Has anyone ever understood sound as deeply as Pauline Oliveros? Likely not. And yet, perhaps no one has taught us as much about the sound of the piano as the composer Annea Lockwood. Unlike Oliveros, whose work abjures a transcendent pianism in favor of a resignedly meditative acceptance of the piano's immutability, Lockwood conjures a series of extraordinary and defiant studies in the art of actually freeing the piano from itself. "Leave it there until it vanishes," she says, in her piece *Southern Exposure*, of the piano we're instructed to anchor to the beach at the high tide mark. Each key a tone disappearing into the waves.

There are four entries in Lockwood's ground (and piano) breaking work *Piano Transplants*, two of which end with the piano's sound submerged in a body of water. In the above quoted *Southern Exposure*, this body is the ocean, whereas *Piano Drowning* is performed in "a shallow pond with a clay/other hard bed." *Piano Garden* begins with our "dig[ging] a sloping trench" into which a piano is partially buried and eventually overgrown with the "fast growing trees and creepers" we're told to plant around it. *Piano Burning* makes plain its combustive intent in the title.

For pianists of a certain time and place, Lockwood's texts have conveyed compelling metaphors about pianism even when no lighter fluid has been at hand. When I was in school, it was common to attend a piano lesson addressing the exact quantity of heat to apply in the opening measures of Prokofiev's *Sonata no. 3* in order to engulf the convulsing audience in a cloud of acrid smoke. How many teachers refused to allow me the simple completion of a phrase from Chopin that I'd begun in too clarion a fashion when what was so certainly required was the burial of the melody under layers of soil and creeping plants? How many pianists my age still practice Ravel next to a large aquarium, periodically dunking their heads into its depths, that they might compare this crude approximation of the sought-after submerged and deliquescent sound of the piano with its air-borne counterpart—back and forth, in and out, until they can no longer detect a difference?

The nature of the piano—each tone so unshakably a key, each key imprisoning a tone—compels these extremes from the artists working in its rigid medium. Yet, as Oliveros demands, is this effort not doomed to repetition and failure? Of course, the generations of practitioners for whom Lockwood's compositions seemed merely poetic—prompts that might enrich their labors in other music-making—might be forgiven for finding the actual realization of her instructions impractical. But the contemporary pianist is fortunate to find herself in an age where burning and drowning pianos are no longer so hard to come by—are, in fact, acceleratingly ablaze and increasingly, if fleetingly, afloat.

How many of you are reading these words in the aftermath of devastation, the waterlogged pages of this book having somehow survived the hurricane that swallowed the rest of a presumably rich and varied musicological library? Did the fleeing owner of that library also leave behind a piano to be sunk, unnoticed, by the blanketing sea? Or did she gather an audience to gasp at the beauty of its sinking sound?

At the time of this writing, the skies over Lockwood's native New Zealand are reportedly intensely aglow, the result of unprecedented fires ravaging the pianos in nearby eastern Australia. And the state of California, where Oliveros taught for many years (and where I was once a determined piano student, struggling to construct gardens of piano-absorbent foliage with only my fingers and turbid imagination)—currently that state, too, is radiant with wildfires encroaching upon and consuming who knows how many living room uprights. Pianists truly dedicated to their craft would, I believe, remember their Lockwood before frantically retreating from these infernos to safety. And anyway, isn't it only a matter of time before the possibility of a safe retreat vanishes completely, like a shoreline, like a species of moth? Why not instead take Lockwood up on her suggestion in the penultimate line of *Piano Burning* and "[staple balloons] to the piano" as if for a child's birthday party? Why not do as she commands in its finale and "play whatever pleases you for as long as you can" on its crackling and erupting keys?

Now is indeed a time for pleasure and celebration, but this propitious state of affairs won't last forever. There are only so many living rooms, so many concert halls, so many pianos in your consumptive town, your teetering countryside. For the pianists who've inherited this enormous opportunity from those, like me, who could only (with Lockwood's help) dimly envision it, I implore you: this moment absolutely cannot come again. Generations of pianists before you have deluded themselves; you have the opportunity to truly do what we could not. Let the civilized sound of the piano gush into the sea. Thrill your swooning listeners with its dissolving evocations of philharmonies, cocktail hours, Ellington, a young boy practicing Bach Inventions, his little legs dangling precariously from the piano bench. Attentively, lovingly disappear each tone into the waves, each key into the flames, the ground. How lucky you are to be alive during this great liberation of the sound of the piano! Practice to attain, here inside the swelling soil, spume, and piano-enveloping smoke, a bravura technique that would make Liszt himself fall breathlessly to the floor, and usher in a new golden age of pianistic virtuosity the likes of which the world has never before heard—and will surely never hear again.

CHAPTER
32

STATEMENT ON TECHNOLOGY AND THE FUTURE OF MUSIC

RAND STEIGER

In October 1998 I presented a *Statement on Technology and the Future of Music* at the Center for Research in Computing and the Arts[1] at UC San Diego. This essay includes that talk in its entirety, along with my reflections on it 22 years later. I engage in a conversation with my former self, assessing the validity of my concerns and the accuracy of my predictions, while also identifying the absences that now, with the benefit of hindsight, strike me as oversights. For the sake of clarity, the passages from the original essay are indented.

1. The Center for Research in Computing and the Arts (CRCA) was originally founded by Roger Reynolds at UC San Diego as the Center for Music Experiment where seminal research in early computer music technology took place. It was disestablished under controversial circumstances in 2012.

At the turn of the century, there was no doubt that new technologies were going to be quite disruptive to the ways in which music was made and disseminated. I was mostly optimistic about this, but I also felt an urgent need to stress to our students that they needed to engage in research and creation of such technologies, lest they be limited by ceding the development of new tools to the commercial sector.

> It is clear that the way music is made and disseminated is changing quickly and will change radically within our lifetimes.
>
> This is not just a question of the opportunities brought about by new technologies as applied to music, although there is much to discuss in that regard. In a much broader sense, a major paradigm shift in society is occurring with the technology of, and the opportunities for communication, in the largest sense of the word. If we fail to recognize the clear signals around us that point to a rapidly changing world, then we will relegate ourselves to the mortuary of history that so much music making resides in today.
>
> I want to ask you to contemplate this purposefully provocative ques-

> tion: If we profess that progress in music is still possible, and if we see ourselves as modernists, then how can we continue to focus our work on the instruments, methods, and venues of the 19th century?

Of course, by 1998 we were already firmly in the post-modern[2] era, but while I admired some of the musical trends asserted by the leading figures in that movement, I considered myself and the program at UCSD to be still strongly committed to experimentalism and the belief that there remained great potential in undiscovered musical ideas and materials. Many of our students at the time considered themselves unapologetic modernists.

2. Jonathan Kramer, "The Nature and Origins of Musical Postmodernism," *Current Musicology* no. 66 (Spring 1999): 7–20.

Much of the classical music world remains focused on the music of the past, but today new music is thriving to a much greater extent. The big institutions (opera companies, orchestras, and presenters) and distinguished soloists have almost all integrated commissions and contemporary repertoire into their programs. And we have seen the establishment of many new ensembles and venues that concentrate on contemporary repertoire and are currently flourishing. In short, we have a much healthier balance between the old and the new, and there is every reason to believe a greater appreciation of new music will continue to grow. I now prefer to think of the music of the past as living in a museum, not a mortuary, wherein the historical works are being recreated with great integrity and inspiration. And, as in the best art museums, classic works are now often recontextualized in creative ways, allowing them to be heard anew.

> What inspires my interest in technology is not just the opportunities of today, but much more my sense of where things will be 10, 20, 30 years from now. I think this long view is very important to take. It allows you to look beyond the limitations and problems of current technology, and to concentrate more on the opportunities that are suggested by contemporary media, and that become extremely exciting when one considers how they may evolve.
>
> I say MAY evolve, because there are many dangers of limitations being imposed, as the technologies mature, if this maturation is only driven by commerce. It is incumbent on us to make sure that the cultural and intellectual communities get deeply involved in the

> maturation of new media so that they evolve in more inclusive, flexible, and even subversive ways.

I think it is safe to say that indeed new media, and in particular music technologies, did emerge in the ways that I hoped they would due to artists and academics inventing and exercising control over them. For example, the *Max/MSP* software environment that so many artists depend on was developed by Professor Miller Puckette at IRCAM and UCSD, where he has also created and continues to refine the widely used, open-source *Pd*. Similarly, Professor Tom Erbe built and has continued to develop his *Sound Hack* tools, making complex signal processing more accessible "for the benefit of the community," while Mark Coniglio's widely used video software *Isadora* grew out of his innovative work with the multimedia dance company Troika Ranch. The influence of these and other innovations have crossed over from experimental music circles to popular genres; for example, *Max for Live* has allowed Puckette's influence to infiltrate the most popular software used for electronic dance music (*Ableton Live*), opening it up to be a much more flexible and potentially user-defined environment.

At the same time, however, the past two decades have seen the consolidation of power into the hands of a few giant companies that own the most-widely used conduits of communication, posing grave dangers to society at large. And while we now have much greater access to music and the means of its production it is easy to imagine how this trend could be quickly and dangerously reversed.

> One thing we know for sure is that computers are playing an ever-growing role in all aspects of life and art. This may cause many to recoil given the clunky presence of computers, and the ugly and unnatural ways we interact with them. But I like to think ahead to what I refer to as mature computing. When the speed of the processor is no longer an issue, and there is enough number crunching, data storage, and network bandwidth to allow us to do anything we can imagine. When the microprocessor will grow so small, and the way we interact with it so seamless, that we will reach what many refer to as ubiquitous computing—that is—computers that are not seen, are all connected, and will interact with us by listening, seeing, speaking, even thinking.

Here, I must admit to being disappointed by a lack of progress. Storage is no longer a factor (due to hard drive capacity growth and price decreases, along with free cloud storage), and network bandwidth allows for better streaming media quality and new levels of fidelity for telematic collaboration.[3] Processor speed has advanced during much of this time at (at least) the rate of Moore's Law,[4] allowing us to do things on little laptop computers that once required a supercomputer. For example, in 2002 my piece *Ecosphere*[5] required two of the most powerful Apple computers, running at close to 100% of CPU capacity, and we still could not realize some of the plans I had for real-time signal processing. (We also occasionally had audible clicks but thankfully no crashes.) Now, I can run this same piece without compromise on my laptop, and it sounds great. Processors will obviously continue to get faster, smaller, and cheaper. This will enable better quality audio and make possible new complex signal processing techniques and far greater polyphony. Reduced hardware costs and open-source software will increasingly provide wider access to new generations of electronic musicians without the means to purchase expensive production resources (for example, *PD* running on a *Rasberry Pi* computer.)[6]

3. See Oliveros, Pauline, Sarah Weaver, Mark Dresser, Jefferson Pitcher, Jonas Braasch, and Chris Chafe, "Telematic Music: Six Perspectives," *Leonardo Music Journal* 19 (2009): 95-96 https://www.muse.jhu.edu/article/363707; and Roger Mills, "Telematics, Art and the Evolution of Networked Music Performance," in *Tele-Improvisation: Intercultural Interaction in the Online Global Music Jam Session* (Springer, 2019).

4. Gordon Moore, a co-founder of Intel, predicted that the number of transistors that could fit on a chip would double every year, leading to great improvements in computing capacity. But the pace slowed, and new ideas would need to emerge to continue the development of computing power. See Tom Simonite, "Moore's Law is Dead. Now What?" *MIT Technology Review*, May 13, 2016.

5. Rand Steiger, *Ecosphere* (2002) for sixteen instruments and electronics (produced in collaboration with Olivier Pasquet), commissioned by IRCAM and premiered by the Ensemble Intercontemporain at the Centre Pompidou in Paris. http://rand.info/rands/text/ircam.html

But computers are still ugly business machines, with counter-intuitive QWERTY keyboards and surprisingly few innovations in the way we interact with them. While some of us use voice assistants on smartphones to do simple tasks, voice recognition and task anticipation are far behind what was expected 20 years ago. Most musicians are still staring at screens, playing conventional midi keyboards, typing, and using a mouse or trackpad.

6. See Puckette on Pd/Rasberry Pi: https://vimeo.com/52265243

There have of course been wonderful developments in new musical interfaces unveiled every year at NIME, the Guthman Competiton, and elsewhere. Composer/performers like Jaime Oliver[7],

7. Oliver, J. "The MANO Controller: A Video Based Hand Tracking System" Proceedings of the International Computer Music Conference, New York, USA, 2010.

Laetitia Sonami, Michel Waisvisz, Pamela Z, and many others have built innovative flexible instruments that they use for their own artistic practice. But the deeper, richer, more elegant, or even invisible interfaces that I had hoped would evolve at the intersection of traditional instrument-building and electrical engineering have not emerged.

> Imagine an oboe that has a tiny sensor and processor in it that will ideally capture, analyze, and transmit wirelessly the signal produced by the oboist, without influencing it in anyway. The oboist can go into any concert hall and know that what they play can be easily transmitted to a digital system for perfectly calibrated amplification and recording. Furthermore, that signal can be sent wirelessly to a computer that will fully understand it, including the subtlest nuances, and then can respond by generating other voices, or processing the signal in remarkably rich ways. We're not far from that day. So don't let the current situation discourage you, while we deal with awkward wires and devices hanging off of instruments like inappropriate prostheses, and then reproduction systems that degrade and distort and cause difficulty when trying to interface this with a dumb computer that understands little more than pitch and rhythm. That may be where we are now, but it is clear that the clutter will fall away, and ideal opportunities will be there for those of us who are prepared to embrace them.
>
> We are still pioneers, and electro-acoustic instruments are still in the amphibious evolutionary state, having not completely abandoned swimming in the water of the 19th century salon, nor completely embraced walking on the land of the digital revolution.

Here too I am disappointed with a lack of progress. There have been some minor improvements to the quality of small, attachable microphones, but they are still analog and continue to require wires and connectors (or perhaps clunky wireless transmitters). The problem persists that when amplifying and applying signal processing to multiple acoustic instruments close placement of super-cardioid mics is required to avoid crosstalk. This in turn produces a less than optimal sound that is not commensurate with the way the performer aspires to sound and does sound in an acoustic environment with natural reverberation and diffusion. While it is theoretically possible to apply signal processing on a close mic signal to simulate what a more distant mic in an optimal acoustic environment would sound like, it is still very difficult to get right and takes enormous time and effort to calibrate in each new performance space. (This is an interesting research problem that I plan to continue to work on.)

20 years ago, I had imagined that new kinds of instruments would be developed in collaborations between instrument builders and electrical engineers that would combine the kind of acoustic instruments that performers are used to playing, with the tactile qualities and sound potential they demand, with built-in sensors and wireless transmitters that would not change the look or feel. I thought this would give us not only an uncompromised digital audio signal, but also much new data about exactly what the performer was doing and how the instrument was responding. My friend and colleague Miller Puckette asserts that we can deduce much of what is going on in the interaction of a performer and instrument through analysis of the signal alone (captured with a conventional microphone) and has made some advancements in that regard. But I continue to maintain that a robust and comprehensive set of sensors imperceptibly embedded in the instrument would lead to new forms of musical expression and creativity, and I'm disappointed that we are not much closer to this goal than we were 20 years ago.

On the other hand, there are promising signs in the application of artificial intelligence research to musical pursuits. While the predictions of Marvin Minsky[8] and others in the 1960s were overly optimistic, incremental progress has been made, and musicians have played an important role.[9]

8. Marvin Minsky (1927–2016) was widely considered the "father of artificial intelligence." See *What Marvin Minsky Still Means for AI* in *MIT Technology Review*, 1/26/16.

9. Michael Edwards: "Algorithmic Composition: Computational Thinking in Music", *Communications of the ACM*, July 2011, Vol. 54 No. 7, pp. 58–67.

Now imagine sitting at your desk with nothing on it but your pencil and a few sheets of paper. You take your pencil and jot down a musical phrase, and it is immediately played back to you. Not only that, but the lines of the paper you are writing on are immediately filled with 100 variations of this phrase based on processes automatically derived from analysis of your previous pieces. Those of you who have experimented with the *Patchwork* environment[10] (developed at the Sibelius Academy) know that the analysis and variation generation are already possible. In

10. Patchwork has evolved into PWGL: http://www2.siba.fi/PWGL/

fact, the only thing that is missing from the realization of this scenario is bi-directional, electro-luminescent paper, something that is predicted to be widely available within our lifetimes. In fact, the long-held dream of communication of large amounts of information without killing trees is becoming more and more likely.

More and more, performers are playing from tablets, and scores are being transmitted as digital files. Music notation on paper is fading away. Notation software continues to improve. A large chunk of the 20th century will be seen as an anomalous period, when much handwritten music was published because engraving had become too expensive, yet computer calligraphy was not yet available. Many composers have found ways to embed their signature style of calligraphy into computer typesetting (even creating their own fonts), and their scores no longer look bland and impersonal. And while we may not yet have the electronic paper interface I envisioned in my old essay, we surely have excellent software tools for the analysis and creation of music. I find the work of Trevor Bača, Josiah Oberholtzer, Jeffrey Treviño and others using Bača's *Abjad*[11] library to be among the most promising examples. These individuals are composing in computer code and automatically rendering the output as elegant musical scores (using the open-source engraving software LilyPond[12]), and creating original, compelling music. There are many other examples, and research and development of software for musical analysis, composition, and improvisation is flourishing.[13] We may still only be scratching the surface in regard to such tools, but they are available and growing more robust all the time.

11. Trevor Ba a, et al., "Abjad: an open-source system for formalized score control." *Proceedings of the First International Conference on Technologies for Music Notation and Representation* (TENOR 2015), Paris, France.

12. http://lilypond.org

13. See: *The Oxford Handbook of Algorithmic Music*, edited by Dean, Roger T., and Alex McLean.: Oxford University Press, 2018-02-22. https://www.oxfordhandbooks.com/view/10.1093/oxfordhb/9780190226992.001.0001/oxfordhb-9780190226992

Authors who bemoan the loss of the paper book will have nothing to worry about anymore. The distinction between paper and computer displays will break down, and we will have wonderful little interfaces that we can hold in our hands as we lay in bed just like a book, but better, for they will also be capable of interactive non-linear text, moving images, and sounds, and combining these and other parameters to produce as yet unimagined new kinds of literary experiences, housed in something that will feel and smell what-

> ever way you like, from that musty old book, to the sleek, space age personal digital assistant.

Of course, we now have tablets and e-readers, but the form they take is not configurable and is much more sterile and inflexible than I had predicted. And for the most part, conventional books are the only thing being read on these devices. I am perplexed as to why the possibilities of hyperlinks, interactivity, and multimedia enhancements have failed to be adopted by most authors and publishers. The technology is available to create non-linear and other novel literary experiences.

> Whether we are talking about books, music, or anything else, publishers are going to be obsolete. Of course, some of us feel they already are, especially in music. In any case, the days of publishers and record companies influencing what music will be performed and recorded, and of centralized broadcasters determining what we can hear, are close to being over. Already, you can easily create an online archive of your own music that can easily be accessed by anyone with a computer and a halfway decent net connection. But the power of self-publishing and broadcasting over the internet is only beginning to be realized.

Publishers and record companies are of course still with us, but things have changed substantially. They are no longer the gatekeepers. Creations of all kinds can be asserted by authors in multiple ways, and in recent years this has raised serious new problems for society at large, particularly in the way news is transmitted and can be used for pernicious political manipulation. But in the musical domain I believe that this decentralization is mostly a good thing. With wide access to the tools of production, distribution, and promotion, a much more inclusive and diverse community of musical artists is now thriving.

I don't mean to dismiss the value of the curatorial role of labels and publishers; I've come to realize that there will always be an important place for this in the music world, especially now that new, small companies are able to emerge and have immediate impact. But clearly there is a pressing need for new curatorial models in the music world beyond what labels, radio stations, and streaming services provide.

> Just two weeks ago (October 1998), a new piece of mine was premiered by the California EAR Unit on a concert in Seattle. The organization sponsoring the concert arranged to broadcast audio over the internet using Realmedia software. My parents in Miami Beach, and my sisters in New Jersey, and San Jose, Costa Rica, all listened to the concert as it occurred with their standard web browser and plugins, or in the case of my parents, their Webtv internet appliance.
>
> Soon much higher quality, multi-channel recordings, with or without video, will be able to be transmitted similarly, live from concerts, or on demand, from low cost computer servers. In fact, every new music forum[14] should be broadcast, just as the EAR Unit concert was, so that anyone interested can listen. Every one of you should have a web page with links to audio files and score images of the pieces you are most proud of. After all, locally the community of people interested in what we do is arguably small, but when our work becomes available to anyone with a net connection anywhere, the community becomes much larger, and it is our responsibility now to reach out and cultivate that potentially expanding community.

14. New Music Forum was the name of a concert series run back then by composers at UC San Diego. Interestingly, due to concerns about privacy and intellectual property law, the Department *still* does not webcast their concerts, although they are finally making preparations to do so.

This has surely come to pass. Many concerts are webcast live, and more and more concerts are documented with high-fidelity audio and video. For the younger generation of composers, if your music isn't available as streaming video, it practically doesn't exist. And due in large part to the work of Dan Tramte and his colleagues at Scorefollower.com, a wonderful new resource has emerged, where one can listen to new works while also reading the score as a scrolling video. If in 1998 it was important to alert young composers to the potential of maintaining a website with information about their music, this is now a ubiquitous prerequisite for any aspiring artist.

In my own case, I have chosen to not only maintain a personal website (for over 20 years now), but also to take an open-access approach to self-publishing driven in large part by bad experiences I had with music publishing companies. During the 1980s and 1990s, I was very active as a conductor focusing on contemporary music, primarily with the *California*

EAR Unit in Los Angeles and *Ensemble Sospeso* in New York. With very few exceptions, my experiences with publishers during that time were preposterously bad. Exorbitant rental charges for scores and parts were extremely problematic for the small organizations that engaged me as a conductor, sometimes making performances impossible, and the quality of materials that publishers sent us, even after paying hundreds of dollars, was often terrible (scores with pages printed upside down, barely legible, torn and tattered parts, etc.)

I once reached out to Donald Martino[15] when the EAR Unit was preparing to perform his 1974 Pulitzer Prize winning piece for chamber ensemble, *Noturno*. The publisher wanted hundreds of dollars to rent us the parts for one performance and would only allow us to have them for two weeks before the concert. We wanted to rehearse for six months and perform the piece many times. When I asked Martino if he could intervene, he responded that he couldn't even get his royalties from them, let alone get them to provide us with what we needed. (He actually encouraged us to bypass his publisher by photocopying the score and making our own parts.) Another time, I was engaged to conduct Boulez's *Le Marteau sans Maître.* At the first rehearsal, the performers told me the greatest obstacle they faced was that they could barely read the awful parts the publisher sent. I was able to reach out to Boulez through his assistant Astrid Schirmer, and within 24 hours an executive with the publisher called me from Europe to apologize and tell me that they had overnighted a brand new set of materials to us. But what if I hadn't had that personal connection? Even with the most distinguished establishment composers, this problem persisted throughout my entire conducting career[16].

15. Donald Martino (1931–2005) https://www.nytimes.com/2005/12/12/arts/donald-martino-74-creator-of-atonal-musical-works-dies.html

16. I chose to stop conducting in 2010 so that I might travel less, and focus entirely on composition.

These and many other experiences convinced me to refuse inquiries from publishers about my own music. I have instead adopted a strategy of making my music as readily accessible as possible to interested performers. My scores are easy to find on my website, and I provide the parts upon request. The previously mentioned advancements in digital files and tablet displays make that simpler than ever.

On the other hand, I am very grateful for the excellent care that small record labels (including CRI, New Focus, and New World) have demonstrated in distributing recordings of my music on CD and through digital services. I'm convinced that whether or not physical media continues to be manufactured and sold, there will always be a place for record labels, particularly those with a point of view and strong curatorial practices. At the same time, current and future platforms that enable artists to directly distribute their own recordings will assure that there will be a means of distribution available to all artists.

> Another reason for the demise of the record company is the decreasing price and increasing quality of the home-based project studio. Soon, dedicated hardware devices like synthesizers, effects processors, mixers, and tape recorders will all disappear, as their tasks will be better executed in software on rapidly improving computers. This assertion is easy to prove if one looks at issues of keyboard magazine over the past couple of years. Hardware companies like Lexicon and Yamaha are increasingly developing and marketing software products, for they themselves realize that the hardware business has a limited lifetime.
>
> Soon, an inexpensive desktop computer will provide a complete, professional quality music production tool. All of the following will be possible with this one device:
>
> —audio synthesis, sampling, signal processing, recording, and editing—CD, DVD, and new types of mastering for a one-off copy—or—to transmit to a factory for mass production
>
> —streaming audio on demand, in other words, world-wide broadcasting
>
> —assisted, algorithmic and notation-based composition with printing, and new means of transmission and display of the score

For too long the only way to make high-fidelity recordings was to work in extremely expensive recording studios, and therefore only projects that were supported by labels (or grants) could be produced, and the cost of creating physical media made it prohibitively expensive to distribute. All of that has changed. The means of production and distribution are now in the hands of artists. Labels continue to play a positive curatorial role, but they are no longer gatekeepers preventing innovation and diversity. And the act of recording, particularly in post-production, has become increasingly a means for new kinds of musical creativity. Composition and improvisation need not be frozen in the earliest stages of the recording but may carry all the way through the editing and mixing processes.

For the first 70 years of its existence, recording served primarily as a means of documenting a performance, but this changed beginning in the 1950s as artists became increasingly creative in the recording studio (musique concrete, early electronic music, Brian Wilson's *Pet Sounds*, the Beatles' *Sgt. Pepper*, etc.). The home studio further opened that up to most artists, and creative production continues to bring about exciting new musical results. A cycle of innovation has developed where new digital tools have emerged that are not copies of old analog devices, and bring new capacities (pitch correction, time compression and expansion, spectral processing, etc.).

What I hadn't predicted is the emergence of a passionate return-to-hardware movement. Analog, a term that was sometimes used pejoratively at the time of early digital optimism, now encompasses fidelity, nostalgia, and even fetishism (as demonstrated by the growing re-adoption of vinyl records). There is an explosion of creativity in the creation of analog modules sharing the widely adopted *Eurorack* format, with far more companies building a much wider range of modular devices than in the period of Moog and Buchla. We have also seen the start of a fascinating trend to reverse the hardware-to-software process; for example, MakeNoise, Inc., has collaborated with Tom Erbe to implement his *SoundHack* software in hardware modules, and Critter & Guitari are producing an elegant little musical instrument (Organelle) that runs *Pd*.

To what extent this is due to the unique qualities of modular systems, the failure of developing better interfaces for digital systems, or both, is an interesting matter for debate.

> Of course, even though the tools will be available to us, it isn't necessarily desirable for us to do all of the things that they make available ourselves. Much can be learned from the role of the producer in popular music. A new kind of musician will emerge, expert and creative in elegantly deploying new technologies in musical situations. We must create space for these new musicians, so they may be educated, employed and respected as essential members of our profession.

Here, too, I am disappointed by the lack of progress. The role of creative producer in popular music genres has still not really found its way into contemporary classical music to the extent I have hoped for. For many years now I have advocated for recognition and support of a new kind of musical profession, one in which the artist would study the full range of recording and computer music techniques, while also acquiring a traditional music education.[17] But even for those who manage to acquire such an education in an ad-hoc manner, compensation for and recognition of the roles these artists now play remains unsatisfactory. Too often computer musicians who play a vital role in large-scale collaborative works are not recognized as the distinguished artists they are.

17. European Tonmeister programs do this to a certain extent but are more focused on educating recording engineers and producers and do not typically include computer music techniques.

Some notable examples of such sustained and fruitful collaborations that took place at IRCAM include Pierre Boulez and Andrew Gerzso, Jonathan Harvey and Gilbert Nuono/Arshia Cont, Chaya Czernowin and Carlo Laurenzi, Philippe Manoury and Miller Puckette, and Kaija Saariaho with J.B. Barriere.[18] When I was a student, I worked as a producer on projects with Joan La Barbara, Morton Subotnick, and others; later on, as a composer I received crucial assistance from Andrew Allen, Olivier Pasquet, and in particular Miller Puckette, all of who have enabled me to do things that went beyond what I could have accomplished by myself.

18. Most of this collaborative work remains undocumented, but some of it is covered in Laura Zattra, *Collaborating on Composition: The Role of the Musical Assistant at IRCAM, CCRMA and CSC*, in *Live-Electronic Music. Composition, Performance and Study*, ed. Friedemann Sallis, Valentina Bertolani, Jan Burle, and Laura Zattra (Routledge, 2018). A more comprehensive book on this subject would be very valuable.

At best, open-minded and respectful collaborations can lead to unpredictable results that would not have occurred to either of the individuals involved when working alone. But at IRCAM this model remains controversial because of a lack of recognition and reasonable compensation for the artists who worked in the role of "Réalisateur," or as it was previously called, "musical assistant." Most of these extraordinary individuals ended up leaving IRCAM. Some went into academic positions, but the model of evaluation and advancement in universities only recognizes journal articles and compositions as publications, not distinguished collaborations like those mentioned, making appointment and advancement difficult if not impossible. This remains a serious disincentive for those who might want to pursue this career path and holds back advancements that might come from sustained collaborations that might otherwise occur.

Gerzso organized a conference at IRCAM in 2007 to examine these issues, and I was among those who presented papers that argued for greater recognition and support for this emerging profession. But 12 years later this is still a serious problem and missed opportunity (and there is no record of this conference on the IRCAM website or anywhere else online that I can find.[19]).

19. Archive.org has some remnants of the original conference webpage (RIM2007.ircam.fr), but IRCAM has erased the proceedings from their servers, including audio recordings of all the papers presented, which had previously been available.

One positive development in this arena is a growing trend for some contemporary music ensembles to include performers with highly developed technical abilities within the ensemble, in some cases in leadership roles. For example, the International Contemporary Ensemble includes among its artists Levy Lorenzo, listed both as a percussionist and sound engineer, as well as co-Artistic Director Ross Karre, who originally joined the ensemble as both a percussionist and video producer. The Switch~Ensemble includes among its ten ensemble members composer Jason Thorpe Buchanon, listed as both Artistic Director and sound engineer. The Talea ensemble includes composer David Adamcyk, with "electronics" listed as his instrument.

While not an official member of any ensemble, the composer/producer/engineer Ryan Streber is another very interesting example. Talea, ICE, the JACK Quartet, and many other ensembles and soloists have worked with Streber at his studio in Mount Vernon, New York, to create a remarkable body of work over the past 15 years. These recordings greatly benefit from Streber's deep understanding of the music, his audio artistry and production creativity, and the trust and collaborative bond he has developed with this generation of New York-based musicians.

At this point in my 1998 essay I returned to the subject of electronic publishing:

> It is easy to imagine how traditional music stands will be replaced by flat computer displays that will allow for traditional, but more importantly, new methods of musical notation, including the use of colors and three-dimensional images. Of course these will be networked, so instead of contacting a publisher, who will take $500 and then send inferior materials a few days before the concert—musicians will hit your web site from their music stand, paying if

you want them to, or not, and displaying the most up to date version of your score, whenever and wherever they wish. The dreaded page turn will be gone forever.

For the most part this has occurred, as more and more musicians are now playing from tablets with wireless pedals used for page turns. But the innovations in notation that these displays make possible have not emerged to the extent I had hoped, and most scores continue to use standard notation in black and white. But there are many notable examples of new approaches being developed and a professional organization (TENOR) has emerged that is about to have their fifth international convention.[20] I find the work of composer James Bean, whose software provides the performer with flexible tools to analyze, annotate and format their parts on their tablet, particularly interesting in this regard.[21]

20. Many of these innovations are documented in the proceedings of the TENOR conferences found at https://www.tenor-conference.org/

21. See James Bean, "DENM (Dynamic Environmental Notation for Music): Introducing a Performance-centric Music Notation Interface," *Proceedings of the First International Conference on Technologies for Music Notation and Representation* (TENOR), Paris, France, 2015.

This also suggests the intriguing possibility of artificial composers—that is—composing agents that we design and program, that will then spontaneously and continuously generate music, either as audio, or even as notation, beamed on to someone's music stand.

As discussed above there have been many advancements in algorithmic and computer-assisted composition. There are also now a number of companies that provide commercial music for film and games generated by algorithm. One company claims that their software will "inspire you to create beautiful music in no time," while another describes itself as "Artificial Intelligence composing emotional soundtrack music." A comprehensive overview of all the AI work being done in popular genres, commercial, and art music circles is beyond the scope of this essay.

Whether generated by us using conventional means, or by an algorithm we design, we can invite the listener, or performer, or both, into the creative process, giving them means for making decisions about the music that they are engaging that goes far beyond the bass and treble control of today, into the sonic detail, and even the structure of the work, should we be so inclined.

> When recording and broadcasting were introduced earlier in this century, they brought about drastic changes to the experience of music. Of course, there were many positive things. But passive music was invented, where for the first time you could have music in your home without playing it yourself or engaging someone to play it. So much has been lost, as people have turned away from folk and chamber music performance and turned increasingly to CDs quietly playing in the background as they wash their dishes and drive their cars.
>
> Another optimistic view of the future of computers and music is their potential to reverse this passive trend. Current Internet and DVD technology invites the creation of new interactive, and far more engaged ways of experiencing music. Among them is the possibility of using telecommunications for long distance musical collaboration. I'll talk more about this issue next time, but I wanted to end my optimistic rant on an even more utopian notion—that as the 20th century draws to a close, passive music is bound to fade away, and may be looked back on as a strange anomalous period in music history. The relationship between music creator, transmitter, and receiver can all begin to interact fluidly in new, experimental relationships. The role of folk and chamber music in the local village can now be taken up by multi-user, visual music collaboration in the global village.

It would seem that my optimism back then that new technologies would encourage new forms of participatory and more deeply engaged listening has not panned out. In all musical genres it seems that most listeners want recordings that are a completed, inflexible product that represents the one ideal rendering of the artists intentions. Here I am reminded of lyrics from the song *Freedom of Choice* by the rock band Devo: "Freedom of Choice is what you got, freedom from choice is what you want."

In popular music there have been some interesting examples of using technology to encourage deeper engagement from the listener, including Peter Gabriel's *Xplora1* and Bjork's *Biophilia.* But despite the initial excitement, attempts to create interactive platforms have largely failed. The Romplr app was available on smartphones for a few years and at its peak enabled remixing of forty songs from various popular artists. But it has now vanished, with very little information about it available online.

I am perplexed as to why there aren't more examples of innovative, interactive recordings in a wider range of musical genres, and why there has been a trajectory towards even more passive listening, with even less audio fidelity (perhaps the convenience of "smart-speakers" is the biggest culprit). Could part of the reason be that by our very nature most composers want complete control of their creations, and this limits our imagination for developing new forms of interactive music?

It seems that those listeners who feel compelled to intervene migrate towards their own creative work, perhaps starting with the tools of remix and DJ culture, with that ultimately evolving into their own creative practice. That of course is not at all a bad thing and has led to some very interesting work. But I still feel as though there should be new musical experiences possible for listeners who do not wish to be creators but who would be intrigued by the possibility of navigating different versions of the same composition. We see this in a limited way when serious listeners curate musical experiences for their friends through the creation of playlists. Opening our music up to interventions such as navigating paths through the music to create different formal structures or rebalancing the different voices in a polyphonic texture, while maintaining the integrity of the composition in all possible outcomes, is possible. And I think it may in fact be *necessary* as a step towards reversing the passive way most people experience recorded music now.

> All that stands in the way of that happening in a rich, and meaningful way, is our willingness to engage in the process of cultivating a desirable future by embracing the problematic technology of today, while looking to the mature technology of the future for inspiration.

It is now over 140 years since the invention of recording and 110 years since the invention of broadcasting. Those revolutionary technologies, along with the migration of innovation in musical instruments from the mechanical, to the electrical, electronic, and finally digital domain, ushered in a century of revolutionary changes to the way music is made and disseminated. But while those disruptions are still unfolding to some degree, I believe we are finally entering into a post-technology period, where the means of production will no longer be the driving force in musical innovation. Incremental improvements and innovations will of course continue to emerge, and commercial interests will attempt to foster excitement around them to generate sales. While it is still valuable and advisable, I no longer feel it is as crucial for artists to engage in the research that drives technological advancement as I did back in 1998.

The tools have matured and proliferated and an abundant new repertoire of musical innovations from a large and diverse community of musical artists is flourishing. There is a wonderful emergence of many new, alternative, decentralized venues for live performance; more academic programs that focus on the present and future of music; a much greater openness to new repertoire among the large institutions, and the emergence of many new performing ensembles. Most importantly, through all these means there have been real efforts to achieve greater diversity and gender parity. There is much to be optimistic about in the state of the musical arts.

But at a time when democracy faces the most serious threats in a generation here in the United States and abroad, when economic justice is regressing, and when we face grave consequences from increasingly irresponsible ecological stewardship, I believe it is much more important for artists to engage in political activism. For the very conditions that enabled the present flourishing of musical life are now threatened.

My final and primary response to my 1998 self is that the era of optimistic technological futurism is over, and the imperative for political activism is urgently upon us.

CHAPTER 33

ENGINEERING NEW MUSIC

RYAN STREBER

I co-own and run Oktaven Audio, a recording studio that specializes in classical and jazz. In this capacity, I'm fortunate to work as an engineer with many incredible and inspiring artists from a wide range of styles and traditions. The projects I engineer largely involve music conceived (and usually written down in some form of notation) by a composer and performed by a soloist or ensemble. Occasionally the composer participates in that performance, but that is the exception. Given that we record a lot of contemporary music, the composer is often directly involved with the larger recording; although, just as often, the composer is absent or has been dead for many years.

I studied composition in a conservatory, and my initial forays into engineering were informed by my biases as a composer—biases that were molded by a modernist, "uptown" perspective. My view was that a composer's ultimate creation is a score, and a recording of a piece would then be just an audio document of an execution of that score. I began engineering recordings with the explicit goal of maximizing accuracy and faithfulness to the score, exercising as much control as possible over the raw audio material so as to hammer it into the most literal sonic translation of the notation as possible. The resultant recording was utilitarian, a means to an end... the most convenient way to experience the composer's intentions.

After working as a professional engineer for 20 years, the past 10 at Oktaven, my idea of the nature and purpose of a recording has changed. I've come to believe that recordings are documents of *performances*, and performance is where players' interpretation creates the end result of the composer's creation. That is, if we're talking about a recording that recreates the sounds made by a person or group of people performing together in some shared space and time, regardless of whether they're improvising or reading notation, then the core of what's being captured is still the sound being made by their performance. The performance of the score is the work, and it needs to stand on its own as a unique creation.

Any recording will probably contain hundreds of edits and all manner of electronic manipulations. But we're still listening to the work that living, breathing performers did in front of some microphones. For a listener who is not reading along with the score, the recording of that performance *is* the piece, and it is our job to make that recording as good as it can be, serving the intentions not only of the composer but of the performer as well.

This shift in emphasis, from a focus on the recording as a document of the composer's work to a shared product of collaboration between composer and performer, is in some ways subtle, but in many ways of vital importance to my work as an engineer. I don't feel less committed to the importance of accuracy or have any less respect for the composer's intentions as communicated on the page. However, years of engagement with the practical problems of music making that we have to confront every time we make a recording, as well as my accumulated experiences with recordings that were satisfying and successful on some level, have led me to an ever-greater appreciation for, interest in, attention to, and care about the performer's role.

The best experiences that I've had in the studio have come not only from a great composition, but from a great performance of that composition, from a composer's and performer's work coming together to result in something about which they both feel some mutual sense of ownership and pride. What can or should composers do in the writing of their music to help promote this kind of relationship? What can I do as an engineer to facilitate this?

Pieces shouldn't be easy or comfortable. Most musicians that I know want to be challenged, and they excel when they're able to push themselves in productive and rewarding ways. But if a composer's intentions for a piece leave little room for (or even work against) the performer's strengths, their creativity and flexibility, their humanity and physicality, then the actual recording likely will be flawed.

As with most things, we can't be simplistic here, and there are composers that make interesting or moving music out of intentionally alienating or disorienting a performer. But in general, I would like for more composers to ask themselves if that is really what they're going for. Do they really want the performer to feel like they're fighting their instrument? Or do they really view the performer as a human substitute for MIDI playback of a sampler? Is their piece really best served by casting a performer (who has probably spent the better part of their waking life practicing and cultivating a highly-refined and sensitive command of their instrument) in the role of an inevitably-imperfect reproducing machine?

This all might seem obvious, and I think there's an extent to which some agreement with what I'm saying would be taken for granted. And yet on countless occasions in the studio, I've seen performers struggle in one way or other to negotiate writing that doesn't give much thought to them, the challenges they're facing, or whether those challenges are "consonant" with the intended musical effect of the piece they're struggling to play. Whether it be careless or unnecessarily-complicated notation, unidiomatic writing, passages that are difficult (or even impossible) in ways that aren't interesting or apparent to the listener and therefore give the performer very little reward for their labor, etc... To see a performer working like mad to play something that would sound mundane through playback in Sibelius or Finale is one of my greatest pet peeves. And it's exceedingly common.

On the other hand, to see and hear a performer play a piece that they can inhabit as if they're improvising, or that they can shape in a way that palpably excites them creatively and expressively—that is not only a joy but usually provides a clear reminder of why we do this in the first place. This is something that is unrelated to style, and I've had this type of elevating experience with pieces that were as conventional or as "out" as one can imagine.

The success or failure of a performance is not solely the composer's responsibility. There are countless reasons why a performer might not give a composer's work its due, and many of those factors may or may not be within the composer's (or performer's) control. It may seem unfair for me to place so much of the responsibility on the composer here. But composers who embrace the role of the performer in a real and meaningful way and give as much consideration to the real-world experience of playing the piece as they give to any other domain of their compositional process will yield compositions that not only serve their intentions better but will also be more rewarding for performers to play and (mostly likely) for audiences to hear.

Working in the studio, we hear everything under a microscope, so to speak. This has a tendency not only to magnify details but also heighten the performer's experience of playing in both positive and negative ways. I've become accustomed to hearing things like breaths, key-clicks, small vocalizations, and so on. To me, so many of these human or mechanical noises (barely noticeable in a live performance but magnified as they tend to be in a recording studio) are parts of the sound of an actual performance... within limits, of course. Anything can be excessive or distracting in excess, and loud snorts, grunts, creaks, and so on are usually undesirable and perhaps better if avoided or attenuated. However, it's strange to me when a composer expects every tiny sonic trace of the physicality of a performance to be removed, or when there's an assumption that an uncomfortable performance of a carelessly-written or awkward passage will be smoothed out and made to sound fluid with digital editing. This can make the performer even more self conscious or minimize their role, and it tends to move attention away from bigger musical questions and goals.

More importantly, I have found that intolerance of these small issues often speaks to a broader attitude towards live performance and a lack of attention to the realities of playing acoustic instruments in the physical world. In my opinion, a composer would better serve both their own work as well as their performer's (and audience's) experience of it by factoring these "realities" into the composition in thoughtful and meaningful ways rather than thinking of them as unfortunate blemishes that are somehow separate from the "real" piece.

For example, if a composer writes a passage in which a violinist sustains a very high double-stop at *ppp* for 20 seconds, this is going to yield a certain kind of sound and texture that might be very different in reality than in one's imagination. There will be elements like bow changes and bow noise that the score doesn't account for, some shakiness and inconsistency in the note's duration, difficulty controlling the attack and release, fatigue and tension that might influence how surrounding material is played, etc.

A composer might write such a thing and wishfully think that the ideal performer will be able to execute it perfectly, and that until that happens someone looking at the score will imagine the sound that the composer had in mind. In a recording situation, we'd probably find a way to edit out the inconsistencies and make it sound very close to the ideal. But this might put the performer in a thankless and compromised role. Why not write it differently or embrace what it actually sounds like and make it meaningful in the context of the piece? That idea could be extended to millions of examples, and such an awareness is a part of the compositional process that I fear is less practiced now than ever.

As an engineer, I find that much of my attention and effort in a session goes towards negotiating many of these issues. I alluded to this earlier, but a recording session, more than a concert setting, can be a stressful and disorienting experience for performers and composers alike. The attention to detail and hyper-awareness of minutiae can be both rewarding and alienating. My job often comes down to finding ways to support the artists in the moment, balancing the need for a sufficient quality and quantity of material to work from with the risks of fatigue and diminishing returns that usually come from driving a performer into an overly-self-conscious head space. This job is made far more easy when the material we're recording is in some way or other inherently rewarding or gratifying for the performer to play.

As a side note, for the sake of this essay I'm focusing on acoustic music and largely ignoring projects using electronics, live processing, lots of studio production, overdubbing, and so on. I'm not a die-hard advocate for purist or minimalist approaches or for viewing classical recordings as some kind of virtual concert experience. Done well and in the right context, such approaches can yield amazing recordings, but that isn't appropriate or practical for many of the projects on which I work. I'm an advocate for the "whatever works" tactic and do my best to adapt my skill set and tools to a specific project's needs.

On virtually every project, it's practically a given that editing work of some kind or other will be a part of the production process. We have a vast array of tools at our disposal to manipulate a recording in every way imaginable, and those tools can serve purposes as varied as refining an already-inspired performance or cobbling together something passable or even excellent from substandard component parts. I don't believe that there is any inherent vice or virtue in the tools or in how we use them, as every project is different and demands its own set of priorities and techniques. There's little room for dogmatism in my world, and nothing is absolute. What might seem heavy-handed or artificial for one record could be too subtle or naturalistic for another.

But I do question the approach of breaking something in order to be able to fix it, an approach that I've seen taken by composers, performers, and engineers alike. For the purposes of this essay, I would simply caution composers against writing in a way that depends upon the technology, upon editing or "fixing it in the mix", without considering how such an approach actually does or doesn't square with the piece's expressive and aesthetic intent. Given the technology available now and surely to an ever greater extent with each passing year, it's almost never a question of what's possible, only of what's artistically successful and satisfying for the people involved in making a recording as well as for those who will hear it.

So many of these questions are peculiar to the specific composer-performer dynamic that has evolved in classical performance practice over the past two centuries. In contrast, it has been something of a revelation for me to work with improvisers. The experience of making recordings where there is no clear distinction between intent and execution and where the divide between composer and performer has been evaded or erased has only underlined the inherent challenges that classical composers and performers face. In the past few years, there seems to have been a refreshing increase in the number of artists who wear both hats, and one would expect that this might lead to a healthy blurring of the divide as well.

Yet, I don't want to suggest that we should denounce or diminish the "composer as specialist." The modernist in me demands a continued appreciation and even reverence for the kind of work that only a composer working at a remove from real-time performance can achieve. And as I've seen over my years as an engineer, there are many instances where a good studio recording is virtually the only way to craft an ideal representation of a piece in all its detail. I would just exhort composers, regardless of their aesthetic or philosophical bent, to appreciate and embrace the practical reality that a performance (whether heard in a concert or on a recording) *is* their work.

ABOUT THE MUSICIANS

Bruce Ackley, 1948, Rochester. Soprano, tenor saxophones, B♭ clarinet. Listening was first: Danny Kaye (!), the oboe and English horn, doo wop, 45s. Choir, glee club, always singing. At 15: COLTRANE. Always records. Studied painting and photography. 1970: first soprano sax. Improvising constant, I got no rhythm section. Blues, pan-African abstraction. LACY, BRAXTON. Sound Clinic, Zorn, Chadbourne, Kaiser, Planet X, ROVA, Actual Size (playing my stuff). Always Rova. Creating music is like creating any art: nothing is pre-ordained; all aspects of a work are subject to inquiry/discovery/open design. Form follows function. Boulez, Stockhausen, Webern, Ives, Xenakis. More listening, more Rova, more improvisation. Nested in community rich with improvisers harvesting meaning in the moments. Touring, recording, playing nightly is key to understanding and movement. LIFE pertains, music sustains. Rova: no end in sight.

Bruce Ackley

John Luther Adams

For John Luther Adams, music is a lifelong search for home—an invitation to slow down, pay attention, and remember our place within the larger community of life on earth. Living for almost 40 years in northern Alaska, JLA discovered a unique musical world grounded in space, stillness, and elemental forces. In the 1970s and into the '80s, he worked full time as an environmental activist. But the time came when he felt compelled to dedicate himself entirely to music. He made this choice with the belief that, ultimately, music can do more than politics to change the world. Since that time, he has become one of the most widely admired composers in the world, receiving the Pulitzer Prize, a Grammy Award, and many other honors. In works such as *Become Ocean*, *In the White Silence*, and *Canticles of the Holy Wind*, Adams brings the sense of wonder that we feel outdoors into the concert hall. And in outdoor works such as *Inuksuit* and *Sila: The Breath of the World*, he employs music as a way to reclaim our connections with place, wherever we may be. A deep concern for the state of the earth and the future of humanity drives Adams to continue composing. As he puts it: "If we can imagine a culture and a society in which we each feel more deeply responsible for our own place in the world, then we just may be able to bring that culture and that society into being." Since leaving Alaska, JLA and his wife Cynthia have made their home in the deserts of

Mexico, Chile, and the southwestern United States. JLA is the author of three books, most recently *Silences So Deep* (Farrar, Straus, Giroux 2020), a memoir of his life in Alaska.

Drummer, composer, and educator Jim Black has become one of the most in-demand drummers in avant-garde jazz and experimental rock since emerging as a key member of the New York downtown scene during the '90s. Born in Daily City, CA in 1967 and raised in the fertile musical scene of Seattle, WA, he moved to Boston and graduated from Berklee College of Music by 1989. During that time Black and his Seattle colleagues Chris Speed and Andrew D'Angelo formed the band Human Feel with guitarist Kurt Rosenwinkel. By 1991, Black and the other members of Human Feel had moved to Brooklyn, NY, where they found a home in the Downtown music scene then centered around the Knitting Factory and rapidly became among the city's busiest sidemen. Black's early years in New York saw him take featured roles in some of the most critically acclaimed bands of the time, like Tim Berne's Bloodcount, Ellery Eskelin's trio, Pachora, and Dave Douglas' Tiny Bell Trio. Thus, began thirty years of near-constant touring and recording, with the above bands as well as artists like Uri Caine, Dave Liebman, Lee Konitz, Steve Coleman, Tomasz Stanko, Nels Cline, and Laurie Anderson. In 2000, Black started the rock inspired quartet AlasNoAxis, recording six albums of his compositions for the German label Winter & Winter. In 2010 he formed the Jim Black Trio with pianist Elias Stemeseder and Thomas Morgan on bass, recording a total of four albums, their latest award-winning release Reckon is available on the Swiss label Intakt.

Jim Black

Martin Bresnick

Carter Burwell

Martin Bresnick's compositions, from opera, chamber and symphonic music to film scores and computer music, are performed throughout the world. Bresnick delights in reconciling the seemingly irreconcilable, bringing together repetitive gestures derived from minimalism with a harmonic palette that encompasses both highly chromatic sounds and more open, consonant harmonies and raw power. Martin Bresnick is also recognized as an influential teacher of composition. Students from every part of the globe and of virtually every musical inclination have been inspired by his critical encouragement. Martin Bresnick's compositions are published by Carl Fischer Music Publishers, New York; Bote & Bock, Berlin; CommonMuse Music Publishers, New Haven; and have been recorded by Cantaloupe Records, New World Records, Albany Records, Bridge Records, Composers Recordings Incorporated, Centaur, Starkland Records and Artifact Music.

Carter Burwell has composed the music for over ninety feature films, including *Blood Simple, Raising Arizona, Miller's Crossing, Barton Fink, Rob Roy, Fargo, The Spanish Prisoner, Gods and Monsters, Velvet Goldmine, Being John Malkovich, Before Night Falls, Adaptation, In Bruges, Twilight, True Grit, Anomalisa, Carol,* and *Three Billboards Outside Ebbing, Missouri.* His theater work includes the chamber opera *The Celestial Alphabet Event* and the Mabou Mines productions

Mother and *Lucia's Chapters of Coming Forth by Day*. In 2005 he developed a concert work for text and music titled *Theater of the New Ear*, presented in New York, London and Los Angeles. The text, by Joel and Ethan Coen and Charlie Kaufman, was performed by a dozen actors including Meryl Streep, Steve Buscemi, Philip Seymour Hoffman, Hope Davis, Peter Dinklage, and Jennifer Jason Leigh. The music was performed by the Parabola Ensemble, conducted by Mr. Burwell. His dance compositions include the pieces *The Return of Lot's Wife*, choreographed by Sara Pearson and Patrik Widrig, and *RABL*, choreographed by Patrice Regnier. He has performed around the world with his own ensembles as well as others, such as The Harmonic Choir. His writing includes the essay *Music at Six: Scoring the News Then and Now*, published in the inaugural issue of Esopus magazine in 2003 and reprinted in Harper's Magazine, and the essay *No Country For Old Music* in the 2013 *Oxford Handbook of New Audiovisual Aesthetics*. He has taught and lectured at New York University, Columbia University, The Sundance Institute, and Harvard University.

ANN CLEARE is an Irish composer working in the areas of concert music, opera, extended sonic environments, and hybrid instrumental design. A recipient of a 2019 Ernst von Siemens Composer Prize, her work has been commissioned and presented by broadcasters such as the BBC, NPR, ORF, RTÉ, SWR, WDR for festivals such as Wittenertage fur Neue Kammermusik, International Music Institute Darmstadt, Huddersfield Contemporary Music Festival, Ultraschall, Rainy Days, and MATA, working with ensembles such as: The International Contemporary Ensemble, ELISION, JACK Quartet, Yarn/Wire, ensemble mosaik, Musikfabrik, and RTÉ National Symphony Orchestra. Ann studied at University College Cork, IRCAM, and holds a Ph.D. from Harvard University. Her scores are published by Project Schott New York. She is Assistant Professor of Music and Media Technologies at Trinity College Dublin. Further information can be found on her website: https://annclearecomposer.com

Ann Cleare

Bram de Looze

BRAM DE LOOZE is a Belgian pianist whose distinct musical vision has found its way through both solo piano projects and collaborations with internationally acclaimed musicians. De Looze's unique technical skill and musical maturity have earned him considerable critical praise and respect from his peers, as his music spotlights his far-ranging interests throughout his continuous quest for artistic depth, momentum and freedom. In his teens De Looze made his entrance to the European scene with LABtrio, a collaboration with bassist Anneleen Boehme and drummer Lander Gyselinck. After having spent 1 year at the New School For Jazz And Contemporary Music in New York, De Looze launched his first international 7-piece band Septych (Clean Feed Records 2015). De Looze currently plays with internationally renowned musicians such as Joey Baron (MiXMONK—Baron/De Looze/Verheyen), Stephane Galland (The Mystery of KEM feat. Ravichandra Kulur) and with multiple improvisation ensembles led by Dré A. Hočevar (Coding of Evidentiality, Verso Doxa). These collaborations have taken him throughout the world to perform at cultural institutions, music venues and celebrated festivals. His solo career took off with *Piano e Forte* (2016), a project for which he approached historical instruments from a contemporary perspective combined with the integration of non-equal tuning systems. The switch to the Chris Maene Straight Strung Grand Piano for *Switch The Stream* (2018) indicated a renewed search for movement, evolution and introspection. Infusing the sound with non-equal tuning stands out even more in his newest solo chapter, *Colour Talk* (2020). It continues this trajectory with another revolutionary piano model, and a continued attempt to renew from within.

ZOSHA DI CASTRI is a Canadian composer/pianist living in New York. Her work (which has been performed in Canada, the US, South America, Asia, and Europe) extends beyond purely concert music, including projects with electronics, sound arts, video and dance. She recently completed *Hunger* for the Montreal Symphony Orchestra with improvised drummer, which accompanies Peter Foldes' 1973 silent film. She also wrote *Long Is the Journey, Short Is the Memory* for orchestra and chorus, opening the first night of the 2019 BBC Proms, with the BBC Symphony, the BBC Singers, and conductor Karina Canellakis at Royal Albert Hall. Other large-scale projects include an evening-length new music theatre piece, *Phonobellow* (co-written with David Adamcyk) for five musicians, large kinetic sound sculpture, electronics, and video in a reflection on the influence of photography and phonography on perception. Her orchestral compositions have been commissioned by John Adams, the San Francisco Symphony, New World Symphony, Esprit Orchestra, the OSM, and the BBC, and have been featured by the Tokyo Symphony, Amazonas Philharmonic, TSO, and the Cabrillo Festival Orchestra among others. Zosha has worked with the Chicago Symphony, the L.A. Philharmonic, and the New York Philharmonic in their chamber music series, as well as with many leading new music groups including Talea Ensemble, Wet Ink, ICE, Ekmeles, the NEM, JACK Quartet, and Ensemble Cairn. She was the recipient of the Jules Léger Prize for New Chamber Music, and participated in IRCAM's Manifeste Festival in Paris, writing an electronic work for the dance company ZOO. Other recent projects include a piece for Yarn/Wire, a solo piano work for Julia Den Boer, a piano/violin duo with Jenny Koh, and a string octet. Zosha was an inaugural fellow at the Institute for Ideas and Imagination in Paris, and is the Francis Goelet Assistant Professor of Music at Columbia University.

Zoshra Di Castri

Ganavya Doraiswamy

Critically acclaimed vocalist GANAVYA DORAISWAMY (b. 1991) lives, learns, and loves fluidly from the nexus of many frameworks. Hers is a deeply profound voice. A transdisciplinary creator trained as an improviser, scholar, dancer, and multi-instrumentalist, she works as a soundsmith and wordsmith. She maintains an "inner library of spi/ritual blueprints" offered to her by an intergenerational constellation of collaborators, continuously anchoring her practice in pasts, presents, and futures. Much of her childhood was on the pilgrimage trail, learning the storytelling art form of *harikathā*, singing poetry that critiques hierarchical social structures. She is a co-founder of the non-hierarchical *We Have Voice Collective.* Ganavya holds degrees in theatre (Broward Community College) and psychology (FIU), with graduate degrees in Contemporary Performance (Berklee College of Music), ethnomusicology (UCLA), and Creative Practice and Critical Inquiry (Harvard). Both as an educator and student, she "wishes to study and bring liberative techniques into this world... study certain dyads: what empowers, who is disempowered; what heals, who is ailing—and wishes to wed the two" in her practice. Recent works include a 64-hour piece titled *Atlas Unlimited: Acts VII–X* (2019) where she continuously generated material from the narrative of Zakaria Almoutlak, a Syrian with refugee status; *Daughter of a Temple* (2019) a 56'51" composition for megaphones, drawing on Alice Coltrane-Turiyasangītānandā's *Monument Eternal*, the sound installation premiering at the 13th Havana Biennial; and *Vimalakīrti Nirdesa Sutrā Chapter 7: The Goddess* (2019) directed by Peter Sellars, featuring Ganavya (composition, voice, electronics) and Michael Schumacher (choreography, dance). Selected forthcoming works include *How To Cure A Ghost: The Album*, songs made from Fariha Róisín's poetry; *Chapter 2: Inconceivable Skill in Liberative Technique,* directed by Peter Sellars, featuring Ganavya (composition, voice), Michael Schumacher (choreography, dance), and Wang Dongling (calligraphy); and *Let's Go Out and Play*, commissioned by Jerome Foundation for Roulette Intermedium.

SAM EASTMOND is a composer, arranger and trumpet player based in London, England. Aged 13 he started his first big band, writing music and drafting in friends to play his pieces. This pattern has continued for 27 years. His big band the Spike Orchestra recorded volumes in *Book Two* and *Three* of John Zorn's *Masada* books. He also runs *Gulgoleth* and Historical Treasures of Atlantis. Projects set up to work with different approaches to composition and ensemble playing. He plays trumpet in TORU and Moss Freed's Union Division, ensembles devoted to free improvisation.

Sam Eastmond

Danny Elfman

DANNY ELFMAN was born 1953 in Los Angeles. His parents were school teachers. At an early age he became a horror/fantasy movie fanatic and more or less spent every weekend of his childhood in his neighborhood theater. Other than an early interest in chemistry, biology and rocket building (which almost cost him some fingers) his youth was mostly unremarkable and ordinary. Upon graduating high school he embarked on what was supposed to be a year-long journey around the world but instead spent the year traveling across Africa. Upon returning to Los Angeles he immediately joined up with his brother Richard in a musical theatrical troupe called The Mystic Knights of the Oingo Boingo. Initially they were a street theater troupe but evolved into a bizarre multimedia musical cabaret ensemble which lasted 17 years. In the late '70s Elfman was taken with the arrival of ska music from London and founded the rock group Oingo Boingo in that model. They recorded a dozen albums over their 17-year run and then retired in 1995. In 1985 Elfman was approached by Tim Burton to score his first feature film *Pee Wee's Big Adventure* and that quickly started his film scoring career that is still active today. He has at this date scored over 100 films including sixteen more films with Mr. Burton. Elfman currently lives in Los Angeles with his wife and son. He also has two adult daughters from a previous marriage.

SASHA FRERE-JONES is a writer and musician from New York.

Sasha Frere-Jones
Leo Genovese
Kate Gentile
Osvaldo Golijov
Russell Greenberg

LEO GENOVESE was born in Argentina in 1979. He moved to the United States in 2001. He has been traveling the world playing music for the last 20 years. He has eleven albums as a leader and dozens as a sideman. He believes in music as a force of change. He practices the saxophone in hotel rooms. He doesn't support MP3 culture. He cooks pretty spicy food, like his music.

KATE GENTILE is a Brooklyn-based drummer and composer. As a leader, Kate released *Mannequins* (Skirl Records) in 2017 with Jeremy Viner, Matt Mitchell and Adam Hopkins. Her current band, Find Letter X, features Mitchell, Viner, and Kim Cass on bass. Collaborative bands Kate is a part of include Snark Horse, in which she co-leads and shares compositional duties with pianist Matt Mitchell, and Secret People, the cryptic jazz/noise rock trio with guitarist Dustin Carlson and saxophonist Nathaniel Morgan. Kate also plays in Mitchell's projects *Phalanx Ambassadors* (Pi Recordings 2019) and *A Pouting Grimace* (Pi Recordings 2017), and Dustin Carlson's septet *Air Ceremony* (Out of Your Head Records 2018). Kate has also worked with Michaël Attias, Tim Berne, Anthony Braxton, Cloud Becomes Your Hand, Steve Coleman, Dave Douglas, Marty Ehrlich, Michael Formanek, God Is My Co-Pilot, Helado Negro, Miles Okazaki, Chris Speed, Anna Webber, and John Zorn.

OSVALDO GOLIJOV grew up in an Eastern European Jewish household in La Plata, Argentina. Born to a piano teacher mother and physician father, Golijov was raised surrounded by classical chamber music, Jewish liturgical and klezmer music, and the new tango of Astor Piazzolla. He lived in Jerusalem before immigrating to the United States in 1986. His blending of genres and seamless integration of voices speak volumes about his approach and style, a musical language that can only be termed "Golijovian." His most recent work is *Falling out of Time*, an 80-minute long song cycle written for the SilkRoad Ensemble. He is the Loyola Professor of Music at the College of the Holy Cross in Worcester, MA, where he has taught since 1991.

New York-based percussionist RUSSELL GREENBERG enjoys exploring creative and unclassifiable music. Internationally sought-after for his singular approach and interpretation, he strives to share his passion for the musical experience with a wide variety of audiences. As a founding member of the piano and percussion quartet, Yarn/Wire, Russell has collaborated with many of today's leading composers to craft a body of new, wide-reaching and vital repertoire. At the vanguard of contemporary music, Russell frequently tours the world, having appeared at the Ultima (Oslo), Tectonics (Glasgow), Lincoln Center (NY), Barbican (UK), and Rainy Days (Luxembourg) festivals among others, and is a regular visiting artist at universities including UC Berkeley, Columbia, Brown, and others. Russell is also member of Either/OR and the Wet Ink Large Ensemble, and has appeared with other prominent groups as well such as the International Contemporary Ensemble (ICE), Argento, and sfSound. He has worked with a many leading composers and conductors including Pierre Boulez, Peter Eötvös, Susanna Mälkki, Enno Poppe, Beat Furrer, and others. In addition to his work with contemporary music ensembles, Russell has toured and recorded with Nate Wooley, Travis LaPlante, Seaven Teares, Kayo Dot, and Hi Red Center.

Originally from Osaka, Japan, Sae Hashimoto is an exhilarating percussionist in New York City. Her versatile performances attract audiences from a wide variety of genres. She has served as guest timpanist with the New York Philharmonic and New York City Ballet Orchestra. She currently serves as the principal timpanist of New Jersey-based orchestra Symphony in C. From 2018 to 2020, she served as the percussionist of Ensemble Connect, a fellowship program of Carnegie Hall for extraordinary young professional classical musicians. As a passionate advocate for contemporary music, she has premiered over ten works by avant garde composer John Zorn, two of which are recorded in a CD titled *Interpretation of Dreams* under Tzadik label. She has performed his music at venues throughout New York and beyond, such as National Sawdust, the Village Vanguard, the Frick Collection, the Guggenheim Museum, the Miller Theatre, Boston's Gardiner Museum, the Art Institute of Chicago and the Silesian Museum in Katowice, Poland. She was a recipient of the Kovner Fellowship at the Juilliard School where she received her BM and MM degrees.

Sae Hashimoto

David Holzman

Pianist David Holzman has won international acclaim for his recitals, recordings and writings. His early studies were at The Chatham Square Music School. He graduated from The Mannes College of Music in 1972, studying piano with Paul Jacobs. His career began soon after as he became involved in New York's new music scene, first as pianist with The Light Fantastic Players, and as free-lance performer. Later, his focus was largely upon the solo repertoire. He has premiered more than 200 solo works and recorded many of them. His reputation is based largely upon his championing of many of the 20th century's most noted and challenging composers. His first Stefan Wolpe CD for Bridge received many awards, both for pianism and liner notes. He has recorded five more CDs for Bridge, most recently *At All Device,* featuring solo works of John McDonald. He has written essays on pianistic, compositional and personal subjects for periodicals such as Sonus and Contemporary Music Review. *The Battle of the Senses* describes his pianistic struggles with hearing loss. His recent film *Deep River,* which also describes pianistic challenges, was shown at the Aural Diversity Conference in England in 2019. His next CD will feature the music of James Ricci and Arnold Schoenberg. He is currently working with Resound Hearing Aids and Cochlear to help them make their hearing devices more helpful for performing artists. For more information, please see *www.battlemuse.com*

Winner of a 2019 Grammy Award in Best Contemporary Composition for his Violin Concerto, 2002 Grawemeyer Award for Music Composition, 1998 Pulitzer Prize, and 2011 Nemmers Award, Aaron Jay Kernis is one of America's most honored and performed composers. His music appears prominently on concert programs worldwide, and he has been commissioned by America's preeminent performing organizations and artists, including the New York Philharmonic, San Francisco, Toronto, and Melbourne (AU) Symphonies, Walt Disney Company, Chamber Music Society of Lincoln Center, Renee Fleming, Joshua Bell, and Sharon Isbin. Recent commissions include his 4th Symphony for the New England Conservatory's 150th anniversary and Nashville Symphony; concerti for violinist James Ehnes, cellist Joshua Roman, violist Paul Neubauer, and flutist Marina Piccinini; a work for the Borromeo String Quartet and a series of commissions for Tippet Rise Art Center. He is the Workshop Director of the Nashville Symphony Composer Lab and, for 11 years, served as New Music Adviser to the Minnesota Orchestra, with which he co-founded and directed its Composer Institute for 15 years. Kernis teaches composition at Yale School of Music, and was inducted into the American Academy of Arts and Letters and the Classical Music Hall of Fame. Leta Miller's book-length portrait of Kernis and his work was published in 2014 by University of Illinois Press as part of its American Composer series.

Aaron Jay Kernis
Ingrid Laubrock
Brandon Lopez

Ingrid Laubrock is a saxophonist/composer based in Brooklyn since 2009. Laubrock is interested in exploring the borders between musical realms and creating multi-layered, dense and often evocative sound worlds. Laubrock has performed with Anthony Braxton, Muhal Richard Abrams, Jason Moran, Kris Davis, Tyshawn Sorey, Mary Halvorson, Tom Rainey, Tim Berne, Dave Douglas and many others. She is a prolific composer who has written for ensembles ranging from duo to chamber orchestra. Awards include Fellowship in Jazz Composition by the Arts Foundation in 2006, the 2009 SWR German Radio Jazz Prize and the 2014 German Record Critics Quarterly Award. She won best Rising Star Soprano saxophonist in the *Downbeat* Annual Critics Poll in 2015 and best Tenor saxophonist in 2018. Laubrock is one of the recipients of the 2019 Herb Alpert Ragdale Prize in Music Composition and has received composing commissions by The Shifiting Foundation, The Jerwood Foundation, American Composers Orchestra, Tricentric Foundation, SWR New Jazz Meeting and The Jazz Gallery Commissioning Series.

Brandon Lopez is a New York-based composer and bassist working at the fringes of jazz, free improvisation, noise and new music. From the New York Philharmonic's David Geffen Hall to the DIY basements of Brooklyn, Lopez has worked beside many luminaries of jazz, classical, poetry, and experimental music, including Fred Moten, John Zorn, Okkyung Lee, Ingrid Laubrock, Tony Malaby,

Tyshawn Sorey, Bill Nace, Steve Baczkowski, Chris Potter, Edwin Torres, Tom Rainey, Cecilia Lopez, Sun Ra Arkestra, Susan Alcorn, Mette Rasmussen, and many others. Lopez was the 2019–2020 Artist in Residence at Roulette, 2018 Artist-in-Residence at Issue Project Room and 2018 Van Lier Fellow at Roulette Intermedium. Recent highlight performances include opening the 2018–2019 season of the New York Philharmonic as a featured soloist in Ashley Fure's *Filament* and a number of works with John Zorn, including the Zorn's 35th anniversary of *Cobra*.

BRIAN MARSELLA is a pianist, composer, bandleader and educator living in New Jersey. A Philadelphia native, Marsella moved to New York in 1998 and has been touring and recording consistently since. Currently Marsella has released eleven albums as a leader or coleader. His projects include the large ensembles iMAGiNARiUM and Gatos do Sul, the jazz quintet The Flail, the psychedelic surf-rock trio The Modulators as well as two acoustic piano trios (one featuring Kenny Wollesen and Trevor Dunn and the other with Christian McBride and Anwar Marshall.) *OUTSPOKEN: The Music of Hasaan Ibn Ali* (McBride, Marshall) was chosen as a Best Album of 2018 by *The New York City Jazz Record*. Brian can also be heard on over thirty other albums including fifteen on John Zorn's Tzadik label (four as a leader). Over the past 5 years, Brian has become a central figure in John Zorn's world as a musician in both his *Masada* and *Bagatelle* projects as well as a member of Zorn's Cobra. Since 2004, Marsella has been of member of Cyro Baptista's Beat the Donkey and Banquet of the Spirits. With Cyro, Brian has toured the world and helped lead workshops in Brazilian rhythms and in the community building project, "Sound of the Community." A passionate teacher, Brian is on the faculty of the Mannes and Jazz and Contemporary Music programs at The New School in NYC. Brian has performed with John Zorn, Cyro Baptista, Matisyahu, Marshall Allen, Nels Cline, Hassan Hakmoun, Jon Irabagon, Ikue Mori, Billy Martin, Meg Okura's Pan Asian Chamber Jazz Ensemble, Jessica Lurie Ensemble, Zion80, Edom, Pharaoh's Daughter, Yemen Blues and Fresh Cut Orchestra.

Brian Marsella

Christian McBride

CHRISTIAN MCBRIDE is a six-time Grammy Award winning bassist/composer and the host of NPR's Jazz Night in America. Since the early 1990s, McBride has appeared on over 350 recordings as a sideman. Aside from various stints with Sting, Chick Corea, Pat Metheny, Roy Haynes, Freddie Hubbard, McCoy Tyner, Joe Henderson and George Duke, he's also been a bandleader since his debut recording *Gettin' To It* in 1995. McBride has served as Artistic Director with organizations such as The Brubeck Institute, The Los Angeles Philharmonic and more. He currently serves as Artistic Director for Jazz House Kids, The TD James Moody Jazz Festival at NJPAC, The Jazz Museum in Harlem and Jazz Aspen. In 2016, McBride was named the Artistic Director of the historic Newport Jazz Festival, taking over the reigns from the festival's longtime Artistic Director and founder, George Wein. McBride manages to tour consistently with his quartet, the New Jawn. He also fronts the Grammy-winning Christian McBride Big Band, whose Mack Avenue recordings, *The Good Feeling* and *Bringin'*

It won the Grammy Award for Best Large Jazz Ensemble Album in 2012 and 2018 respectively. In addition, McBride hosts *The Lowdown: Conversations With Christian* on Sirius/XM and DJs at clubs as DJ Brother Mister.

Bill Nace is an artist and musician based in Philadelphia, PA. He has collaborated with a wide range of musicians, including Michael Morley, Graham Lambkin, Samara Lubelski, Joe McPhee, Chris Corsano, Jooklo Duo, Chris Cooper, John Truscinski, Greg Kelley, Jake Meginsky, Jessica Rylan, Paul Flaherty, Wally Shoup, and Kim Gordon, with whom he regularly plays as one half of the duo Body/Head. Their latest LP *The Switch* was released on Matador in 2018. His first solo LP *Both* will be released on the Drag City label in the Spring of 2020. He has been a featured musician in festivals such as ATP (curated by Jim Jarmusch and held in Monticello, NY), Colour Out of Space (Brighton, UK), Supersonic Festival (Birmingham, UK), International Festival Musique Actuelle (Victoriaville, QC), and Homegrown (Boston, MA). He has performed in a wide variety of venues, running the gamut from the Musee d'Art Contemporain (Strasbourg, France) to The Stone (NYC) to Bennington College (Vermont). Recordings can be found on Ecstatic Peace (Northampton, MA), Ultra Eczema (Belgium), Holidays (Italy), 8mm (Italy), Throne Heap (VA), HP Cycle (Toronto, ON), as well as on Nace's own label Open Mouth.

Bill Nace

Miles Okazaki

Miles Okazaki is a NYC-based guitarist originally from Port Townsend, a small seaside town in Washington State. He has released five albums of original compositions over the last 12 years and is an artist on the Pi Recordings label. In 2017 he released a six album recording of the complete compositions of Thelonious Monk for solo guitar. His sideman experience over the last two decades covers a broad spectrum from standards to experimental music (Kenny Barron, Stanley Turrentine, Dan Weiss, Mary Halvorson, Matt Mitchell, Jonathan Finlayson, Jane Monheit, Amir ElSaffar, Nasheet Waits, Rajna Swaminathan, Darcy James Argue, and many others). He was seen prominently with Steve Coleman and Five Elements from 2009–2017. Okazaki has taught guitar and rhythmic studies at the University of Michigan since 2013, and his first book, *Fundamentals of Guitar*, was released on Mel Bay Publications in 2015. He has also taught at the Banff Institute, The New School, the School for Improvisational Music, Queens College, The Juilliard School, Amsterdam Conservatory, and many other institutions. Outside of guitar, his past teachers include Anthony Davis (composition), Ganesh Kumar (Carnatic percussion), and Kendall Briggs (counterpoint). His awards and grants include Chamber Music America's *New Works* (2007), Chamber Music America's *French-American Jazz Exchange* (2009), the Jazz Gallery and Jerome Foundations Residency Commission (2010), the American Music Center's Composer Assistance Program (2011), the Mid-Atlantic Arts Foundation's US Artists International grant (2012), the Rockefeller Brother's Fund Artist Residency (2012), the Jazz Gallery Mentorship program (2015), and the Shifting Foundation (2019). He holds degrees from Harvard University (B.A.), Manhattan School of Music (M.M.), and The Juilliard School (A.D.), and lives in Brooklyn, NY with his wife and three children.

CHRIS POTTER A world-class soloist, accomplished composer, and formidable bandleader, Grammy Award nominated saxophonist Chris Potter has emerged as a leading light of his generation. Potter's music showcases limitless creativity and a vibrant sense of swing, prompting critics, musicians, and fans alike to cite him as the one of the finest saxophonists today. With his 2019 Edition Records release, *Circuits*, Potter makes a return to groove, echoing music from his *Underground* era. Joined by keyboardist James Francies and drummer Eric Harland, Potter's new music thrives on the band's chemistry, blending a vibrant soundscape of electronics, melodies with unforgettable hooks, and surprising turns of phrase, all played with relentless energy.

Chris Potter

Tomeka Reid

Jorge Roeder

Cellist and composer TOMEKA REID has emerged as one of the most original, versatile, and curious musicians in Chicago's bustling jazz and improvised music community over the last decade. Her distinctive melodic sensibility, always rooted in a strong sense of groove, has been featured in many distinguished ensembles over the years. Reid grew up outside of Washington D.C., but began her musical career after moving to Chicago in 2000. Her work with Nicole Mitchell and various Association for the Advancement of Creative Musicians-related groups proved influential. By focusing on developing her craft in countless improvisational contexts, Reid has achieved a stunning musical fluency. She is a Foundation of the Arts (2019) and 3Arts Awardee (2016), and received her doctorate in music from the University of Illinois, Urbana-Champaign in 2017. In 2019 Tomeka Reid received a teaching appointment at Mills College as the Darius Milhaud chair in composition. Reid has been a key member of ensembles led by legendary reedists like Anthony Braxton (Zim Sextet) and Roscoe Mitchell (Roscoe Mitchell Quartet, Art Ensemble of Chicago), as well as a younger generation of visionaries including flutist Nicole Mitchell (Black Earth Ensemble, Artifacts), vocalist Dee Alexander (Evolution Ensemble), and drummer Mike Reed (Loose Assembly, Living By Lanterns, Artifacts). She co-leads the adventurous string trio Hear In Now, with violinist Mazz Swift and bassist Silvia Bolognesi, and in 2013 launched the first Chicago Jazz String Summit, a semi-annual three-day international festival of cutting edge string players held in Chicago.

Originally from Lima, Peru, bassist JORGE ROEDER has become renowned as one of the most versatile and expressive bass players in jazz today. Combining a symphonic imagination with the intimate lyricism of a folk musician, the aggressive energy of a raw rocker with the buoyant rhythmic sensibilities of his Afro-Peruvian roots, Roeder conveys a wide spectrum of influences within a resolute foundation. Roeder has enjoyed long-standing partnerships with Julian Lage, Sofía Rei, Shai Maestro and Ryan Keberle, and shared stages with such innovators as John Zorn, Gary Burton, and Nels Cline. He's been recognized with a number of awards, including the 2007 International Society of Bassists

Jazz Competition and semi-finalist status in the 2009 Thelonious Monk Bass Competition, as well as a Grammy nomination for the Julian Lage Group's debut album.

DAN ROSENBOOM (b. May 7, 1982) is a musician at the forefront of the thriving Los Angeles creative music scene, who has garnered an international reputation for boundary-pushing projects and relentless productivity. A trumpet virtuoso equally at home in improvised and classical music, and a prolific composer-producer entrepreneur, Rosenboom has been featured on stages and festivals all over the world. To date, Rosenboom has produced over twenty-five albums under his own name and with his internationally-acclaimed bands, Burning Ghosts, DR. MiNT, and PLOTZ!. He has also appeared as a featured collaborator on albums by Vinny Golia, James Newton, Anthony Wilson, MAST, Harris Eisenstadt, Kubilay Üner, the Jon Armstrong Jazz Orchestra, Jose Gurria-Cardenas's Gurrisonic Orchestra, Trevor Anderies, Dorian Wood, David Rosenboom, RootSystem, Geoff Gallegos's NineNet, Killsonic, Got Monk?, Orkestar Mézé, the Industrial Jazz Group, and more. As a Hollywood studio recording artist, he has worked with such notable film composers as John Williams, Hans Zimmer, Alan Silvestri, Danny Elfman, Alexandre Desplat, James Newton Howard, and many more, and has toured the world as multi-platinum pop singer Josh Groban's trumpet soloist. As a classical musician and noted interpreter of modern and avant garde music, he has performed with many of the elite groups and musicians in Los Angeles, including the Los Angeles Philharmonic, Los Angeles Opera, Los Angeles Chamber Orchestra, Monday Evening Concerts, Southwest Chamber Music, the Long Beach Opera, and is the founder of Orenda Records.

Dan Rosenboom

Joel Ross

Cory Smythe

Chicago native and newly minted Blue Note artist JOEL ROSS is a sophisticated jazz performer with a sound steeped in the post-bop tradition. Joel has performed with many of jazz's most lauded artists including Ambrose Akinmusire, Christian McBride, Marquis Hill, Gerald Clayton, Louis Hayes, Melissa Aldana, Wynton Marsalis and Herbie Hancock, among others. He leads his own group Joel Ross' Good Vibes, among other projects, and recently released his debut album *KingMaker* on Blue Note in 2019. He is currently based in New York City.

Pianist CORY SMYTHE has worked closely with pioneering artists in new, improvisatory, and classical music, including saxophonist-composer Ingrid Laubrock, violinist Hilary Hahn, and multidisciplinary composers from Anthony Braxton to Zosha Di Castri. Smythe has been featured at the Newport Jazz, Wien Modern, Nordic Music Days, Approximation, Concorso Busoni, and Darmstadt festivals, as well as at Lincoln Center's Mostly Mozart festival, where he was recently invited to premiere new work created in collaboration with Peter Evans and Craig Taborn. He has received commissions from the Trondheim Jazz Orchestra, Milwaukee's Present Music, the Banff Centre for the Arts, the International Contemporary

Ensemble, of which he is a longtime member, and the Shifting Foundation, which supported his 2018 release, *Circulate Susanna*. Smythe received a Grammy Award for his work with Ms. Hahn and plays regularly in the critically acclaimed Tyshawn Sorey Trio.

RAND STEIGER was born in New York City and lives in San Diego, where he draws inspiration from the natural landscape and the long history of experimental music in Southern California. Many of his compositions combine orchestral instruments with digital audio signal processing. They also propose a hybrid approach to just and equal-tempered tuning, exploring the delicate perceptual cusp between a harmony and a timbre that occurs when tones are precisely tuned. Some examples include: Ecosphere, developed at IRCAM and premiered by the Ensemble Intercontemporain in Paris; Traversing, premiered by the Southbank Sinfonia in London; Cryosphere, premiered by the ACO at Carnegie Hall, A Menacing Plume, premiered by the Talea Ensemble, and the Coalescence Cycle, premiered on a Miller Theater Composer Portrait Concert by the International Contemporary Ensemble. More recently he created a series of works for the Arditti, JACK and Flux Quartets, and was commissioned by the Los Angeles Philharmonic to create an installation with Yuval Sharon that embedded thirty-two loudspeakers in clouds hanging in W.D. Concert Hall that played a series of compositions throughout the day for the entire 2016/17 season. Soloists he has composed for include Maya Beiser, Claire Chase, Peter Evans, George Lewis, Susan Narucki, and Steven Schick. Steiger was also active as a conductor and led a series of critically acclaimed concerts with the Ensemble Sospeso in New York City in the early 2000s, and the California EAR Unit in Los Angeles in the 1980s and '90s. He holds the titles of Distinguished Professor and Conrad Prebys Presidential Chair in Music at U.C. San Diego. A former Guggenheim and Rome Prize Fellow, he also served as Visiting Professor in 2009 at Harvard University, and was Composer-in-Residence at the California Institute for Telecommunications and Information Technology from 2010 to 2013. For more information, please see http://rand.info

Rand Steiger

Ryan Streber

RYAN STREBER is a composer and audio engineer based in NY. As an engineer and producer, Ryan co-owns and operates Oktaven Audio in Mt Vernon, NY. He has worked with a wide range of artists and ensembles on hundreds of studio recording projects including albums released on the New Focus, Kairos, Tzadik, Naxos, New Amsterdam, Mode, Innova, Hot Cup, Warner, Parma, and Intakt labels among many others. Ryan engineered and produced Aizuri Quartet's Blueprinting (New Amsterdam) and Publiquartet's Freedom and Faith (Bright Shiny Things) both of which were Grammy nominees, and he and Oktaven were also a part of Grammy-nominated recordings by Fred Hersch, Du Yun and ICE, Mike Holober and Gotham Jazz Orchestra, and Missy Mazzoli and Olivia DaPrato. Ryan's compositions have been performed in the United States and abroad by ensembles such as counter)induction, ACME, Line C3, New Juilliard Ensemble, and Flexible Music. Ryan received his BMA and MMA from The Juilliard School, studying composition with Milton Babbitt and

Christopher Rouse. He served as the director of Juilliard's Composers Forum and coordinator for the composition department from 2005 to 2012, and he has also taught composition in the school's Evening Division. He is a recipient of the ASCAP Morton Gould award and Juilliard's Palmer Dixon prize. Born in 1979 in Rochester, NY, Ryan currently resides in Yonkers, NY and Sharon, CT.

John Zorn Born and raised in New York City, composer/performer JOHN ZORN has been a central figure in the Downtown scene since 1975, incorporating a wide variety of creative musicians into various compositional formats. His work is remarkably diverse and draws inspiration from Art, Literature, Film, Theatre, Philosophy, Alchemy and Mysticism as well as Music. Honors include a MacArthur Fellowship, the Cultural Achievement Award from the National Foundation for Jewish Culture, the William Schuman Prize for composition from Columbia University and honorary doctorates from the University of Ghent, SUNY Purchase and New England Conservatory.

RECOMMENDED LISTENING

Bruce Ackley

(w./Twins) Parachute
Cinema Rovaté Metalanguage
Favorite Street—Rova plays Steve Lacy Black Saint
Long on Logic—Rova plays Frith, Kaiser and Rova Sound Aspects
The Eye Cassette
The Hearing Avant
No Favorites!—A tribute to Lawrence D. "Butch" Morris New World
In Transverse Time Victo

John Luther Adams

Become Desert Cantaloupe
Become Ocean Cantaloupe
The Light That Fills the World Cold Blue
In the White Silence New World
Canticles of the Sky Rvng Int'l
Strange and Sacred Noise Mode
The Wind In High Places Cold Blue
Ilimaq Cantaloupe
Inuksuit Cantaloupe
Everything That Rises Cold Blue

Jim Black

AlasNoAxis Winter & Winter
Splay Winter & Winter
Habyor Winter & Winter
Dogs of Great Indifference Winter & Winter
Houseplant Winter & Winter
Antiheroes Winter & Winter
Somatic Winter & Winter
Actuality Winter & Winter
The Constant Intakt Records
Reckon Intakt Records

Martin Bresnick

Parisot Bandcamp
Prayers Remain Forever Starkland
Caprichos Enfáticos Cantaloupe Music
Every Thing Must Go Albany Records
The Essential Martin Bresnick Cantaloupe Music
Martin Bresnick: My 20th Century New World Records
High Art: Chamber Music for Solo Flute Albany Records
Works of a Poor Music CRI
Conspirare: Chamber Music for Solo Flute CRI
Martin Bresnick: Music for Strings CRI
Long Distance CRI
The Monticello Trio: Bresnick, Ives and Shatin CRI
CDCM Computer Music Series Vol. 2 Centaur Records
New York Woodwind Quintet Plays Bresnick, Powell, Roseman, Shapey New World Records

Carter Burwell
Carter Burwell—Music for Film, The Brussels Philharmonic conducted by Dirk Brossé Silva Screen Records
Carol Varese Sarabande Records
Wonderstruck Lakeshore Records
Howl Lakeshore Records
Being John Malkovich Astralwerks
Fargo/Barton Fink TVT Records

Ann Cleare
eyam v (woven)
to another of that other
Earth Waves
teeth of light, tongue of waves
fiáin
eöl
I should live in wires for leaving you behind
anchor me to the land
I am not a clockmaker either
Dorchadas

Bram de Looze
Colour Talk Sdban Records/ N.E.W.S. Records
Switch the Stream Outhere Music/ Outnote Records
Piano e Forte Outhere Music/ Fuga Libera
Septych Clean Feed Records
MiXMONK Universal
Nature City Outhere Music/ Outnote Records
The Mystery of Kem Outhere Music/ Outnote Records
Stephanos Chytiris Flux Project PYR|N
Coding of Evidentiality Clean Feed Records
Collective Effervescence Clean Feed Records

Zosha Di Castri
Tachitipo New Focus Recordings
Life Reflected—NACO—Alexander Shelley Analekta
Canadian Composers—Gruppo Montabello—Henk Guittart Etcetera

Sam Eastmond
Splintered Stories Tzadik
Binah: The Book Beri'ah Tzadik
Cerberus: The Book of Angels Vol. 26 Tzadik
Ghetto Bandcamp
Gulgoleth Chant Records
TORU: Anthology 1 Chant Records
Meltdown EGR/Bandcamp

Danny Elfman
Violin Concerto: "Eleven Eleven" Sony Classical
Serenada Schizophrana Sony Classical
Rabbit and Rogue Sony Classical
The Unknown Known La La Land Records
Standard Operating Procedure Varese Saraband
Alice and Wonderland Walt Disney Records
Tim Burton's Nightmare Before Christmas Walt Disney Records
Black Beauty Giant Records
Milk Decca Records
Music For a Darkened Theater Original release: MCA Records

Sasha Frere-Jones
Body Meπa, Butler Bandcamp

Calvinist, Calvinism Vol. 1 Bandcamp
Calvinist, "Yo-Yo" DFA
Ui, Lifelike Southern
Uilab, Fires Duophonic/Bingo

Leo Genovese
Haikus Ii Fresh Sound New Talent
Unlocked Ropeadope
Shaman Independent
Legal Aliens I & Ii Independent
Seeds Palmetto
Argentinosaurus Newvelle
Hidden People Independent
Piano Tuerto Independent
Reflejos De Sal Independent
Haikus I Independent
Oxidation Independent

Kate Gentile
Mannequins Skirl

Osvaldo Gollijov
St Mark Passion DGG
Ainadamar DGG
Azul Rhino Warner Classics
The Dreams and Prayers of Isaac the Blind Nonesuch
Ayre DGG
Tetro DGG
Youth Without Youth DGG
Oceana DGG
Yiddishbuk EMI

Russell Greenberg
Yarn/Wire Currents Volumes 0–5 self-released
Images of Duration Northern Spy
Eliminated Artist Distributed Objects
Negotiation of Context WERGO records
Tone Builders Carrier Records

Sae Hashimoto
The Interpretation of Dreams Tzadik

David Holzman
Music of Wolpe, Pleskow and Maxwell Davies Centaur
Visions—Bloch, Ben-Haim, Avni, Schoenberg, Wolpe Albany
Music of Martino Albany
Music of Wolpe Bridge
Music of Sessions and Shapey Bridge
Music of Sessions Bridge
Music of Poul Ruders Bridge
At All Device—Music of John McDonald Bridge 9528

Aaron Jay Kernis
Violin Concerto Onyx
Three Flavors, Two Movements (with Bells), Superstar Etude #3 Naxos
String Quartet #3 ("River") Sono Luminus
Colored Field, Air, Musica Celestis Virgin Classics
Three Concertos: Dreamsongs, Viola Concerto, Concerto in Echoes Signum
Second Symphony, Musica Celestis, Invisible Mosaic III Phoenix
String Quartets 1 ("musica celestis") and 2 ("musica instrumentalis") Arabesque
Lament and Prayer, Air, Double Concerto for violin and guitar ARGO
Goblin Market, Invisible Mosaic II Signum
Brilliant Sky, Infinite Sky; Love Scenes; Morningsongs Recordings

Ingrid Laubrock
Kasumi Intakt

Channels Intakt
Contemporary Chaos Practices Intakt
Utter Relative Pitch
Serpentines Intakt
Roulette of the Cradle Intakt
Ubatuba Firehouse 12 Records
Zürich Concert Intakt
Blood Moon Intakt
Union Cleanfeed

Brandon Lopez

violent starts at the tongue NeverNotAGraveDigger
Live in Zurich NeverNotAGraveDigger
quoniam facts sum vilis Astral Spirits
The Industry of Entropy Relative Pitch Records
The Church of Plenty Empty No Rent Records

Brian Marsella

MountAnalogue Tzadik
Hierophant Tzadik
OUTSPOKEN—The Music of the Legendary Hasaan Tzadik
chapter one: The Clocks Have Gone Mad Red Palace
Buer Tzadik
Caym Tzadik
Banquet of the Spirits Tzadik
Gatos do Sul Tzadik
Winged Serpents Tzadik
Calculus Tzadik

Christian McBride

The Movement Revisited Mack Avenue
Gettin' To It Verve
Live at the Village Vanguard Mack Avenue
New Jawn Mack Avenue
Bringin' It Mack Avenue
Conversations with Christian Mack Avenue
Kind of Brown Mack Avenue
Out Here Mack Avenue
The Good Feeling Mack Avenue
People Music Mack Avenue

Bill Nace

No the Sun Open Mouth Records
Last Notes Open Mouth Records
The Switch Matador Records
Scratch LP Holidays Records
Stolen Car Golden Lab Records
Live at The Stone Open Mouth Records
S/T Open Mouth Records
Live at Disjecta Open Mouth Records
Live at Rotunda Open Mouth Records
BAND Open Mouth Records

Miles Okazaki

The Sky Below Pi Recordings
Work: The Complete Compositions of Thelonious Monk self-released
Trickster Pi Recordings
Figurations Sunnyside
Generations Sunnyside
Mirror self-released

Chris Potter

Gratitude Verve
Traveling Mercies Verve
Underground Sunnyside
Song for Anyone Sunnyside
Follow the Red Line Sunnyside
Ultrahang ArtistShare
The Sirens ECM
Imaginary Cities ECM

The Dreamer is the Dream ECM
Circuits Edition

Tomeka Reid
Old New Cuneiform
The Mouser Relative Pitch
Geometry of Distance Relative Pitch
Ithra Aeorphonic Records
Geometry of Caves Relative Pitch
Not Living In Fear Anthem
Signaling Nessa Records
Live at the Hungry Brain Veto Records
Artifacts 482 Records
Tomeka Reid Quartet Thirsty Ear Records

Jorge Roeder
Love Hurts Mack Avenue
The Dream Thief ECM
The Hope I Hold Greenleaf Music
De Tierra y Oro Cascabelera

Dan Rosenboom
Absurd in the Anthropocene Gearbox Records
Trio Subliminal Orenda Records
American Circus Orenda Records
Kakistocracy self-released
Fine Dining Orenda Records
Reclamation Tzadik
Voices in the Void Orenda Records
Burning Ghosts Orenda Records
Book of Storms Orenda Records
Astral Transference & Seven Dreams Orenda Records

Joel Ross
KingMaker Blue Note
Flight Blue Note
In Common Whirlwind Recordings
Visions Motema Music
Universal Beings International Anthem
Modern Flows Vol. 2 Black Unlimited Music Group
Global Blue Room Music
Anomaly Fresh Sound New Talent
Being & Becoming More is More Records
The Concert: 12 Musings For Isabella Giant Steps Art

Cory Smythe
Accelerate Every Voice Pyroclastic Records
Channels Intakt Records
Circulate Susanna Pyroclastic Records
Weatherbird More Is More Records
A U T O TROPHS Not Art Records
Planktonic Finales Intakt Records
Pluripotent self-released

Rand Steiger
The Coalescence Cycle, Volume 2 Tundra/New Focus Recordings
The Coalescence Cycle, Volume 1 Tundra/New Focus Recordings
Wittener Tage Für Neue Kammermusik 2017 WDR
Metafagote New Focus Recordings
A Menacing Plume New World Records
Ecosphere, Music for instrument and electronics EMF Media
Flue Einstein Records
Beneath Breath New Dynamic Records
New Electro-Acoustic Music Centaur
Woven Serenade CRI

Ryan Streber
Concentric New Focus Recordings

Mirrored Spaces New Focus Recordings
Hanging Gardens New Focus Recordings
The Hierophant Tzadik
Le Memoire Dolorose Olde Focus
TISM Rogueart
Healing Modes In a Circle Records
A Howl, That Was Also A Prayer New Focus Recordings
American Rage Warner Classics
Torrent NWR
Meshes Amulet
American Dream Cantaloupe

John Zorn
The Urmuz Epigrams Tzadik
Nove Cantici per Francesco d'Assisi Tzadik
Tractatus Musico-Philosophicus Tzadik
Encomia Tzadik
The Hermetic Organ Tzadik
The Book Beriah Tzadik
Beyond Good and Evil Tzadik
Calculus Tzadik
Baphomet Tzadik
Les Maudits Tzadik